The Eternal Wisdom of Anandamayi Ma

Guidance for Spiritual Seekers on the Path to Realization: A Commentary on Words of Sri Anandamayi Ma

The Eternal Wisdom of Anandamayi Ma

Guidance for Spiritual Seekers on the Path to Realization: A Commentary on Words of Sri Anandamayi Ma

Swami Nirmalananda Giri
(Abbot George Burke)

Light of the Spirit
Press
Cedar Crest, New Mexico

Published by
Light of the Spirit Press
lightofthespiritpress.com

Light of the Spirit Monastery
P. O. Box 1370
Cedar Crest, New Mexico 87008
OCOY.org

ISBN: 978-1-955046-45-9 (paperback)
978-1-955046-46-6 (ebook)

Library of Congress Control Number: 2026940321
Light of the Spirit Press, Cedar Crest, New Mexico

Bisac categories:
REL032000 RELIGION / Hinduism / General
REL062000 RELIGION / Spirituality
PHI033000...PHILOSOPHY / Hindu

First edition, (April 2026)
04252026

Contents

Dedicated to the blessed, holy and living memory of
Sri Swami Muktananda Giri: the Mother of Sri Anandamayi Ma.

SRI SRI MATRIKA DHYANAM

(MEDITATION ON SRI SRI MA)

Samadhi donned with natural ease,
An aura of golden luster spreading,
Serene and kindly Her lotus eyes,
Abounding Grace by loving glances shedding.

To consecrated hearts with love devoted,
A blissful state of Joy bestower,
Her smile vanquishing the Autumn moon:
We pray and meditate on Her–our Mother.

Her feet like embodied rays of sunshine,
Very like the heavenly Kalpa Vriksha* tree,
Which save from the shackles of pain and suffering
All who come for refuge–and surrender.

Placed in the center of my heart
In deep and diverse ways to meditate
The pair of Mother's feet so holy
I adore and most ardently supplicate.

* Kalpataru–the wish-fulfilling tree.

Hymn To Ma

(Bhaiji–Sri Jyotish Chandra Roy)

Victory to You, pure, eternal indweller of the heart: Sri Anandamayi Ma!

Your luster, Mother Nirmala, illumines the universe with the radiance of all heavenly virtues.

Rajarajeshwari, swaha, swadha, Gauri, Pranava, are Your forms, O Mother.

You are, Mother, ever divinely graceful to all eyes and minds, ever-abiding and supremely beautiful, ultimate reality behind the manifested universe.

The sun and the moon are Your twin ear-drops, the great expanse of the sky is Your hair, the entire universe is Your form. Mother, You are the glamor of all the riches of the world, sweetness incarnate, and radiant with all splendor of life.

You are enchanting as Lakshmi, You are peace, rest, and mercy. You are the embodiment of all the gods and goddesses, O Mother. You are the giver of happiness, the granter of devotion, knowledge, and salvation, O Mother.

You are the birth-giver of the universe, the nourisher of the universe, and the destroyer of the universe, O Mother. You are the embodiment of the devotee's life, the image of divine grace, and the deliverer of the three worlds, O Mother.

You are the well-spring of all actions; You express Yourself in all activities, are beyond all synthesis and differences, and are the supreme deity, O Mother. All wisdom derives its charm from the sweet words of Your lips, O Mother. You are the charmer of all saints; all terrors of the world vanish at Your glance.

You are the essential soul of mantras. You are the illuminator of the Vedas, you pervade all, O Mother. You are all qualities and all forms. You are without qualities and without forms. You are the embodiment of the highest supreme state, O Mother.

All creation constantly gracefully hymns Your sweet qualities, O Mother. Our breath and life are united in bowing to Thy holy feet. Victory, victory, victory to Thee, O Mother.

Foreword

This is a book I never thought I would write. Though I have written several commentaries on various sacred texts, I could not have imagined myself becoming so bold as to comment on the words of the Infinite–for Sri Sri Anandamayi Ma was the Infinite Absolute in manifestation.

Anandamayi Ma–Sri Nirmala Sundari Devi Bhattacharya–was born in the latter part of the nineteenth century in rural Bengal, but became renowned through the world among students of Hindu Dharma–especially through Paramhansa Yogananda's *Autobiography of a Yogi*. In India Ma most certainly became the most widely known spiritual figure, both through personal contact with aspirants throughout India through Her constant travelling and through publications of the Anandamayi Sangha, an association of devotees dedicated to spreading Ma's divine teachings. To many people Ma was a perfected being, and to very many others She was considered an avatara, literally an incarnation of the Supreme Consciousness: Parabrahman Itself.

Having read about Ma in Yogananda's autobiography and various publications of the Anandamayi Sangha, I went to India at the end of 1962 and met her and travelled with her. Throughout the following nineteen years until her departure from this world I went several times to do the same. During the last fifteen years of Ma's earthly manifestation our Atma Jyoti Ashram in America was under Her direct supervision. (She even told me how to set up our ashram kitchen.) Someone once asked Ma, "Who are you?" and She simply answered "Purna Brahma Narayana," indicating that She was a manifestation of the Absolute Being, Parabrahman. This was evident to me through experiences of Ma's being and blessing when I was in America, and even more so when I met Her in India.

Several books were written about Ma in Bengali and Hindi, but little was produced in English. Eventually *Matri Vani*, a small collection of quotations from Ma's correspondence with various persons was printed in English. Later, a book of Ma's discourses, *Words of Sri Anandamayi Ma*, was printed in English. This is a commentary on that book.

When Ma was just becoming known in India during the first quarter of the twentieth century, Sri Jyotish Chandra Roy wrote a book simply entitled *Matri Darshan*: Mother's Darshan. When an English translation was printed, it was titled *Mother As Revealed To Me*. This was wise, because it implied the truth that Ma herself was a Swarupa–a Revealed Form–of the Supreme Existence, Parabrahman Itself. Actually, Ma often said that a person could not even see Her if there was not the will (kheyala) on Her part for them to see Her. When asked as to "Who" She was, Ma would reply: "I am whatever you think I am." This itself was a statement of Her divinity, because it is Brahman that is appearing as every thing; and in Her was embodied the entire range of being/manifestation. For this reason, seasoned devotees of Ma were never upset or angered when they heard Ma defamed or denounced: because if the defamers or denouncers were sincere, Ma *was* whatever they thought or said She was. Devotees knew that unless Ma revealed herself to someone, they could have no insight regarding Her nature. Really, Ma had no "nature" because She was the embodiment of That which manifests as nature or form.

Sri Ramakrishna told a parable about a dyer who had a single vat for dyeing cloth. When a person brought him a cloth to dye, he would ask them what color they wanted. When they told him, he dipped it in the vat and it came out the exact color they desired. But one day, someone told him: "I want the color of the dye in your vat itself." Therefore I once was so bold as to say to Ma: "I want your color."

A sannyasi devotee of Ma once told me that he had met three people who had known Sri Ramakrishna Paramhansa, who is considered an incarnation of God (avatar) by millions. They all three declared that Ma and Ramakrishna were virtually identical–that they even spoke in a kind of verbal shorthand that Ma herself referred to as "broken speech." Once some intellectuals were speaking with Swami Akhandananda, a disciple of Ramakrishna. They said to him, "We are studying his teachings and trying to understand him." Akhandanandaji replied: "You may try to understand him if you wish. But we lived with him and never tried to understand him." This was wisdom. I never for a moment attempted to understand or comprehend Ma. From my first sight of Ma I was aware that I was in the presence of Infinity, and that my only intelligent response would be to do my best to simply be affected by Her mere presence, to somehow touch Her very Being as the very essence of my own being. Therefore I have often told people who wanted me to tell them about Ma: "The only thing I can say about Ma is that I cannot say anything about Ma."

Nevertheless I always tried to be like soft wax and "take an impression" from being in Her presence. That Ma and I are one is certainly true. And I can say nothing more about it. If I understand Her words that I am now going to attempt to comment on and explain, it is only because She wills it.

Note: The comments in italics and the section/chapter headings are those of the original compiler. The words in bold type are the words of Ma herself.

Anandamayi Ma

ONE

Solan, September 12, 1948.

From Sri Ma one can but rarely get a definite decision on any problem. That is why I wondered of what use it was to write down Her utterances? I asked Sri Ma about it.

Ma was beyond definition and prediction. She stated that She did not have a mind–or therefore a will. Rather, everything She said or did was a "kheyala," a spontaneous movement resulting in action that was not an act of thought, will or desire, or even definition. It simply occurred. A kheyala might be termed a divine movement. Mother never wanted or desired anything. Yet She told people what to do on occasion or declared what She was going to do. It was a revealing of divine will, not a personal desire. It was simply Truth and Reality in external expression. Ma often said: "This body is a drum. According to how you beat it determines what you get in response." Therefore the determining factor was the inquirer–not Ma. It was also unwise to ever say: "Ma *always* does," or "Ma *always* says." Certainly there were things that She usually said or did. But they were not absolutes. Therefore the devotee would always be ready for the unanticipated in word or deed.

Several times over the years, when I mentioned something Ma had said to me, or had told me to do, Atmananda, the translator-compiler of this book, would vehemently declare that Ma never said such or did things–that She always said or did the opposite. I would simply tell her to go ask the translator who relayed Ma's words to me. She always found Ma had said or done those things. So she was wise in consulting Ma about writing down what eventually became *Words of Sri Anandamayi Ma.*

At least you have understood that there is a state, "where" problems are no longer settled in any particular way.

The word "where" implies that states of mind are not just conditions, but actual "places" that are both within and beyond spatial existence simultaneously. This is not fully graspable to the ordinary person, but learning it should prepare us for eventually experiencing it to some degree. It also gives us some understanding that Ma was always living in another dimension than we were. We were living in–and as–just a part, a fragment of reality, but Ma both lived in and was Herself the totality of Reality.

Human beings are creatures of habit and like consistency and predictability. But when we are endeavoring through yoga sadhana to expand our consciousness into the level of Unconditioned Consciousness that is the Divine Self, the Atman which is inseparable from the Paramatman, we have to realize that we are not going to remain in our previous and present state of consciousness. We even now must be prepared to think, will and act in that dawning expansion of both our inner and outer lives.

The ultimate answers lie in the area of consciousness where inner and outer do not exist: only unity. Since this is outside of ordinary awareness, predictability is only possible after thorough experience of that otherness. Therefore the wise sadhaka does not expect any thing, but is prepared for virtually everything.

Ma did not just live and move in a transcendent state of consciousness, She was the embodiment of that consciousness. Early on in my first pilgrimage to India and Ma I met a great yogi-adept (yoga-siddha) named Sri Dattabal. He told me in our very first conversation that I should realize that I was not seeing the real Ma. Rather, I was seeing a kind of projection of Ma's will which I could experience, relate to and communicate with. "If we saw Ma's true being, we would instantly dissolve, because we are unreal and She is The Real. Her body is like a thin skin or veil which protects us and enables us to communicate with Her." I readily understood and believed him because of what I had experienced when I first met Ma and She touched me–as I relate in my autobiography *An Eagle's Flight*.

In the course of your life you have after careful consideration come to a decision on many questions, have you not? But now you will have to realize that no solution is ever conclusive; in

other words, you will have to go beyond the level where there is certainty and uncertainty.

We are existing and actively living in the present moment and in eternity simultaneously, which is possible since there is really at all times only The One of which we are an inseparable "part" and which IS Ma even now. To our conditioned minds this seems contradictory, but that is the nature of relative existence. Ma was a demonstration that experience of this contradiction was possible. Ma was the unity that yet embraces duality–our relative experience–because it includes it as a reality, not a mere appearance. Since everything is a part of infinite Life it is both absolutely unmoving and in fluctuation simultaneously and yet, according to Ma, it is neither in the highest sense. Even illusion in one aspect is real: it is existing in our mind as an image or concept. This is why we speak of relative and absolute reality.

To sum up what Ma is saying: We must come to understand that words and concepts are certainly real and relate to lesser (lower) reality, but they cannot embrace the whole, the totality of anything due to our innate limitation of consciousness–both depth and breadth. So we can speak the truth about something, but that truth is of necessity always partial, not all-embracing/all-encompassing. We must come to understand that our intellectual understanding/comprehension cannot encompass the entire reality of anything, but we certainly can comprehend or intellectually encompass it partially. Just as language is irrevocably limited, so is our intellectual comprehension. And when we add the realization that we can partially or totally misunderstand something, then we are ready to "make some sense of things." We can understand while realizing that we cannot understand totally or flawlessly. So we work with what we have. We use words in definition and explanation, but realize that both uses are inherently limited and not absolutes at any time.

It is true that we can acknowledge that at all times Ma was incomprehensible, inexpressible and indefinable. But to some degree She was also comprehensible, expressible and definable. That is why the Eastern Orthodox Christians speak of apophatic theology: we may not be able to say precisely what God is, but we can certainly say what God is not. But of course, since we can say what God is *not*, we are at the same time saying what he *is* in a backhanded manner. In other words: Words cannot suffice.

And this what Ma is saying: We will have to realize that no solution is ever conclusive. We will have to go beyond the level where there is certainty and uncertainty. In other words, we must go beyond duality even in the intellectual realm.

> **The resolution of a problem arrived at by the mind must of necessity be from a particular point of view; consequently there will be room for contradiction, since your solution represents but one aspect. What then have you actually solved?**

The fundamental viewpoint is that no matter what is said or done, there will always be a counter-reaction either positive or negative. Therefore sometimes a sure and permanent result or resolution cannot be gained–only provisionally acted upon. I think that what Ma is pointing us toward is the recognition that "there is no rest for the weary." Change is the permanent condition of samsara which is also manifesting as tides which move in opposite directions cyclically. So nothing in relative existence is sure or permanent. Yet the human being instinctively seeks for permanent resolution or resolve since changelessness is our fundamental condition, even if overlaid by constant movement and contradictory tides. So the only solution is to turn our attention from the outer, unending and unavoidable fluctuation to the permanent peace of the inmost condition of the Self, our own inmost, unchanging being.

> **You will find a complete and final solution of each particular question from its own particular angle of emergence; and you will also find that there is a place where all problems (actual and possible) have but one universal solution, in which there is no longer any room left for contradiction.**

Now this is something very unique: Ma says that the answer to every question is in its point of emergence–the answer to a question is inherent in its arising. Therefore someone who can return to the point where something arose in his mind will find the revelation of all its aspects. Since duality is an absolute in our relative existence, the question and the answer arise simultaneously, though the ordinary mind may not perceive that. No only is the answer inherent in the question, the question is inherent in the answer! What is needed to unravel this mystery is to enter into the state of consciousness from with all such dualities both arise and resolve themselves: the inherent unity of our Self. Naturally, this seems incomprehensible to the ordinary mind, but the mind of the yogi which is always oriented toward that unity can reach out and perceive it. This is why the yogis of all ages have said that the answers to all questions arise simultaneously with the questions, but only a mind clarified by sadhana can perceive and experience that.

> **The question of solution or non-solution will then cease to arise: whether one says Yes or No–everything is THAT.**

Ma was living proof of this principle. The only step toward resolution of anything is the step that leads to unity. And this is a matter of consciousness, not philosophy or code of behavior. Yoga alone is the key to both the intuitional and the intellectual insight that illumines the reality of anything and can result in illumined thought and action in relation to anything.

Two

Solan, September, 1948.

Concerning the value of religious and philosophical discourses, Sri Ma said:

By listening repeatedly to discussions and discourses on topics of this kind, the path to first-hand knowledge of what has been heard gradually opens out.

Now this is really to be marked out in our minds, because it is virtually unanimously considered that "mere words" count for very little and that intellectual consideration and discourses are of little–or contrary–value. Now Ma does not say such things will produce first-hand knowledge, but She does inform us that by fixing our intellects on the consideration of such things, their very source and psychic vibration as intentional, intellectual entities in their own right will enable the intellectual opening which can result in our becoming able to engage in the path which will culminate in first-hand knowledge: yoga sadhana. The mind is a field of vibrating energy, and the scope and quality of its perceptions is determined by the quality and the extent of its thoughts and intellectual perceptions. As the adage says: Thoughts Are Things. Concepts are actual entities in the subtle energy field of the mind and intellect. And by their "satsang" higher awareness can first become a potential and then eventually, if the mental focus is not ended or deflected, an actualized force of realization. That is why Sri Krishna declared to Arjuna: "Great is that yogi who seeks to be [one] with Brahman, greater than those who mortify the body, greater than the learned, greater than the doers of good works: therefore, Arjuna, become a yogi" (Bhagavad Gita 6:46).

You know, it is as when water uninterruptedly dripping on a stone finally makes a hole in it, and then a flood may suddenly surge through which will bring Enlightenment.

Therefore reading words of spiritual wisdom and listening to discourses on spiritual wisdom, when done with true, inner attention and aspiration, can bring about a literal breakthrough in understanding and awareness.

Be it the perusal of Sacred Texts, listening to religious discourses, engaging in kirtan–God must be the alpha and omega of whatever is done.

Personal self-realization must be the ultimate aim of all religious and spiritual activities, inner and outer. For God is the Self of our Self, and therefore the ultimate goal of all the sadhaka thinks or does–especially japa and meditation.

When reading, read about Him, when talking, talk of Him, and when singing, sing His praises.

This intentional, one-pointed focusing of the mind and heart on God and God alone must be the constant activity and condition of our mind and intellect. The ego-mind and its worshippers will instantly panic at its consideration and begin frantic and even hysterical rejection of such "fanaticism" and "unbalanced mentality." Compromise with ignorance and delusion is the fundamental mentality of most supposedly philosophical or religious people. "A balanced life" is their ideal which is, as I say, compromise, neither balance nor reason. Since God is The All That Is, it is only practical good sense that the genuine spiritual aspirant will consider God his sole focus and aspiration, that everything in his life must be in conformity with divine reality–his own sole reality. Saint John Vianney used to tell people: "Go to God like a shot out of a cannon!" That is intensely single minded. And Ma is indicating the same intensity.

> **These three practices are intrinsically the same; but because people respond differently, the same is expressed in three different ways to suit each person's temperament and capacity for assimilation.**

So each person must engage in them according to his own intellectual and spiritual character and aspiration. Therefore spiritual aspirants will not be identical in their personal spiritual pursuits, and that it as it should be. In the Bhagavad Gita (3:35) Krishna says: "It is better to do your own duty [dharma], however imperfectly, than to assume the duties of another person, however successfully." Each sadhaka is a distinct individual in touch with his own inner being, and should live his life, both secular and spiritual, as an expression of that interior reality. So Ma is telling us to conform ourselves to the highest spiritual principles, but in conformity with our own inmost being–which is far above our personal inclinations and personalities. Ma is not saying, "Suit yourselves." She is saying, "Conform yourselves" to spiritual principles, but in the manner that reflects and expresses the truth of our inner being–not ego-personality.

> **Essentially there is only He and He alone, although everyone has his own individual path that leads to Him. What is the right path for each, depends on his personal predilection, based on the specific character of his inner qualifications.**

In my Fundamentalist Protestant childhood I heard a song that said: "On the Jericho Road there is room for just two. No more and no less: just Jesus and you." In the Gospels Jesus worked some life-changing miracles as he journeyed on the road to Jericho. So the Jericho Road is the path of encountering Divine Reality. And there is no room for anyone but the seeker and the Sought on that journey. Ma is saying the same. Each seeker must walk the path in the unique, individual way that is his personal swabhava: his own inherent disposition, nature, or potentiality–the state of his inner being.

So the sadhaka conforms to two elements: his nature and God's nature–but on that level where they are the same, even though one is finite and other infinite. So we walk two ways that are one in their nature. Our conscious mind is essential, but so is our subconscious and superconscious minds. Though we are one, we have all three minds, practically speaking. And our entire life must express their unity that will eventually result in their identity. Swami Sivananda used to say: "Bhakti [devotion] begins with two and ends with one." So also does any spiritual path that is genuine. For that ultimately-perceived unity is the truth, the reality, behind the unreality of duality. Therefore Ma continues:

> **Take for instance the study of Vedanta. Some seekers become completely drowned in it. Just as others may so lose themselves in kirtan as to fall into a trance, a student of Vedanta may become wholly absorbed in his texts, even more so than the one who gets carried away by kirtan.**

The path of jnana–knowledge that is the path of the Vedanta, Non-dualism–being the path leading to the Ultimate Reality, will naturally culminate in total absorption in the awareness of Unity, since Unity is the only Reality. Perception of duality is a temporary state only, the unreality that is dispelled by realization of the true, eternal Unity.

> **According to one's specific line of approach, one will be able to achieve full concentration through the study of a particular Scripture, or by some other means.**

Therefore Ma was insistent that each person follow in a single-minded focus whatever line of approach was natural to him–in keeping with his personal swabhava. And an essential part of that path was his own personal recognition and realization of his true path–an insight that could only legitimately arise from his own Self or Atman, not from any external factor, including a supposed teacher or guru, although an external person can point out to the seeker the path that will lead to his own self-discovery.

First comes listening, then reflection, and last of all the translation into action of what has been heard and pondered over.

These are the stages of truly rational action. First a person listens, looks and learns–gathers the facts. Then he ponders what will be the likely result of acting on those facts and opinions or any conclusions he has come to in his analysis, for intelligent consideration is an absolute requisite in responsible thought and action. But thought must then be expressed in action, either momentary action or action that becomes a habit, the expression of resolution, permanent or momentary. As Saint Paul said: "Faith [thought] without works [action] is dead" (James 2:26).

All the noble thoughts in the world mean nothing if there are no correspondingly noble deeds. This is extremely important as a principle of living, for it is particularly a foible of philosophers–and especially of Advaitins–to assume that intellectual principles of wisdom guarantee a wise mind or a wisely-lived life.

This is why one has first of all to listen, so that later on each may he able to select Vedanta or kirtan or whatever else be in his own line.

So however much some supposed aspirants may decry intellectual endeavor and thinking, it is absolutely essential for the sadhaka to learn: and learn a great deal through study, listening to spiritual discourses, and pondering deeply over what has been read or heard. This is not being merely intellectual, it is being intelligent–*practically* intelligent.

Also, varying opinions and disciplines will be presented to the aspirant, all of which must be processed by him both intellectually and intuitively. (This second intuitive aspect is crucial, though usually unconsidered and unrecommended.)

Ma presents two choices that may be made as the aspirant's personal approach: Vedanta or kirtan. It should be noted that Ma does not designate which Vedanta: Dwaita (Dualism), Vashishtadvaita (Qualified Non-Dualism), or Advaita (Non-Dualism). Kirtan usually means singing the various

Divine Names over and over in a certain sequence, but it also means repeating a particular Divine Name constantly–usually mentally. This is done while moving about and engaging in ordinary actions or while sitting with closed eyes in meditation. Obviously Ma is presenting two approaches: an externalizing, devotional approach and an internalizing meditational approach. Both can be considered jnana or bhakti according to the inner disposition of the devotee-yogi.

> **Have you never come across people making light of kirtan, saying: "What is there to be gained by it?" Nevertheless, after listening to it for some length of time, they actually develop a liking for it.**

Fake "jnanis" are always disdainful and express contempt for bhakti–devotion toward God. "Bhakti is for the babies," I heard one arrogant, false "jnani" declare. This is an easy reaction of the unintelligent who consider themselves the epitome of wisdom. Those who are "invincibly ignorant" will retain this perspective all their life, but Ma says there are those who by hearing–and thereby absorbing the spiritual vibrations of–the Divine Names develop an affinity and a liking for them. And this is only reasonable, since the yogi-siddhas of India have for millennia declared this principle: God and His Name are One. So the inner divinity, the life, of the mantra or Divine Name becomes revealed to them inwardly since all Divine Names are one with the Supreme Consciousness and the inmost individual consciousness that is their own Self. So love of the Divine Name is the first step to Self-realization. They "develop a liking for it" because they are awakening into their Self which is one with–and is–that Divine Name.

In a striking passage in his epic *Savitri*, Sri Aurobindo describes this process:

> As when the mantra sinks in Yoga's ear,
> Its message enters stirring the blind brain
> And keeps in the dim ignorant cells its sound;
> The hearer understands a form of words

And, musing on the index thought it holds,
He strives to read it with the laboring mind,
But finds bright hints, not the embodied truth:
Then, falling silent in himself to know
He meets the deeper listening of his soul:
The Word repeats itself in rhythmic strains:
Thought, vision, feeling, sense, the body's self
Are seized unalterably and he endures
An ecstasy and an immortal change;
He feels a Wideness and becomes a Power,
All knowledge rushes on him like a sea:
Transmuted by the white spiritual ray
He walks in naked heavens of joy and calm,
Sees the God-face and hears transcendent speech.
(Book IV Canto III)

Therefore one must listen before one can reflect, and then later, what has been heard and reflected upon will take shape in action suited to the person concerned.

This is exactly what Sri Aurobindo expressed so beautifully in the preceding words.

To listen to discourses on God or Truth is certainly beneficial, provided one does not allow oneself to be moved by a spirit of fault-finding or disparagement, should there be differences of outlook to one's own.

Such an ego-based negativity, which is essentially intellectual darkness, will by its nature blind the individual and render him incapable of inner understanding–even of any perception that would illumine his understanding. So pernicious is this, that Ma explains the damaging effects of indulging this reflexive, negative rejection.

To find fault with others creates obstacles for everyone all around: for him who criticizes, for him who is blamed, as well as for those who listen to the criticism.

This is a sobering declaration by Ma, yet clearly understood.

Whereas, what is said in a spirit of appreciation is fruitful to everybody.

And equally uplifting and heartening.

For only where there is no question of regarding anything as inferior or blameworthy (asat) can one call it Satsang [a play upon words: Sat means True Being, the Good]. Satsang means the company of the good, and also a religious gathering. Asat, the opposite of sat, means non-being, wrong, evil. Therefore to find fault (asat) in a religious meeting (satsang) is a contradiction in terms.

This is plain-speaking indeed.

Who is known as a Vaishnava? One who sees Vishnu everywhere. And as a Shakta? One who beholds the Great Mother, and nothing save Her.

It is a matter of divinized consciousness. And the process of divinization is one: sadhana.

In truth, all the various ways of thought spring from one common source–who then is to be blamed, who to be reviled or suppressed? All are equal in essence.

Everything that exists–including all the dualities, half of whom we consider should be rejected as false since we are in the grip of dual consciousness as an absolute–is really only the One, the True and the Real.

Ma then expresses the right view–which should be based on our own inner awakening:

> **Thou art Mother, Thou art Father, Thou art Friend and Thou art Master, Truly, Thou art all in all. Every name is Thy Name, Every quality Thy Quality, Every form Thy Form indeed.**

This is easy to say and think we believe, but if it is not based on our own insight, our own inner illumination of that which seems outside us, it is mere words without substance–in other words: ignorance. Ma spoke from the Absolute Reality that was Her very Being. But we can glibly recite them and mean–and be–nothing thereby. Without personal experience, personal inner awakening, we are like illiterate people saying (and usually mispronouncing) words we do not understand at all.

> **Yet He is also where no forms exist, as pure unmanifested Being–all depends on one's avenue of approach.**

Because duality is an essential of relative existence, we must realize that even though immature, half-baked Vedanta may say otherwise, formlessness and form, unmanifest and manifest are both true. But without personal and complete experiential realization of this, we are only halfway understanding this. So speaking words of wisdom does not make us wise. We must have *realized* what we say.

> **Is it not said that what is viewed by the Shaivas as the Supreme (Parama) Shiva, and by those who inquire into the Self, as the One Self, is none other than the Brahman Itself? In reality there is no contradiction.**

I once heard the egotism of a modern religious group described as: More Liberal Than Thou. And the ego loves duality, even it if preaches non-duality. Again: Talk is cheap. Realization is not.

So long as the slightest difference is perceived, even by a hair's breadth–how can one speak of the state of Pure Being?

And how can there be a possibility of genuinely believing in non-duality, in Advaita? It is not a matter of belief, but of knowing based on direct perception. Again: only the yogi truly knows these things.

Ma herself went through a period of sadhana. Once at about two or three in the morning in Dehradun, Ma told me that during Her sadhana period She practiced every spiritual method of every religion of the world. She said that She did this so that She should be able to give advice to sadhakas of any religion that might come to Her for assistance.

Ma was omniscient in the most practical matters.

For this reason, no matter what path anyone may choose, it is THAT.

Therefore we cannot say that anyone is wrong. Once Edison told some visitors to his laboratory that in his attempt to create the light bulb he had tried over four hundred substances to use as a filament. When the inquirer expressed shock at the seeming tremendous waste of his time, he replied: "It was no waste at all. Now I know over four hundred things that cannot be the filament in a light bulb." If a sadhaka discovers he has been wasting his time in a practice it is not a complete waste because he, too, knows what will not work as a sadhana.

Therefore, whatever path we choose, it will end in our gaining of knowledge: it works or it does not work.

Even if they discover the chosen path is mistaken and does not lead to jnana, yet it is a part of reality, which is based on duality, true and untrue, real and unreal.

Who could say it better?

> **Vedanta actually means the end of difference and non-difference.**

Ma is employing a play on words. "Vedanta" means the end of the Veda in the sense of it being the end or culmination of Vedic wisdom. She was also making a play on words in Bengali where B is used for the Sanskrit V. So in Bengali Veda is pronounced as "bheda" which means "difference." Also, "anta" means "end," so Vedanta [Bhedanta] means both "end of the Veda" and "end of difference."

> **While engaging in sadhana one must concentrate in a single direction; but after it has been completed, what comes then? The cessation of difference: distinction and disagreement. Differences do indeed exist on the path, but how can there be a difference of Goal?**

This is extremely important, absolutely essential, for the sadhaka to know. Sadhana itself must become the main focus of the sadhaka's life, and all the adjuncts of sadhana, especially Sanatana Dharma, the philosophy on which it is based and by which it is justified and comprehended, must be observed and fostered always. There is never any letting-up or relaxation for the genuine yogi. As Christina Rossetti wrote:

Does the road wind up-hill all the way?
 Yes, to the very end.
Will the day's journey take the whole long day?
 From morn to night, my friend.

Spiritual practice and discipline must be maintained at every moment of the yogi's life–and beyond. And it is truly a life-long endeavor, for nothing less than Infinity is the yogi's goal. The yogi's entire life must have sadhana as its center and purpose.

At first the sadhaka must be very single-minded in his interests and resolves regarding spiritual life. His focus must be total. But Ma tells us something I have never found anywhere else: that after we have attained siddhi by single-minded endeavor we will come to see that all ways lead to the One Way. But at first we must have the blinders of entire focus on our mind. Those who successfully attain siddhi will find that although it was necessary to engage in sadhana as though there was only one way to success, indeed many paths lead to the same goal. First we must become wisely narrow; then we can be all-encompassingly wise in our outlook. Indeed we *must* be so.

The wise use of diversity opens the way to unity. Samsara itself becomes the way to nirvana. The closer the sadhaka comes to the Goal, the clearer he perceives that many ways lead to the One. But he also realizes that the following of a single path is sure to most quickly lead to the One Goal. Therefore he cherishes and holds unfalteringly to his chosen path while valuing all others as he does his chosen one.

THREE

Solan, September 16, 1948.

A member of a well-known Indian family, who had distinguished herself by devoting her life to social service, came for Sri Ma's darshana and asked: "Does the capacity to meditate come by practice in this life, or is it an aptitude acquired in former births?"

> **It may be the result of either of the two, or of both combined.**

Ma always gives the complete picture, never just a part or a fragment. The sadhaka must himself become complete in order to be a part of that complete picture. Total Self-realization is the absolute requisite. Ma was always practical, never just theoretical. So She reveals the means to become fully adept in meditation.

> **Meditation should be practiced every day of one's life.**

This is the only way to follow the previously-cited advice of Saint John Vianney to go to God like a shot out of a cannon. Meditation is itself the cannon and our aspiration is the force by which the transformation of our consciousness reaches the target as the means to total Self-realization.

> **Look, what is there in this world? Absolutely nothing that is lasting. Therefore direct your longing towards the Eternal.**

To realize that the world is insubstantial and even empty is a great blessing–not a disillusionment that leaves us sad and hopeless. It is a blessed insight that brings us onto the path to the ultimate and absolute beatitude and fulfillment: Self-realization. It is the turning from the No Thing to The All.

Sometimes we hear the question: "But isn't the desire for Self-realization a desire?" No. It is the only way to absolute fulfillment–and therefore elimination–of all desire. Ma often said that the desire for God was the way to God. For the "longing towards the Eternal" She calls us to is not a desire, but an aspiration arising from the awakening Self. For sadhana truly is, as has been said: The flight of the alone to the Alone: the Ekam [one], Evam [only], Adwitiyam [non-dual] Brahman.

Pray that the action done through you, His instrument, may be pure.

God alone is truly *vishuddha*–supremely pure. How, then, can our actions, even the highest in purpose, be pure with divine purity? By the truth that Ma keeps pointing us to: we are ourselves divine in nature. Our divinity is finite as contrasted with God Whose divinity is infinite, but on the level of our inmost being, that is the only difference between us and God.

However, we find ourself enmeshed in the dualities of samsara–something impossible to God. Therefore in samsara we act in the bondage of ego and ignorance. But if we keep our consciousness fixed on our own divine nature through sadhana, especially Soham japa, then we can act with divine purity and thus produce divine karma which results in the advent of atma-chaitanya: the consciousness that *is* the Self.

First we unite our consciousness with the Divine: then our thoughts and deeds will be manifestations of the Divine. This is a high state, but if we do not attain it we will remain "of the earth, earthly" (I Corinthians 15:47). So it is not really a choice for the awakening individual, the sadhaka. Rather, it is a necessity of an urgency that ultimately cannot be denied but must be fulfilled and made manifest. And how is this awakening produced and maintained?

In every action remember Him.

And that Ma always insisted was managed by a single thing: japa–the repetition of a mantra that has within itself the potential to awaken the divine consciousness which is our own essential being. Many are the mantras which bear within themselves as vibration the potential to awaken the divine consciousness of the Self. Japa is the way to manifest the divine life inherent in the mantra. As can be seen by the words of Ma given in this collection of Her teachings, this is the entire purpose of japa sadhana. And I have found after decades of practice and observance that the most direct and immediately effective practice and mantra is the japa of Soham. (Again, see *Soham Yoga: The Yoga of the Self.*)

The purer your thinking, the purer will be your action.

Though it may not seem so at first glance, this too is about japa. Japa of the Divine Name is the mental process by which divine consciousness is literally invoked into the mind. What could be more pure than the mind and will that is absorbed in repetition of the Divine Name which itself is described as *vishuddha*–supremely pure? Nothing could be surer or more effective. From a pure mind proceeds pure action. Therefore: The purer the thinking, the purer will be the sadhaka's action. It is simple cause and effect. Experience will bear this out. The Divine Name effects the divine alchemy that transmutes the mind of earth into the mind of the Divine.

I will never forget the moment I first read the statement that God and His Name are one. The inner recognition and conviction of that truth was a trumpet blast of permanent awakening. Japa both awakens, empowers and guides the consciousness toward the goal of Realization. Japa, too, begins with two and ends with one. The life does not just become pure, it becomes divine. Ma affirmed this constantly.

In this world you get a thing, and by tomorrow it may be gone. This is why your life should be spent in a spirit of service. Feel that the Lord is accepting service from you in whatever you do.

This is the way to divinize every moment of our life. If we do all our actions directed toward others with the understanding that it is God we are relating to and acting for–seeing them as living embodiments of God as divine selves or atmas, then truly what we do to and for others is done to and for God. Such karma is supernatural association with the Absolute. In *A Christmas Carol* the ghost of Jacob Marley tells Scrooge: "Mankind was my business." Sri Krishna declared in the Gita: "I am the Atman that dwells in the heart of every mortal creature" (Bhagavad Gita 10:20). Every karma we create with others, we create with God. Therefore it is literally true that "the Lord is accepting service from you in whatever you do."

If you desire peace you must cherish the thought of Him.

There is no peace in samsara, but there is infinite peace to be gained if we fix our consciousness in That which is within and enlivening samsara while at the same time being beyond it. The very thought of God, the mental repetition of the Divine Name, unites us with God. Peace must come to us as a natural result if we maintain the flow of that Name within our minds and hearts. Remembrance of the Divine Name–*nama smarana*–is joining our consciousness with the Divine Consciousness, eventually turning two into one. Just do it and see.

Question: When will there be peace on earth?

Well, you know what the present state of affairs is; things are happening as they are destined to be.

Years ago I made my own adage in Russian: *Nyet mir vo mir*–there is no peace (*mir*) in the world (*mir*). But within God Who is seated in our heart there is eternal peace. In the world troubles and wars and conflicts are inevitable because it is the nature of the world. But God is above and beyond the world, and Ma often said that God and His Name are one and the same. Therefore those that live in japa of God's Name are living in union with God. We can experience this by following Ma's urging to continually repeat the Divine Name within. Then the Divine Life becomes our life.

Question: When will this state of unrest come to an end?

> **The fact that many of you feel concerned about it and ask: 'When will it end?' is also one of the ways of His Self-manifestation.**

So to be truly desiring inner peace is itself a manifestation of our inmost Self which is ever living in God. Ma often said that the desire for God was the way to God.

> **Jagat (world) means ceaseless movement, and obviously there can be no rest in movement. How could there be peace in perpetual coming and going? Peace reigns where no coming exists and no going, no melting and no burning. Reverse your course, advance towards Him then there will be hope of peace.**

But where is God? In His Name. For Ma and the wise have told us that God and His Name are ONE.

> **By your japa and meditation those who are close to you will also benefit through the helpful influence of your presence.**

In metaphysical writings there are references to the "astral" and "causal" bodies that are within the physical bodies of all living embodied beings. These are centered in the physical body, but extend beyond it invisibly in what is known as the "aura." These energies are the forces that manifest as the life of the material body. In the yogi, these bodies are developed by his sadhana and become stronger and extend further beyond his physical body. The more developed the yogi, the further the subtle bodies extend beyond the physical body. Highly developed yogis may have auras composed of these subtle vibrations extending even forty or more feet beyond the physical body. So when you come near a yogi you become inside his astral and causal bodies. Naturally, this affects you, and you may even be able to feel it to some extent. Because of this, people's mental states can be elevated if they are near a yogi, and in some instances their physical bodies may be strengthened and even healed of disease or defect. Those who are not just physically close to a yogi, but have personal ties with him through some factors such as blood relationship or friendship definitely are affected by him–even from a distance. So the yogi blesses his family, friends and associates by his spiritual vibrations. I knew a woman with a long-established lower back trouble that gave her real pain. But when she met a very advanced yogi she had the sudden sensation that she was lifted up off the ground and at the same time the chronic pain vanished permanently. I have known people to be mentally and spiritually healed and uplifted by the mere presence of very advanced yogis. And this is what Ma is referring to. People very mentally close to a yogi can be affected by him even when at a long distance from him. So Ma is indicating that our sadhana will definitely benefit those who are close to us.

> **In order to develop a taste for meditation you have to make a deliberate and sustained effort, just as children have to be made to sit and study, be it by persuasion or coercion.**

It is the nature of the mind to be restless and therefore distracted and shallow in its functioning. The mind is like a hyperactive child–mostly through conditioning and a preference for constant movement and external experience. Then there is the fact that the mind is conditioned toward–and even addicted to–both distraction and negativity. For example, I once took a little cousin to a motion picture theater on a weekend where there were mostly children in the audience. Therefore there was noise and confusion throughout–except when there was violence on the screen. Then there was complete quiet and attention. It was a terrible thing to witness the seemingly natural affinity for cruelty and violence.

Therefore Ma is telling us that we must train ourselves to have "a taste for meditation" to make it a desired part of our life. And "a deliberate and sustained effort" is necessary, just as with a restless child. In the book *Dracula*, Professor Van Helsing, the adversary of the vampire, refers to "his so great child-mind." Evil is childish and foolish because it is instinctual rather than intelligent and reasonable. The yogi has to be his own disciplinarian and condition his mind to be an instrument of insight and peace rather than instinct, ego and chaos. The mind and will are "brats" that have been allowed to run wild and function chaotically and impulsively. But if they are taken in hand and shown the way of discipline and peace they will happily go in that direction. The essential guru is our own intelligent will, and meditation and its supporting disciplines are the only means to peace and a meaningful life. Once the yogi gets a taste of the positive effects of meditation he develops a liking for it and arranges his mind and outer life to accommodate and facilitate it. Then his ego no longer seeks fulfillment of its whims, but his Self rules and brings order and peace into his whole being.

> **By taking medicine or having injections a patient may get well; even if you do not feel inclined to meditate, conquer your reluctance and make an attempt. The habit of countless lives is pulling you in the opposite direction and making it difficult for you–persevere in spite of it!**

Medicine often tastes terrible and being stuck by a hypodermic needle hurts. But that is the way to health. Yogananda said that reluctance to meditate was the strongest weapon of our delusional nature. Our struggle is with the negative habits developed through "countless lives." This is a real and serious war! That is why the wise Solomon said: "He that rules his spirit is better than he that captures a city" (Proverbs 16:32). The ego and its delusions and illusions is to be conquered, tamed and made our best friend. Yoga meditation is the way. *Banat, banat, banjai!* Doing, doing, done!

> **By your tenacity you will gain strength and be moulded; that is to say, you will develop the capability to do sadhana.**

Just hold on and keep on keeping on. Since the Self is our eternal nature, it is really the most natural thing about us. But delusion and ego have us fooled into thinking that sadhana is some awful laborious struggle to the death, when it really is the only door to life. Under the domination of the ego we are unable to realize that. As a child I heard a song that said: "Let me lose myself and find it, Lord, in Thee." What I did not know then was that God is my ultimate Self. For we and God are ever one, though eternally distinct. There is no need to try and figure it out intellectually: meditation will reveal it as a reality. All our suffering and confusion come from our ignorance of that reality. But as Buddha said: "Just turn around and behold: The Other Shore!"

Make up your mind that however arduous the task, it will have to be accomplished.

Do not think of the effort that is necessary–think of the absolute necessity to put it forth and succeed. Self-realization is the ultimate goal, and therefore the only real goal we can attain. It is our nature. As Yogananda wrote: "I was made for Thee alone."

Recognition and fame last for a short time only, they do not accompany you when you leave this world.

But the Self has been with us always and will be there through countless lives until we wake up and really do Face Reality.

If your thought does not naturally flow towards the Eternal, fix it there by an effort of will.

We have conditioned ourselves to pursue the mirage of the unreal, turning from the Reality that is our Self. So we got ourselves into this mess and therefore can get ourselves out. The same key that locks the door can unlock it. And that key is our will.

Some severe blow of fate will drive you towards God. This will be but an expression of His Mercy; however painful, it is by such blows that one learns one's lesson.

We have been so negatively polarized by countless lives in the delusion of samsara that it is sometimes necessary for pain to drive us onto the path of peace and joy. And it is true: all our pain in this world is really divine mercy trying to awaken us to seek out the way that leads us from the unreal to the Real, from darkness to the Light, from death to Immortality. It really does work. The saints and masters of all ages have demonstrated it.

The obstinacy of the mind must be curbed with resoluteness.

Why talk about free will if we do not use it for our own liberation? Arjuna said to Krishna on the battlefield of Kurukshetra: "Restless man's mind is, so strongly shaken in the grip of the senses: gross and grown hard with stubborn desire for what is worldly. How shall he tame it? Truly, I think the wind is no wilder" (Bhagavad Gita 6:34).

And Krishna replies: "Yes, Arjuna, the mind is restless, no doubt, and hard to subdue. But it can be brought under control by constant practice, and by the exercise of dispassion. Certainly, if a man has no control over his ego, he will find this yoga difficult to master. But a self-controlled man can master it, if he struggles hard, and uses the right means" (Bhagavad Gita 6:-35-36).

Whether the mind co-operates or not, you must be adamant in your determination to do a certain amount of practice without fail–simply because sadhana is man's real work.

I can assure you that in the beginning the mind will not cooperate! But you are not the mind: you are the eternal, immortal Self. And free will is your fundamental nature and faculty. So by the force of your will every day put forth the effort to raise your consciousness through sadhana.

A lot of people deliberately defeat themselves by setting too high a goal or discipline. Usually they do this with at least the subliminal intention to fail by overdoing it and then say: "Well, I tried." But Ma does not tell us to try: She tell us to DO it, however small it may be. Start out with a little time spent in meditation–even a few minutes. Then as you get used to it, gradually increase the time. A lot of people jump in and overdo and burn themselves out and then say: "Well, I gave it a chance." But they did not. They intentionally burnt themselves out so they could have an excuse. Be aware of your own tricky mind.

Note Ma's last statement: Sadhana is the human being's true work. "Sadhana" comes from the Sanskrit word *sadh*, which literally means: "to go straight to the goal" or "make something straight." That is exactly what yoga meditation does. It is like aiming an arrow and sending it straight to the target: our own Self. Sadhana is Self-knowledge, and includes both the entire knowledge of our relative self and our eternal Self. Since liberation is our only purpose in existing, yoga sadhana is our only true and natural activity. When we mediate we are completely "real." And outside meditation when we do japa we continue to be real. When we do not meditate or do japa we are only a mirage, a hint of what we should be. So for a true human being meditation is not an option but the One Essential.

> **For so long you have been accustomed to perform actions that fetter, therefore from sheer force of habit you feel the urge to bind yourself by activity again and again. But if you try hard for some time, you will be able to see for yourself how you are caught in your action, and that the more you engage in sadhana the quicker will be your advance.**

For so long you have been accustomed to perform actions that fetter, therefore from sheer force of habit you feel the urge to bind yourself by activity again and again. It is like people who after a time in prison feel fearful and purposeless when they are free and faced with putting forth their will to continue their life.

But if you try hard for some time, you will be able to see for yourself how you are caught in your work, and that the more you engage in sadhana the quicker will be your advance. Only by effort do we realize the true nature and extent of our bondage and compulsion, and by continuing that effort they are automatically loosened and then dissolved. First we must see our bondage, but only sadhana reveals that bondage fully. And only sadhana frees us from the perceived bondage. Sadhana is both diagnosis and cure.

The more we walk the farther we go. Everyone knows that, but the yogi must apply his external experience and understand that the more he engages in sadhana–meditation and japa–the further he travels on the path to Self-realization.

As to self-surrender: by constantly endeavoring to live a life of self-dedication, it will come about one day. What does self-surrender mean, if not to surrender to one's very own Self!

There is a lot of hot-air talk by fake yogis and "spiritual seekers" about "surrender" in the hope that sterile passivity will be the result or else a rebellion against having to surrender one's freedom and will. But real self-surrender is surrendering the delusions of the ego to the true knowledge of the Self that is attained through constant sadhana (for japa must become constant through continual endeavor) and frequent meditation.

Keep in mind what this little daughter of yours is asking you to do!

And do it. Always.

FOUR

Solan, September 11, 1948.

A Government Official and his wife had come for Sri Ma's darshana. They were meeting Her for the first time. To a question of theirs, Sri Ma replied:

> **If you say you have no faith, you should try to establish yourself in the conviction that you have no faith.**

Why? Because most people are so busy putting on an act that they have not really thought through, they end up being nothing: no thing.

Self-definition is absolutely essential for self-knowledge. When I was eight or nine years old I had willful nonentities say to me with great indignation: "You are too young to have such strong opinions!" Why? First of all, like all of us I had lived many lives. We are all thousands of years old if we add up all the years we have lived in physical embodiment. And we all have subconscious minds in which are stored the samskaras, the impressions created in our subtle bodies by those many lives. Should they not be accessed?

A person who does not believe in reincarnation is utterly incapable of comprehending life in this body and mind which are both the results of karmas and samskaras–products of past life experience. It is now time to learn–not just follow instinctual impulses and behavior that are rooted in past lives of which we are completely unaware.

But back to Ma's intriguing statement that if you say you have no faith, you should try to establish yourself in the conviction that you have no faith. If you do what Ma says, this will bring you face to face with that statement and necessitate your seriously considering if that is really true. Since people lack clear and detailed self-knowledge or self-understanding as a rule, they need to follow Ma's injunction and literally face themselves. But how many do? Most are immersed in ego-knowledge, not even the lower-level self-knowledge of simply being aware of their thoughts and feelings–and their implications, including what they reveal about their inner character. This is why some people cannot endure silence, so much so that elevator music was at one time a necessity.

But Ma now clarifies the purpose and result of Her counsel.

Where 'No' is, 'Yes' is potentially there as well.

Again we see the absoluteness of duality in the realm of relative existence. No implies the existence of Yes–is actually the presence of Yes in the sense that it implies the possibility of Yes. Therefore it is impossible to be beyond either negation and affirmation; rather it is a matter of the preponderance of one or the other.

To have faith is imperative.

The word Ma is using, translated "faith," is *shraddha*, which means: trust; faith; belief; confidence; religious faith; and faithfulness. Therefore She continues:

The natural impulse to have faith in something, which is deep-rooted in man, develops into faith in God.

This development can only take place when there is already at least a provisional conviction of the existence of God and the acceptance of the principles which must be adopted if the faith is both sincere and intelligent: a result of intellectual and intuitive insight.

This is why human birth is such a great boon.

Only in the human being is there both intelligence and intuition that make the arising and conviction of faith possible. Therefore human birth is itself the natural and inevitable doorway to the supernatural opening of the individual's intellect and fundamental consciousness.

It cannot be said that no one has faith. Everyone surely believes in something or other.

But the object of that faith need not be immaterial, psychic, or spiritual. For example, A. A. Milne, the author, said that he was profoundly grateful to his father for giving him atheism. So he had faith and believed in unbelief.

It is only the insecure in their faith that insist no one is an atheist. My religion, Sanatana Dharma (Hinduism), even considers the materialistic Charvaka philosophy a legitimate darshan (viewpoint) within itself. The Charvaka writings are the only really intelligent atheism I have ever found. Western writings in support of atheism are particularly childish and simplistic.

Since Sanatana Dharma holds that God (Brahman) is absolutely beyond definition it does not believe that God "exists" in the usual, intellectual concepts of God. It holds that God is beyond both existence and non-existence. You cannot say that God exists; and you cannot say God does not exist. This is why some consider Advaita to be atheism. Ma was a supreme Advaitin, but Her Advaita included theism.

The word *manusha* (the Sanskrit word for "man") is derived from *man* (mind) and *hus* (conscious), which denotes the mind's awareness and vigilance. This shows that man's natural calling is to attain to Self-knowledge.

For that is his inherent nature.

I well remember Brahmachari Paramachaitanya, an American disciple of Swami Akhandananda, the great disciple of Sri Ramakrishna, saying to me about God: "He meditates on human beings and they evolve–they can't help it!" The profound joy in his face and in the very vibration of these words as he spoke them was wondrous and unforgettable.

When children learn to read and write, they have to accept rebuke and censure. God, too, now and again administers to man a mild beating–this is but a token of His Mercy.

God meets us on our own level and therefore does very "anthropomorphic" things to get our attention. It is called KARMA. And it is ours exclusively, just as an echo is our own voice coming back to us. It is truly mercy, but so much more: it is a call to Awakening, not mere retribution. Therefore, Ma is saying that God does indeed "punish" human beings. But it is really an act of mercy intended to awaken them to the nature of their very own actions. For all that happens to us is an echo of our own previous thoughts and deeds. And its purpose is to enable us to understand and not repeat our errors. It empowers our own free will.

> **From the worldly standpoint such blows are considered extremely painful, but actually they bring about a change of heart, and lead to Peace: by disturbing worldly happiness they induce man to seek the path to Supreme Bliss.**

See? I told you.

> **It is of course true that the human body lives by breathing, and hence there is suffering. Human life, in fact animal life in general, depends on breathing, which is a sign of disturbance in the universal equilibrium. The entire creation is characterized by this disturbance. The process of breathing implies a dual movement, inward and outward, and a periodic rest between the two. The state of harmony can be reached by getting rid of this urge for movement, by attaining to repose, calm and peace. This is possible through yoga. When one is in a state of perfect poise, there is no longer any need to breathe.**

This is the experience and the insight of the adept yogi. Duality is the path to Unity for the yogi, but for the non-yogi it is a continual immersion in disturbance, bondage and suffering. The breath of the non-yogi binds him to samsara and suffering. But the yogi employs his breath to free himself from samsara and suffering. To understand this, read *Soham Yoga: The Yoga of the Self.*

There are two kinds of pilgrims on life's journey: the one, like a tourist, is keen on sight-seeing, wandering from place to place, flitting from one experience to another for the fun of it. The other treads the path that is consistent with man's true being and leads to his real home, to Self-knowledge. Sorrow will of a certainty be encountered on the journey undertaken for the sake of sight-seeing and enjoyment. So long as one's real home has not been found, suffering is inevitable.

This is simple truth, but it must be understood and acted upon: "Become a yogi" (Bhagavad Gita 6:46).

The sense of separateness is the root cause of misery, because it is founded on error, on the conception of duality. This is why the world is called "du-niya" (based on duality).

The error of duality is only dispelled by the experience of unity, of reality. So again: "Become a yogi."

A man's belief is greatly influenced by his environment; therefore he should choose the company of the Holy and Wise.

This is what is meant by Satsanga: Company With Truth. For the holy and wise embody the holiness and wisdom–the Reality–that is The Truth. That is why Yogananda often said: "Company is greater than will power." This is a fundamental truth that should never be absent from our awareness.

Belief means to believe in one's Self, disbelief to mistake the non-Self for one's Self.

Acceptance or rejection of philosophy or religion is meaningless. The true Theism is belief in the Self, and action–a life lived–according to that belief. Whereas ignoring the reality of the Self in our practical life is the true atheism.

> **There are instances of Self-realization occurring by the Grace of God, whereas at other times it can be seen that He awakens in some a feverish yearning after Truth. In the first case attainment comes spontaneously, in the second it is brought about by trials. But all is wrought solely by His Mercy.**

But there is another one whose mercy we also need: our own Self. Otherwise even the existence of God has little practical meaning for us.

> **Man thinks he is the doer of his actions, while actually everything is managed from "There." The connection is "There," as well as the [connection with a] power-house. Yet people say: "I do." How wonderful it is!**

Yet more wonderful than that illusion is the truth that every one of us is a part of "There," that It is our essential being. So "connection" and "disconnection" are myths. There is no improving the Mahavakya: Tat Twam Asi–Thou Art That. So as our true Self we *are* the doer. Delusion is possible only for the ego-mind.

> **When in spite of all efforts one fails to catch a train, does this not make it clear from where all one's movements are being directed? Whatever is to happen to anyone, anywhere, at any time, is all fixed by Him; His arrangements are perfect.**

So all that is needed is to awaken into our Self which is inseparable from Him. Again we see the necessity to realize: Tat Twam Asi.

Ma's final statement is illustrated in the story *Appointment in Samarra*: "There was a merchant in Baghdad who sent his servant to market to buy provisions and in a little while the servant came back, white and trembling, and said, 'Master, just now when I was in the marketplace I was jostled by a woman in the crowd and when I turned I saw it was Death that jostled me. She looked at me and made a threatening gesture; now, lend me your horse, and I will ride away from this city and avoid my fate. I will go to Samarra and there Death will not find me.' The merchant lent him his horse, and the servant mounted it, and he dug his spurs in its flanks and as fast as the horse could gallop he went. Then the merchant went down to the marketplace, he saw Death standing there in the crowd and he went to him and asked, 'Why did you make a threatening gesture to my servant when you saw him this morning?' 'That was not a threatening gesture,' Death replied, 'It was only a start of surprise. I was astonished to see him in Baghdad, for I knew I had an appointment with him tonight in Samarra.'"

An eternal relationship exists between God and man. But in His Lila it is sometimes there and sometimes severed, or rather appears to be severed; it is not really so, for the relationship is eternal.

First we need to understand the relationship between God and human beings. Fundamentally it is not a relationship at all. Rather, God and all sentient beings are ONE. There is no separation between them. There is only absolute, eternal Identity. Any perception or experience of separation is illusion. That is why the heart of yoga sadhana–the original yoga of the original yogis, the Nath Yogis–is Soham: I Am That.

What makes the seeming difference is our own misperceptions and our mistaken identity with them. Also the lack of spiritual realization on our part throughout the creations-long chain of our incarnations in countless forms. We have not forgotten what/who we are: *we have never known it*! Then at some time in our chain of lives we heard it said. At first we surely did not even comprehend the meaning of the concept when it was presented to us. It took a lot of inner growth through many lives to even develop the intellectual capacity for the needed understanding of the dictum Tat Twam Asi–Thou Art That. And when we first had some dim comprehension, we no doubt mocked it as supreme foolishness and egotism, if not outright blasphemy. It takes aeons to develop the ability to even ask: Who Am I? And more aeons to develop the ability to comprehend or consider the answer. Tat Twam Asi is the Great Answer to the Great Question whose mere arising is an indication of the dawning ability to ask it ourself and attain the answer. For it is attained through evolution of inmost awareness. It is not at all an intellectual inquiry, but the dawning of an inmost urge: K'oham: Who Am I? Then there has arisen the possibility of there arising from within us the reply: So'ham: I Am That. It is a seed-concept that must grow into a total realization. This is possible and inevitable.

> **Again, seen from another side, there is no such thing as relationship.**

Or course not. There is only eternal identity outside of which there is no reality of any kind.

> **Someone, who came to meet this body, said: "I am a newcomer to you." He got the reply: "Ever new and ever old indeed!"**

In the beginning is the ending. In the meeting is the separation. This is Samsara; this is Duality. And both are illusion. Since time is a basic illusion there is nothing new; and that which exists is eternal and new/old simultaneously while embracing and transcending both. That is why in the ultimate sense we can say nothing. Therefore the great sages are munis–not speaking. For silence alone is the only wisdom. The nature of Reality is such. It both Is and Is Not–and is beyond both.

> **The light of the world comes and goes, it is unstable.**

Because it is unreal.

> **The Light that is eternal can never be extinguished.**

Because it is real.

> **By this Light you behold the outer light and everything in the universe; it is only because It shines ever within you, that you can perceive the outer light.**

Enlightenment is not just a tentative potential, it is the eternal nature of every single sentient being. Nothing is more natural than Self-realization and the means to attain/reveal our inmost condition as the Self. We have always been the Self at every rung we have climbed in the evolutionary ladder. In the seed is the entire tree in potential form. The same is true of us. Perfect Self-realization is at the core of our being and IS our being. We do not even need to attain it: only perceive/realize/recognize it. This is what sadhana is all about–and only that.

Our true nature is irrevocable perfection, and sadhana is the process of perceiving/realizing it. When we are asleep we do not need to go somewhere else to awaken. We only need to awaken and perceive the Self. But we must realize that this is not true of our real Self–it only relates to our conditioned, relative perceptions that are all illusions.

For ages yogis have used the simile of the thorn that is used to remove a thorn from our hand or foot. Our ignorance is the thorn that is removed by the thorn of insight and sadhana. Then both "thorns" are discarded as the mirages they both are. This is the very essence of the divine Lila whose only goal is realization-liberation.

> **Whatever appears to you in the universe is due solely to that great Light within you, and only because the Supreme Knowledge of the essence of things lies hidden in the depths of your being is it possible for you to acquire knowledge of any kind.**

No comment is needed–just awakening to the experiential truth of these words.

> **The human brain may be compared to the root of a tree; if the root is watered, nourishment spreads to every part of the plant.**

The brain is the physical manifestation of the Sahasrara Chakra, the Thousand-petaled Lotus at the core of which the Self shines forth as Consciousness both relative and absolute. The watering of this "root" is Soham Sadhana. This is a plain and simple fact and applies only to Soham Sadhana, which culminates in the revelation of Soham as our absolute reality. When Soham Sadhana becomes the sole focus and inner activity of the awakening yogi his ultimate realization becomes possible. Soham Sadhana is not one of many: it is the one and only factor of awakening/realization.

Soham Sadhana takes place in the Sahasrara from the first moment and continues there until Self-realization is revealed in the sadhaka's consciousness. Please see *Soham Yoga: The Yoga of the Self* to understand how to apply and realize this for yourself. What I say is not narrow-mindedness or sectarian bigotry any more than the statement that one and one make two is narrow or bigoted. It took me sixty years to discover Soham Sadhana, and I hope my words save you from such a waste of time. Just try it. And be sure you are doing it right. Nothing more is needed.

> **There are occasions when you say your brain is tired. When does this happen? When you are very busy with outer things. But as soon as you return home and talk to your loved ones, your head feels light and you are full of joy. For this reason it is said, because your brain belongs to yourself, your own action [swakriya, swakarma, swadharma] does not produce weariness.**

Therefore rest and refreshment are produced by continual sadhana–not as a labor or straining but as a calm relaxation into the consciousness that is your Self: "open vision direct and instant" (Bhagavad Gita 9:1).

> **Really speaking, all action is your action–only how can you understand this?**

Only by the highest action: *ceasing to act* in "open vision direct and instant" that is the very nature of the Self.

Indeed the whole world is yours, of your Self, your very own–but you perceive it as separate, just as you see "others."

To know it to be your own gives happiness, but the notion that it is apart from you causes misery.

The duality of ignorance is the source of unhappiness and delusion, but the experience of the true Unity that is our individual Self and the Supreme Self ends all duality and therefore ends all ignorance, unhappiness and delusion. The principle is simple and so is the means to that ending: Soham Sadhana. For it does not bring the unity about, but reveals the unity that is the truth of our very being, and always has been.

To perceive duality means pain, conflict, struggle and death. Pitaji [Father], do take to some kind of sadhana!

For the only ending to pain, conflict, struggle and death is the permanent experience of ever-present unity that is Self-realization itself. And this only comes about through diligent sadhana.

Always bear this in mind: Everything is in God's hands, and you are His tool to be used by Him as He pleases.

In a sense we do nothing: all is done by the divine power, Mahashakti. Yet, since it is an act of intentional will, our aspiration and sadhana enable that Shakti to act and bring the Eternal Destiny into realization through experience. At the same time nothing really happens: it is the revelation-realization of that which is even now ever-present. In a sense it is not a journey at all, but as Buddha said: "Turn around and behold! The Other Shore."

Try to grasp the significance of "all is His," and you will immediately feel free from all burdens.

Before commenting this I want to point out that authentic spiritual life is the embodiment of sattwa guna. Those lacking sattwa cannot possibly even intellectually understand the principles of spiritual life, and the meaning of Ma's words are open only to those in whom sattwa guna is predominating. And sadhana is the only way that sattwa arises in anyone.

As Ma is saying here, once we understand with a sattwic intellect the reality that everything is His and is He–Infinite Consciousness–then we are freed of all illusory conditions and obligations. But only the sadhaka can experience that revelation, for his consciousness alone is purified and prepared for such realization.

> **What will be the result of your surrender to Him? None will seem alien, all will be your very own, your Self.**

What do we surrender? Our illusion, our very insistence, that we are in any way separate from Him. For our egos are actively working to maintain the illusion of separation so we can continue in the pathetic condition that is only a creation of our minds. As the figure in a newspaper comic said many years ago: "We have met the enemy and he is us!"

> **Either melt [dissolve?] by devotion the sense of separateness, or burn it by knowledge–for what is it that melts or burns? Only that which by its nature can be melted or burnt; namely the idea that something other than your Self exists. What will happen then? You come to know your Self.**

The sense of separateness is an illusion, a mirage, produced by our minds through our own efforts. This is the Satan within that is only a lie told by us to ourselves. It is as Yogananda said: "People are so skillful in their ignorance."

Ma indicates that bhakti and jnana equally have the power to dispel illusion. But if it were not the very nature of illusion to be dispelled nothing could do so. Therefore, when illusion ripens by the passing of time, it dissolves itself. This is the nature of both the deluded and the deluding: they are one and rooted in Reality. Maya is just the Real sporting with Itself. Delusion is a play, sadhana is a play, and realization is the ending of the play. All along it has been the play of The Real pretending that Maya is real. But the nature of the drama is only revealed when the play is ended and the jiva-spectators leave the theater of samsara and go home to Absolute Being–Where they have been all along. Do not try to understand this condition: Become it.

Since all names are His Name, all forms His Form, select one of them and keep it with you as your constant companion.

Of course Ma is referring to the many Divine Names and Divine Forms that the Absolute has assumed within the play of samsara so we can engage in the play of sadhana and end it in Self-realization. By the Real we turn from the unreal and enter into the Real. "Therefore, become a yogi" (Bhagavad Gita 6:46).

At the same time He is also nameless and formless; for the Supreme it is possible to be everything and yet nothing.

Since God is everything, He is also nothing: No Thing. Why does Ma tell us this? Because She is urging us to sadhana by which we can pass beyond name into the Nameless and beyond form into the Formless. And the Nameless and Formless, being one, is our own Self. So we are ourselves everything and no thing, named and unnameable. Everything we can say about the Absolute can be said of ourselves as waves in the ocean of Reality. Decades ago before I met Her, I wrote some praises to Ma in English. One phrase was: "Thou art all and Thou are nothing. To Thy mystery we bow!" And that is the mystery of ourselves.

Adhere to the name or form of Him that appeals to you most, and ceaselessly pray that He may reveal Himself to you as the Sadguru.

That name and form which evokes the strongest inner response or affinity from us when ceaselessly invoked and meditated upon will reveal itself as our own Self, the sole Sadguru. For only truth can lead to Truth. And if as our sadhana progresses we find that another form and name begins to exercise that interest and appeal, we should not hesitate to adopt that, for all names and forms are of The One. Some yogis in their sadhana are tying up loose ends of the sadhanas they had practiced in previous lives. So such change is beneficial to them. The yogi must always employ insight and intuition in his sadhana.

The last statement, "ceaselessly pray that He may reveal Himself to you as the Sadguru" indicates that though we might have many gurus–upa gurus, adjunct gurus–finally the sole, the Absolute Guru, is revealed in and as our own Self.

In very truth the guru dwells within, and unless you discover the inner guru, nothing can be achieved.

The Self is the inner guru, and only when that inner consciousness is awakened can any true or lasting realization be attained.

If you feel no desire to turn to God, bind yourself by a daily routine of sadhana, as school children do, whose duty it is to follow a fixed timetable.

Deluded people sometimes protest that since they do not want to meditate or engage in spiritual disciplines, then to do so will be hypocrisy and will not get them anywhere. But that is not the way to view it. Ma does not say to wait until we get some inner call or desire to take up sadhana. Rather we are to take ourselves in hand like foolish children that need to be coerced to go to school and learn.

The worthy parent does not ask the child if he feels he is ready to go to school. He sends or himself takes the child to school. So the worthy sadhaka does not follow his feelings or inclinations, but acts upon his knowledge and insights to direct his feelings and inclinations into the right channels that will result in his learning and thereby becoming able to pass into higher and higher levels until All is known.

And it is essential for the yogi develop a fixed and invariable routine of sadhana.

When prayer does not spontaneously flow from your heart, ask yourself: "Why do I find pleasure in the fleeting things of this world?"

The problem is not in the things of the world, but in the attractions and delusions of samsara in our samsara-addicted minds that are barriers to wisdom and freedom. We must not foolishly say that we are being honest and realistic and therefore to engage in regular, disciplined sadhana would be hypocritical or useless. We must realize that this lack of spontaneous attraction and urge towards spiritual life indicates great danger for us. For inner death is drawing us away from inner life.

We must realize that we prefer the shallow and fleeting things of this world because we allow ourselves (not our Selfs) to be shallow and fleeting. And we must ruthlessly and intently reverse this negative condition by forcing ourselves to engage in sadhana. And I am do not mean the old ploy of the ego where the slacker starts kicking and castigating himself and forcing himself to overdo everything like some sadistic drill sergeant in the army. The intention of that is to burn out and then virtuously say that spiritual discipline is unhealthy and even hypocritical.

I knew a woman who forced herself to spend hours in meditation as punishment for looking at the clock to see how much time had passed. (For every peek at the clock she added thirty more minutes to the meditation time.) When this negatively affected her health she quit mediation and would very proudly announce: "Well, I gave it a chance!"

As Sri Ramakrishna used to say: "Be a devotee, but why a fool?" But some people prefer being a fool if it helps them avoid spiritual discipline and awakening.

If you crave for some outer thing or feel specially attracted to a person, you should pause and say to yourself: "Look out, you are being fascinated by the glamour of this!"

It is a good thing for the spiritual aspirant to talk to himself. That means he is separating his intelligent will from his lower, delusion-loving mind. Realistically, our life is in our hands. We must control and direct it. Therefore we must give our ego a good shaking occasionally and demand: "What are you doing? And why are you doing it?" and extract the truth from our deluded and delusive mind and will. Objectivity is an absolute requisite for the sadhaka to realistically perceive and direct his mind. So we must warn and even lecture ourselves on occasion. As I say, this deliberate objectification can be very good for us as an exercise in spiritual intelligence.

Is there a place where God is not?

How about our own mind?

What Ma is indicating is that there is no place and no situation where God is not present, and therefore no place and no situation where we should not maintain awareness of the divine presence and through that awareness infuse ourselves with the will and wisdom to think, will and act according to our own divine nature. For that is the only useful aspect of the divine presence that will aid us in becoming established in increasingly higher levels of consciousness until we become ourselves the very presence of God. This is the practical application of the upanishadic dictum: Tat Twam Asi–Thou Art That. Be That.

It is because Ma has such faith in us that She urges us to the realization and personal embodiment of The Highest.

Family life, which is the ashrama [stage of life] of the householder, can also take you in His direction, provided it is accepted as an ashrama. Lived in this spirit, it helps man to progress towards Self- realization.

For centuries spiritual slackers in India–and now outside India, too–have liked to plea that being a grihastha, a "householder," prevents them from following dharma with exactitude and having the requisite attitude of indifference to materiality and the discipline that is supposedly very easy for the yogi and the sannyasi. But that is cowardice and hypocrisy.

Every ashrama leads to higher life and consciousness when it is lived and maintained in the fulness of its aims and observances. That is what Ma means by accepting a mode of life as an ashrama–which includes scrupulous observance of the disciplines and obligations of that ashrama. No ashrama is a life of laxity and indulgence. Observance–which necessarily includes self-discipline–is the essence of each ashrama.

In the true observance of Sanatana Dharma, the grihastha ashram is only undertaken after years in the brahmacharya ashram. So discipline will have become a second nature, a basic personality trait, before the grihastha ashram is even entered. But the grihastha ashrama is used by the unworthy as an excuse for being unworthy. Not so!

Every element of Sanatana Dharma bears within itself the power of spiritual awakening, spiritual development and spiritual increase. All genuine Sanatana Dharmis are continually moving forward and upward in spiritual development and consciousness. They literally are gods upon the earth. And I write this because I have known and lived with them and shared in their life. And every one of them was living the life of their proper ashrama in scrupulous observance. Sanatana Dharma is the not just the path–it is the Highway To The Infinite because it is the presence of the Infinite.

Nevertheless, if you hanker after anything such as name, fame or position, God will bestow it on you, but you will not feel satisfied.

When I was young I heard someone say: "You can have anything you want. So be careful about what you want!" I never forgot that, for it is a fundamental fact of life.

We are all gods. Therefore we have the will power of gods. So eventually we will all have whatever we want–even it if takes a future life for some desires to be fulfilled. So desire is a net, a snare, in which we entangle ourselves. And though the desires are fulfilled our inner being, our hearts, will not be fulfilled. They will be prisoners of desire. But we who desire freedom must make the right choice and choose desirelessness–which entails renunciation–instead.

The Kingdom of God is a whole, and unless you are admitted to the whole of it you cannot remain content.

In genuine spiritual life, which is the fulness of truth, the entire mode of life must be embraced and assimilated until we are the embodiments of that Kingdom–ourselves kingdoms of God. Now this means that all virtue must become ours personally, all knowledge must be obtained personally, all laws must be observed personally, all enlightenment and liberation (moksha) must be attained personally. Since unity is our fundamental character, without the whole we have nothing. To possess the all-embracing inner, divine realm and kingdom we must have–and be ourselves–all-embracing, inner-centered, divine and a kingdom of God. This is a very high ideal, but we are that by nature. So we only need to uncover and reveal it. But that revelation must be complete–one hundred percent. Not a mote, not a mite can be lacking. Otherwise we cannot be content and fulfilled–ourselves complete.

He grants you just a little, only to keep your discontent alive, for without discontent there can be no progress.

Every relative desire ultimately become a disappointment, both in gaining, failing or losing its fulfillment. There is such a thing as "divine discontent" which takes the form of being dissatisfied with our present situation or dissatisfied with what we have obtained in hope of satisfaction and found it does not fulfill our hope. Just as a bit of grit in the oyster's shell irritates it and causes it to emit the fluid that will solidify into a pearl, so wise, spiritual discontent can keep leading us ever onward in a chain of fulfillments unto the Ultimate Fulfillment which results in the Ultimate Satisfaction: Knowledge and Experience of the Self.

Consider the incredible attention and caring that this implies on the part of the Infinite Reality, the Ultimate Self.

You, a scion of the Immortal, can never become reconciled to the realm of death, neither does God allow you to remain in it.

More divine–and divinizing–discontent! It is ultimately a matter of our own essential nature which is rooted in the Divine and therefore is itself divine.

He Himself kindles the sense of want in you by granting you a small thing, only to whet your appetite for a greater one. This is His method by which He urges you on.

Skill in anything begins with us doing it just a little bit, perhaps no more than a touch. But a chain of increasingly stronger actions and experiences both urges and keeps us moving onward toward encompassing–and discovering ourselves as–Infinity Itself.

The traveller on this path finds it difficult and feels troubled, but one who has eyes to see can clearly perceive that the pilgrim is advancing.

Ma is revealing the severest difficulties and puzzles confronting the sadhaka: 1) Not advancing on the path to enlightenment. 2) Advancing on the path, but not perceiving it. Of course it is even worse to have the third possible outlook: considering he is advancing when he is not. Having "eyes to see" an aspirant is advancing is the fundamental necessity for him and his associates.

All progress of any kind necessitates a progression of endeavors and successes. But it is Eyes To See and the resulting Seeing that are absolute necessities. Sadhana alone opens the inner eyes and the faculty of inner sight. Seeing True is the assured result and brings self-knowledge and peace.

The distress that is experienced burns to ashes all pleasure derived from worldly things. This is what is called "tapasya."

That distress is the experience of discomfort and pain that inevitably accompanies "all pleasure derived from worldly things" when their true nature as pain-bearers becomes revealed by personal experience or observation or by their dissolving away and leaving only pain and emptiness behind. Also distressful is the disillusionment that arises from such experience or observance of its presence in others that pursue pleasure derived from earthly (material) things.

> **What obstructs one on the spiritual path bears within itself seeds of future suffering. Yet the heartache, the anguish over the effects of these obstructions, are the beginning of an awakening to Consciousness.**

What obstructs one on the spiritual path bears within itself seeds of future suffering. These obstructions are almost always mistakenly seen as benefits and pleasures easily grasped by turning from the spiritual path or adopting a false and delusive seemingly spiritual path. Suffering is the sole and inevitable–and usually long-lasting–result.

The Bhagavad Gita describes it this way: "Senses also have joy in their marriage with things of the senses, sweet at first but at last how bitter: steeped in rajas, that pleasure is poison" (Bhagavad Gita 18:38), bearing that inevitable, future suffering. But such pain eventually awakens and educates the individual and causes him to turn from the pain-bearing.

Yet the heartache, the anguish over the effects of these obstructions, are the beginning of an awakening to Consciousness. For it produces a turning from the source of pain to the awaking of consciousness that leads to the joy of the Self. The Gita expresses it this way: "Who knows the Atman knows that happiness born of pure knowledge: the joy of sattwa. Deep his delight after strict self-schooling: sour toil at first but at last what sweetness, the end of sorrow" (Bhagavad Gita 18:37).

FIVE

Solan, September 21, 1948.

A young girl was talking to Sri Ma. She said:

"When I sit down to meditate I do not intend to contemplate any form, but how is it possible to meditate on the formless? I have noticed that at times, when I try to meditate, images of deities come floating before my mind."

Sri Ma replied:

> **Whatever image arises in your mind, that you should contemplate; just observe in what shape God will manifest Himself to you.**

Spontaneity is an absolute necessity here. If no image arises of itself without any attempt to produce one, then absence of any image should be contemplated.

But now Ma begins speaking of the voluntary, intentional rising or creation of a divine form by the meditator, and gives advice on that.

> **The same form does not suit every person. For some, Rama may be most helpful, for some Shiva, for others Parvati, and again for others the formless.**

This implies that what arises spontaneously, or is willed by the sadhaka, should be meditated on.

The formless is considered by some, especially the advaitans, to be the best object of meditation. But Ma wants the sadhaka to be sure that formless meditation is spontaneous on her part and not deliberately produced. So She continues:

> **He certainly is formless; but at the same time, watch in what particular form He may appear to you in order to show you the way.**

Peaceful, alert and persistent attention should bring about the needful: either meditation on the divine formless or on a divine form.

> **Consequently, whichever of His forms comes into your mind, that you should contemplate in all its minute details.**

That which arises of itself is the correct way to proceed. Therefore:

> **Proceed as follows: When sitting down to meditate, first of all contemplate the form of a deity. Then imagining Him to be enthroned on His seat, bow down before Him and do japa.**

Now it is not clear if these instructions presuppose the preceding as to whether there should be spontaneous or deliberate meditation on a divine form. But since Ma says, "When sitting down to meditate, first of all contemplate the form of a deity," it seems clear that in this instance She is instructing the sadhaka to deliberately bring a divine form to mind through visualization. And maintaining that visualization throughout, the sadhaka should mentally do continuous japa of the deity's mantra.

> **When you have concluded the japa, bow down once more and, having enshrined Him in your heart, leave your seat.**

Of course, the japa should be mentally continued throughout the rest of the sadhaka's day. Ma was very insistent on what She termed "maintaining the flow" of the mantra always.

> **This, in short, may be your practice if you are not able to meditate on the [formless] Brahman.**

To those who wished to meditate on Brahman without form, Ma gave explicit instructions. But rarely did She recommend doing either form or formless meditation at personal preference. Usually one or the other should be the usual manner of meditation. And of course Ma would tell the sadhaka which should be done–including alternating both forms as they desired if that applied to them. I know that Ma did tell some to meditate only on the mental sound of the mantra and not bother with the form. It was a mistake to say: "Ma *always* says." Those with experience would say, "Ma *usually* says."

> **Be ever convinced that at all times and without exception He will do and is doing what is best for you.**

A Roman Catholic priest wrote a short booklet called, *Think Well Of God*. In it he discussed the fact that some people (for some reason) held opinions and attitudes about God that implied He was not always either good or nice. But that was their mistake. And he tried to correct it.

> **Reflect thus: In order to aid me, He has revealed Himself to me in this particular guise.**

Holding this ever in mind, the sadhaka looks upon each of his encounters with others as a meeting with God. This evokes the divine nature in both the meeter and the met.

> **He is with form as well as without [form]; the entire universe is within Him and pervaded by Him. This is why it is said: "The Sadguru is the World-teacher and the World-teacher the Sadguru."**

But what is meant by "Sadguru"?

It was a mistake to think we always understood Ma completely, because Her words proceeded not from a mind–for Ma said that She did not have a mind–but apparently directly from Infinity. And we could not always be sure we understood everything Infinity was saying to us. I often recall the words of Swami Akhandananda about Sri Ramakrishna to some people: "You may try to understand him if you wish. But we lived with him and never tried to understand him." To live with Ma! That was the necessary thing. She was with us, but were we with Her?

> **The aforesaid is especially meant for you. The same does not apply to every person.**

This is very important also. Just as there were those who were guardians of orthodoxy about Ma, who knew what She always said and did, there were those who wanted to make everything She told one person applicable to everyone. But here we see this was not so. More than once Ma said virtually the same words to me, and I am sure She said the same to many others.

> **The more you contemplate Him, the more rapid will be your progress.**

This is so brief it is easy to almost ignore or forget. But it should be mentally engraved in every sadhaka's mind. It is so (literally) divinely simple and so absolutely crucial to never forget.

> **If any image arises in your mind, it is He, just as He is also the formless; mark what comes spontaneously.**

This, too, has immeasurable value. However, this cannot be applied to all, because some people's minds are so chaotic they never stop claiming a chain of divine and profound experiences. Actually, I think this is part of advice regarding japa and what may arise in the mind while doing japa. The person to whom these words were addressed obviously was an adept, perhaps even a siddha. We must be cautious in applying to ourselves Ma's words to others.

SIX

Benares. August 18, 1948.

When meditation (dhyana) occurs spontaneously, then only is it real meditation. It must come of itself, effortlessly.

Ma is not telling us to only meditate when suddenly the urge overwhelms us! She means that meditation practice must become a regular part of our daily life, and in time if we faithfully and regularly meditate we will find that on occasion meditation will spontaneously occur–we will effortlessly pass into the meditative state and remain there for a significant amount of time. Not that the only time we should meditate is only when it "just happens."

I am making a point of this because I have known spiritual slackers that would aggressively quote Ma completely out of context to justify their lack of practice and discipline. And this statement about spontaneous meditation would have been their delight. I knew a woman of that type who would quote Ma as supposedly having said: "When have I ever told you to do anything?" But she never showed the source to anyone. I knew another person who would ask: "If I don't feel like meditating, what good will it do?" Regarding people like this who worship their own spiritual whimsy, the prophet Hosea said: "Ephraim is joined to idols: let him alone" (Hosea 4:17). We should do the same. God does.

Furthermore, when you say the mind subsides (laya), from where does it originate?

First we will have to decide what the mind actually is. And what either arising or subsiding of the mind means. What Ma wants us to realize is that our talk about something does not necessarily make it true or real. People love to spin spiritual fantasies, feel inspired, virtuous and self-aware. But it is all talk, and cheap talk at that.

> **You say you cannot grasp the all-pervasiveness of the mind. Quite naturally so, because it is not a thing to be grasped it is neither a thing, nor can it be grasped.**

Here is a situation in which we are greatly hindered by not knowing the word Ma is using that is translated "mind." Two words might be used in this context: manas and buddhi. Manas is the sensory mind, the perceiving mind. Buddhi is the intellect, the reasoning, analyzing mind. The manas sees something, and that is the end of it. But the buddhi knows what is being seen and thereby enables the person to respond according to its understanding.

> **You experience the pleasures and pains of the world; again, you enjoy temporary happiness or bliss while in meditation. This also is an experience, is it not? Yet it is of a slightly different nature from the former.**

But the experiences have this in common: they began and they ended. So where is their value in the final analysis? At first there was nothing and now there is the same nothing.

People used to come and relate to Sri Ramana Maharshi their visions of deities. To each one Sri Ramana made the same response: "Did they eventually go away?" To those who of course replied Yes, he would ask: "When are you going to forget about gods that only come and go?" For the only thing that never comes or goes is the ever-abiding, ever-existent Self.

> **When a man says that he describes or refers to an experience after he comes down from the heights of divine ecstasy (samadhi), it implies that ascent and descent still continue to exist for him, otherwise why should he use these expressions? But there is also a state where ascending and descending are out of the question.**

The "state where ascending and descending are out of the question" alone is real, for that is not just a description of the Self, it is the very state of being that *is* the Self: Reality Itself.

> **You may maintain that the mind should be held as existing in samadhi, although in an absorbed state; otherwise how can a person, on issuing from samadhi, speak of the experience he had in that state? You may further maintain that his mind is a purified mind.**

And then what do you have and where are you?

> **I am speaking from your standpoint. Experiences occur on the path. Between the two types of experience that have just been mentioned, there is a difference. Nevertheless, they are both of the mind, though on different levels, even what you call samadhi.**

The Self is described as *bhavatitam, trigunarahitam*: beyond all bhavas or states of mind, and beyond the three gunas which manifest as states of the mind, or "color" the mind. It is essential to understand this–not through the mind but by getting beyond the mind in direct, immediate experience.

The crux is to know the Seer as the Sole Reality and recognize the seen as essentially unreal in that context. But at all times we must remain aware that the True, the Real, is beyond all concepts and words, so what can we say about It? Nothing. That is why a sage is called a muni–a silent one. As the upanishadic dictum says: "He who knows tells it not. He who tells knows it not." The only "definition" we can give of Reality is: *Neti Neti*–Not This. Not That. Yet the upanishadic sages have told the aspirant: *Tat Twam Asi*: You Are That.

> **However, there is also another state of being where one cannot speak of ascent and descent, and consequently not of a body either. Should the question of the body or of action, or**

any question whatever, still arise, it means that this state has not been reached.

Actually, that is both simple and clear. Now we must attain it by becoming adept yogis.

Where destruction is destroyed, there is THAT. Do you call the annihilation of the ego-mind (*manonasa*) its dissolution (*laya*)?

If you shoot at a ghost can you kill it? So if the ego-mind is an illusion, so is its destruction. It is like trying to silence an echo by shouting.

It is not a matter of Doing or Becoming anything. It is a matter of BEING. Only the yogi can begin to comprehend this.

It is for you to keep on practicing [sadhana] faithfully. But the fruit comes spontaneously in the form of Self-revelation.

Sadhana makes possible the Self-revelation that is simply experiencing the ever-present, eternal nature of the Self. Nothing happens, but Something is revealed.

The power to make you grasp the Ungraspable duly manifests itself through the guru.

But what/who is the guru? Since the sages tell us nothing exists but Brahman, it is The Reality alone that in time begins to interact with/upon sentient beings that is the guru. And yet the guru is just a channel. For what? For the revelation of our own Self. Both guru-Brahman and disciple-Self are eternal and inseparable. And unchanging.

Where the question: "How am I to proceed?" arises, fulfillment has obviously not yet been reached.

So long as there is a question, no answer is possible. But what is needed is found in the words of a Sanskrit hymn: "How amazing! The guru remains silent but the disciples' questions are all answered." Only in Silence does Knowledge arise.

My friend Swami Bhumananda told me that his best friend had once accumulated a store of "crucial" questions that he felt only the master-yogi and philosopher Sri Aurobindo Ghosh could answer. Once a year at the ashram in Pondicherry there was Darshan Day on which Sri Aurobindo could be seen. So his friend went there armed with his queries. There was a large auditorium at the front of which was a curtained platform. The doors were closed and locked. Then the curtains opened to reveal Sri Aurobindo simply sitting there. Beginning at the first row, he began looking into the eyes of each person. There was total silence. When Sri Aurobindo's eyes met his, every one of that man's questions were instantly answered! After some time the curtains closed and everyone left.

The Bhagavad Gita (9:1) speaks of "that innermost secret: knowledge of God which is nearer than knowing, open vision direct and instant."

> **Therefore, never relax your efforts until there is Enlightenment.**

The Absolute Itself is described as Akhanda: indivisible; whole; complete; unending; always one. Therefore to reach It one must become equally as whole and endlessly one.

> **Let no gaps interrupt your attempt, for a gap will produce an eddy, whereas your striving must be continuous like the flowing of oil, it must be sustained, constant, an unbroken stream.**

Relative existence is a field of ever-changing shakti. Continuity is the secret of unity and cohesion. Oneness becomes automatic because unity is the nature of the One.

The flowing of oil has some interesting and instructive aspects:

It does not appear to be moving.
It appears as a single entity.
It is silent.

These are the qualities of the Self, therefore reproducing them in ourselves is the beginning of–or the door to–the revelation of the unmoving/unchanging, unitary and essentially silent Self. Authentic sadhana has all these qualities inherent in it, therefore it directly and naturally reveals the Self. Conformity to and establishment in these qualities is the direct way to success in sadhana.

That you have no control over the body's need of food and sleep does not matter.

Spiritual slackers like to make excuses for their neglect of sadhana or of success in sadhana. Naturally, the body comes in for blame, its supposed demands, weaknesses, failings and "needs." I use the word "supposed" because the effects and defects of the body are often created or fostered and increased by these lazy hypocrites. Even faked or exaggerated illnesses are used by them as excuses to do little or no sadhana. These are also the people that like to present "prior commitments" as the reason for justifiably being what they are: spiritual nonenties. They are like Cousin Minnie Pearl's Uncle Nabob: they started at the bottom and decided they liked it there. (If this means nothing to you, look up Cousin Minnie Pearl on youtube.)

Your aim should be not to allow any interval in the performance of your sadhana.

This entails a great number of factors. Briefly stated, every aspect of the sadhaka's inner and outer life affects his sadhana in various ways. But just moving ahead and not allowing ourselves to be hindered or distracted or even momentarily slowed or paused in our sadhana is absolutely necessary. Even a slowing down of previously established momentum can be significantly harmful. Just writing this sentence there popped into my mind a line from a Strauss operetta, *The Gypsy Baron*. One of the characters sings:

"So we plunged pell-mell through the shot and shell" and were victorious. The sadhaka has no time for gentility and diplomacy in dealing with his inner delusions, illusions and deterrents. He applies his will and the power of sadhana to win the day. And there is no time for a ceasefire or a palaver with the enemy. As George C. Scott says in *Patton*, victory is not won by dying for your country, but by making the opponent die for his country. There is no such thing as partial Self-realization. It is either total or not at all. Therefore the yogi cannot allow any dead spot in his sadhana practice. Steady, unbroken persistence is itself virtually a guarantee of ultimate success.

Just as the path to hell is paved with good intentions, so the path to failure in spiritual life is paved with noble resolves to sometime in the future "really get busy and knuckle down and apply myself." I have never seen even one person who talked like that come anywhere near succeeding in sadhana. They were self-doomed from the very beginning. The wise yogi is thoroughly self-motivated, self-supported, self-empowered and self-reliant. There is no team work, only unbroken self-application. Satsang, association with like-minded sadhakas, is very encouraging and beneficial, but you had better make sure that others truly are like-minded and not just dreamers and talkers. It is true: talk does not cook the rice.

It really is a matter of Do Or Die. And the Doing has to be Right Now and Always.

The sadhaka cannot allow anything or anyone whatsoever to delay or diminish his sadhana. Oftentimes the only one a sadhaka can really trust is himself.

> **Do you not see that whatever you require in the way of food and sleep, each at its own appointed hour, is without exception an ever-recurring need? In exactly the same manner must you aspire at uninterruptedness where the search after Truth is concerned.**

We rarely decide to not eat or sleep according to our usual routine. In just the same way we should not even consider omitting any sadhana practice or time for sadhana. Nor can delay be considered.

There is a most interesting passage in *The Gospel of Sri Ramakrishna.* Someone once described to Sri Ramakrishna the following dream:

"I saw the whole world enveloped in water. There was water on all sides. A few boats were visible, but suddenly huge waves appeared and sank them. I was about to board a ship with a few others, when we saw a brahmin walking over that expanse of water. I asked him, 'How can you walk over the deep?' The brahmin said with a smile: 'Oh, there is no difficulty about that. There is a bridge under the water.' I said to him, 'Where are you going?' 'To Bhawanipur, the city of the Divine Mother,' he replied. 'Wait a little,' I cried. 'I shall accompany you.' The brahmin said: 'I am in a hurry. It will take you some time to get out of the boat. Good-bye. Remember this path and come after me.'"

This is a most valuable symbol of spiritual life and its principles. First, we must find the path beneath the appearance of this chaotic world. Second we must immediately and rapidly journey over it and never look back or even delay in traveling that path.

A nun, Sister Maddaleva, wrote:

Know you the journey that I take?
Know you the voyage that I make?
The joy of it–one's heart could break.
No jot of time have I to spare,

Nor will to loiter anywhere,
So eager am I to be there
For that the way is hard and long,
For that gray fears upon it throng,

I set my journey to the song.
And it grows wondrous happy so
Singing I hurry on for–oh!
It is to God, to God I go.

Once the mind, in the course of its movement, has felt the touch of the Indivisible–if only you can grasp that moment!–in that Supreme Moment all moments are contained, and when you have captured it, all moments will be yours.

The mind–the combination of the manas, the sensory-oriented perceiving mind, and the buddhi, the discriminating and self-illumining intellect–is ever-moving. When it is engaged in the process of sadhana, which itself is necessarily a matter of movement, it is possible for it to enter into that state which Ma calls "the touch of the Indivisible." But for this to happen, it must become indivisible itself in the Unity that *is* the Indivisible. And that moment must be grasped and become continuous through sadhana. Since all moments are contained in that Unity, past, present and future become fully present and comprehended by the adept sadhaka in his meditation. Nothing is left out to be further attained and known. Ma has wondrously encapsulated what no one else could have brought into the compass of our understanding. Ma was unique at every moment since She was beyond all "moments."

We must realize that there is The Moment which being Eternity is always right at hand. Why do we not reach out and grasp it? Because we do not perceive just where it is. Its existence we may believe, but believing is not seeing, to reverse the adage. And besides that, it is not outside us to grasp. It is in the depths of our being which we Are. So it is within us and *is* us. How can this become known except through meditation?

In Her early life Ma went through a sadhana phase. Why? Because that which She not only embodied, but which She WAS, could not be manifested or perceived outside the context of sadhana. And that perception was Self-Realization itself which She was revealing to the world as much as was possible

One time in the Delhi ashram Ma began singing a divinely exquisite melody over and over again. It was captivating, and all who heard it wanted to sing it with Ma. But no one could! They found themselves incapable of grasping it in their minds. Brahmachari Vibhu, a renowned singer, was called to do the needful. But he could not, because at the mere hearing of it he entered into an inward ecstatic state. Ma simply said: "No one can do what a child can do." When Ma referred to herself as "this little girl" She was not being humble or cute. She was the Divine Kumari [Virgin], the Universal Being, the Indivisible Itself.

> **Take, for example, the moments of confluence (sandhiksana) at dawn, midday and dusk, in which the power inherent in the contact-point, where coming and going meet, becomes revealed. What you call "electric discharge" is nothing but the union of two opposites; thus does the Supreme Being flash forth at the moment of conjunction. Actually IT is present at every single moment, but you miss it all the time. Yet this is what you have to seize; it can be done at the point of juncture where the opposites fuse into one.**

The moments of dawn, noon and dusk (sunset) are called sandhyas (joinings, junctures) because they are the points in which the previous state and the arising-arriving state touch each other and in that way are joined to or merged into one another. For just a brief period neither state is "present" in a kind of neutral passing from one to the other. Such times are considered ideal for practices which in the consciousness of the sadhaka and his surroundings are in a state between a state–a kind of neutral moment in which both the preceding and the succeeding are present and absent: perfect neutrality. Such a moment is considered ideal for practices which lift the sadhaka's mind beyond the ordinary and puts it into a higher condition–or is the natural prelude to a higher condition of both vibration and consciousness. It is the ideal moment in which the sadhaka can produce a balanced and rarified state of mind which is still yet filled with dynamic potential. Obviously this is not a material phase, but a profoundly subtle phase of consciousness-awareness in which the inmost being of the sadhaka can be revealed and "polarized" to a higher condition and function. That is the best I can do to explain it. Experience is still the best teacher for the sadhaka.

At the time of the sandhyas the sadhaka usually recites the Savitri Gayatri Mantra which invokes the principle of enlightenment within the individual doing the recitation. This is a potentially vast subject, so I refer you to a marvelous source of knowledge: Wikipedia. Look up the words/articles: Gayatri and Sandhyavandanam. That should be sufficient.

> **Nobody is able to predict when for any particular individual this fateful Moment will reveal itself; therefore keep on striving ceaselessly.**

Ceaseless sadhana is the needed impulse toward Realization.

> **Which exactly is that great Moment depends for each one upon his particular line of approach. Does not the moment at which you are born determine and rule the course of your whole life? Similarly, what is important for you is the Moment at which you will enter the current that is the movement of your true being, the Going Forth, in other words, the Great Pilgrimage. Unless this happens, perfection cannot be attained.**

This is so perfect and so awesome I am simply not able to add anything to it in comment.

Now Ma is going to give teaching regarding the sadhana of those who have adopted or accepted an adept sadhaka as their guru. It is also possible to follow the written teachings of enlightened masters, considering them as gurus leading to encounter with the ultimate guru: God.

> **This is why, for some disciples, the guru fixes special times for sadhana, such as dawn, dusk, midday, and midnight; these are the four periods usually prescribed.**

No comment needed.

> **It is the duty of the disciple to carry out conscientiously the guru's orders, which vary according to the temperament and predisposition of the aspirant.**

This is why sadhana must necessarily be based on the individual sadhaka's inner and outer makeup. It is also necessary to realize that God is the ultimate guru, and by aligning our consciousness with God through sadhana we become a true disciple.

The same method does not suit everyone.

It is incredibly necessary to understand and observe this principle.

Foolish people either try to copy others' sadhana or impose their personal sadhana on others. This only leads to confusion and failure.

Intuition and practical intelligence are essential for the sadhaka whether in the beginning, middle or final stage of his sadhana.

Ultimately each sadhaka's intelligence and intuition must become his guru, though listening to or consulting those with experience in sadhana is not amiss.

> **The average person can have no knowledge of the particular combination of factors that are necessary to bring to completion the hitherto neglected facets of his being; for this reason it is essential to obey the guru's instructions. The decisive Moment is bound to manifest as soon as by your attitude of mind, as well as by your actions, you are ready for it. Therefore try to follow closely the path indicated by the guru, and you will see how everything just happens spontaneously.**

The teachings of Self-realized teachers can become the guru of an aspirant without personal instruction from those teachers. So also can a sacred text such as the Bhagavad Gita or the Upanishads.

> **Within the twenty-four hours of the day, some time must be definitely dedicated to God. Resolve, if possible, to engage regularly in japa of a particular Name or mantra while sitting in a special posture, and gradually add to the time or the number of repetitions. There is no need for a daily augmentation. Fix the**

> **rate and the interval at which you will increase, say fortnightly or weekly. In this way try to bind yourself to the Quest of God; wherever you may be, take refuge in Him, let Him be your Goal.**

Ma is giving very necessary and beneficial instruction to those who consider God or their own Self to be their guru.

Of course it must be understood that those who choose to follow Ma's instructions certainly become Her disciples according to their own volition.

> **When by virtue of this endeavor you become deeply immersed in that current and devote ever more time to it, you will be transformed and your appetite for sense enjoyment will grow feeble; thus you will reap the fruit of your accumulated efforts. You may also come to feel that the body is liable to depart at any time, that death may arrive at any moment.**

This, too, is very applicable to those who consider God as their guru.

Awareness of the fragility and instability of the sadhaka's body can be very beneficial if it enables him to realize that he must be at every moment striving toward enlightenment and its consequent freedom.

> **Just as there is ever-new creation in the universe, so also does your mental and psychological reaction to it undergo constant change. If you proceed in the manner indicated, you will observe that as a result your outer interests will gradually fall away and your vision turn inward.**

Constant involuntary change is a fundamental trait of the world and of all the sentient beings in the world. There is constant alternation of dissolution of life and form and arising of new life and new form. Death and birth are fundamental conditions, the very nature, of relative existence. Those who aspire to freedom from constant birth and death have only one option: total awakening and functioning of the immortal principle within each sentient being–and therefore within themselves–that is beyond the reach of change and death.

Those who persevere in sadhana will witness that automatically, and therefore inevitably, all that is not of their Self will dissolve and vanish and all that is of their Self will arise and become not only dominant but the sole remaining factor both within and without.

Sadhana is the beginning and the perfecting of true Life.

> **The more ardent your pursuit, the vaster the possibilities that will open out for you, and in proportion to your advance, suffering will diminish and not increase again. It is also said, is it not, that karma is extinguished by karma–that is to say, the effects of past actions are neutralized by counter actions.**

The sadhaka's inner and outer life becomes utterly transformed and glorified by his sadhana. No one can even imagine the wonder that his life and he himself becomes through diligent sadhana. As one Buddhist sage wrote: "I pass through this world and no one knows that Paradise is within."

> **Indeed, if it be anyone's destiny, this may be achieved in a very short time.**

Even in the matter of diligent sadhana, karma is a determining factor, though not the only one.

What is karma? The force created by both external action and internal intention that is also a form of action. Karma is a derivation of *kri*, which means "to act." Karma is the continuation of action in the form of reaction or a furtherance of the original action.

Therefore, sadhana being both internal and external action, it creates a reaction we can call "sadhana karma." This produces the immediate reaction-result from the sadhana karma and determines the quality of the sadhana karma that extends into the future.

There is not an iota of our life that is not the creation-result of our past action, our past karma. The future is the extension or result of karma, therefore karma is a potent creative force in everyone's life. But sadhana karma, being based on our inmost being, is the most potent form of karma and possesses an incalculable power. The sadhaka wields this power through his sadhana and thus creates or recreates his life and may affect the lives of those close to him with which he possesses significant karmic ties. That is why it is said that when a sadhaka attains moksha it affects generations of both his ancestors and his descendants. This is why in India we encounter families of yogis that for a vast number of years have produced adept yogis. Therefore the printed lives of great yogis usually begin with their family history and recount the yoga siddhas in their ancestry. In my pilgrimages to India several times I was very subtly and diplomatically questioned as to my own spiritual antecedents, because if there were no such figures in my past it was not likely that I merited serious consideration. I understood this from the first and was relieved that I had ancestors on my family tree that were renowned and highly regarded for their spiritual character. (I won't relate them here lest you think I would be boasting. And I would be.)

> **Look, even when the body is not given food, it does not stop the assimilation of nourishment; we are told that in such a case it starts consuming its own flesh. Therefore, just as you keep your body well nourished, so must you take equally good care where your spiritual well-being is concerned; then only will you flourish in that respect.**

The body lives on food, the mind lives on wisdom-knowledge, and the Self–for its manifestation and liberation–lives on sadhana and its fruit-effects.

> **Who can tell at what moment the flame of illumination will blaze forth? For this reason, continue your efforts steadily without flagging.**

Ma frequently spoke of the Great Moment in which, as a result of our sadhana, liberation can be grasped, and the necessity for us to continually be watching for its advent and be both able and prepared to take hold of it and enter into its sublime potential.

> **Gradually you will get more and more deeply absorbed in Him–He and He alone will preoccupy your thoughts and feelings. For the mind ever seeks that which gives it proper sustenance, and this cannot be provided by anything save the Supreme Being Himself.**

This is the basic outline-sketch of the unfoldment of the yogi's consciousness through diligent and continuous sadhana.

> **Then you will be carried away by the current that leads to your Self.**

This is why it has been said that the desire for God is the way to God. It is our will directed unceasingly and unstintingly to the attainment of Self-realization that guarantees our success. If our will is not engaged profoundly and unceasingly in our sadhana, nothing can ultimately result. That is why when some spiritual slackers asked Yogananda to bless them, he replied: "You already have God's blessing and my blessing. What is missing is your blessing."

In reality, we ourselves carry ourselves to God by the current-power of our own will. Nothing else succeeds. We need *our* blessing!

> **You will discover that the more you delight in the inner life, the less you feel drawn to external things.**

This is simple cause and effect. The more we approach the light, the further we leave the darkness behind. But notice that Ma speaks of *delighting* in the inner life. We do not engage in sadhana like an ill person taking bitter medicine, but with happiness and even joy. For sadhana is itself the fulfillment of our Self. Therefore we must engage in sadhana with the perspective of the Self uppermost in our mind and aspiration.

This affinity for and attraction to the inner life ensures that we will turn from and abandon the material, ego-bound life, and immerse ourselves in the light and delight of the Self. For the two attractions cannot exist together: they negate each other by their very nature.

> **In consequence the mind becomes so well nourished with the right kind of "food," that at any moment the realization of its identity with the Self may occur.**

This is Ma's guarantee. We can trust it. And act upon it.

> **As regards laya: if you meant the mind's dissolution into THAT, then what you said was correct.**

There is what is called Laya Yoga. In time various misunderstandings and misinterpretations have arisen and distracted aspirants from attainment of this state–which is not mere dissolution of the ego-mind, but a merging of and a transmutation of the mind into the Self which is nothing but pure Consciousness itself.

> **Jada samadhi is not desirable.**

"Jada samadhi" is a satirical expression for the condition in which the meditator passes out in an unconscious state like dreamless sleep and then upon awaking decides that he has experienced real samadhi and experienced the non-duality that is the nature of the Self–when actually he has experienced nothing but unconsciousness and non-Self. In my early yogi days I met a few delusionals who boasted of attaining this state and therefore considered themselves accomplished yogis. It is very kind and diplomatic of Ma to put it in this way. As a satirical song I once heard said: How can you be in two [or all] places at once when you are not anywhere at all?

> **On the contrary, you have to realize what the mind is, who it is.**

And what and who it is not. The mind can be a master deceiver.

I am reminded of a man that offended a whole group of what a friend of mine called "Sunday-evening metaphysicians" when he said: "We all know that twenty minutes after N. [he named a very renowned local metaphysician] leaves the body he will show up at a seance, enter the body of the medium, and say: This is Jesus Christ your Master speaking!"

There are people who love self-deception because it makes them feel so assured, wise and admirable. But the process of attaining the state of Reality necessitates the awareness and insight into what is not real or reality. And the prerequisite is willingness to experience and acknowledge that awareness and insight. For the false, ego-bound mind will fight for its life–a life that true knowing and seeing will utterly negate and dissolve.

This negative predisposition for self-deception is presently revealed in those that are supposedly involved in Vipassana Meditation. They unanimously use the expression "Insight Meditation" as though it was a kind of opening to self-analysis and knowledge of the mind. But Vipassana does not mean Insight–it means Clear Sight. There is a great difference.

The mind subsides into THAT–is this what you intended to express?

Well, whether the person addressed meant to express that or not, the sole truth is: The mind subsides into THAT.

Laya may signify either that the mind has nowhere to go to, in other words, can no longer find its way and hence subsides into latency; or else it merges into THAT, which is Self-revelation, and consequently there can be no possibility of a separate existence of the mind.

The mind then becomes potentially all-pervading.

Where Self-revelation is, how can the question as to whether the mind gets dissolved or not, arise at all?

Since Self-revelation is a revealing of the fullness of the Reality which is the Self, all else is dispelled, including the mind which depends on the Self for its very existence. Consequently such a question as the possible dissolution of the mind cannot arise since there is nothing for it to arise from. And since that which is truly Real always exists, then that which can be dissolved is by that very fact revealed as unreal.

> **This has been replied to from the standpoint from which you asked.**

Therefore Ma's words in reply were a kind of reflection or even a production of the questioner's own mental status or standpoint. And those qualities or limitations affected or perhaps even produced in a roundabout way the very reply Ma gave. Therefore the reply came from the questioner–or at least conditioned it. What Ma said to one person might not at all apply to another. Because of this no conscientious devotee of Ma would ever cite Her words to others with the implication that because Ma said them they personally should be expected to follow or conform to them.

But neither would any true devotee reject or disagree with Ma's words because they did not like, understand or agree with them. I vividly remember a European woman come stalking out of an interview with Ma fuming and sputtering: "Oh! How hard it is to have a guru!" I very much wanted to say to her: "It is especially hard if you think the guru does not know what She is talking about and you don't like what She says!" But I did not.

In just two or three weeks I learned that Ma had told her to immediately go to Bombay to see a specialist in case her cancer returned. She fussed and fumed that there was no need until one of the translators said to her: "Can't you do this simple thing Ma has told you? What harm will it do you?" So she went to Bombay and discovered the cancer had indeed returned! (The denouement is interesting: I alerted her to a drugless therapy that she could obtain free from a brilliant natural therapist I knew. She agreed and in three weeks she was permanently cancer-free.)

At the same time there were those who went into a tailspin if they were told that Ma had said something they did not like or want to accept.

Perhaps because of this there were times when Ma would tell someone that Her words were specifically for them and not for all.

> **You began by enquiring how meditation on a particular part can lead to meditation on the whole. Surely, the whole is contained in the part; it is in order to arrive at the realization of this truth that you have to do so.**
>
> **The aforesaid gives but a faint idea of only one aspect of the whole matter.**

In India there is a common comparison of disciplines being like a thorn by which a thorn embedded in one's body can be removed. Sadhanas that seem partial or limited to the inexperienced or unwilling will in time through their practice reveal a far vaster scope or more profound effect than was at first imagined. Ma on occasion advised a person to do or eat something that would logically have harmed them, but they benefitted from them immensely. Ma told one man to eat what his physician declared would kill him. He ate it and was immediately healed. I have heard of several similar instances. By obeying Ma's directions we came in line or synchronization with Her kheyala, Her spontaneous response. (Kheyala is perhaps impossible to satisfactorily translate or even explain. It means a spontaneous impulse or movement of will. But the bulk of the meaning is that it came from within Ma directly with no thought or will or attitude behind it. Literally it arose from Ma's Being. Therefore it was divine.)

> **Again, look: There are instances when one loses consciousness while sitting in meditation. Some people have found themselves swooning away, as it were, intoxicated with joy, remaining in this condition for quite a long time. On emerging they claim to have experienced some sort of divine bliss. But this is certainly not Realization.**
>
> **A stage does exist in meditation, where intense joy is felt, where one is as if submerged in it. But what is it that gets submerged? The mind of course.**

It is extremely crucial that these words of Ma are understood and made the context in which the sadhaka engages in meditation. The ananda experienced in profound meditation is great and the mind wishes to never leave it. But it is only a symptom of drawing near to the Self. The divine Ananda that *is* the Self is another thing altogether, and those who experience the lesser should not mistake it for the greater. But it can lead to the greater.

> **At a certain level and under certain circumstances this experience may prove an obstacle. If repeated time and again, one may stagnate at its particular level and thereby be prevented from getting a taste of the Essence of Things.**

How do we prevent this? By continuing to intensely and constantly practice sadhana-meditation which by its nature, its inherent momentum, will keep us moving forward-upward-inward (there are many words for it) toward the ultimate goal. This alone will keep us from mistaking the part for the whole or the middle for the end. In the beginning days of the comic strip B.C., there was one episode in which a caveman climbed a high mountain, looked around in all four directions, and then climbed back down, saying: "Well, so much for the whole world!" We must not make that mistake. Since every atom is essentially infinite, it is easy to mistake the part for the whole. Perseverance in sadhana is the only safeguard against making that natural mistake.

> **Once genuine contemplation (dhyana) has been established, worldly attractions lose all their appeal.**

This statement has two indispensable messages.

First is that dhyana must not just occur every so often, but must become established–made a constant, ever-present state, not just of mind, but of essential being: the state of our Self that *is* the Self.

Second is that when we no longer just occasionally experience our Self that is of the nature of ananda, we experience it permanently. As a result, everything else outside us in the world is clearly seen as not our Self and therefore devoid of the ananda that is us. So to go after anything outside our Self–even if we mistake it for the Self–is to leave our true Ananda-Self and so lose its experience. That is why the yogis insist that the sadhaka must become permanently established in–and as–the Self. Nothing less, nothing more. For there is really only The One. And the one essential truth is: Tat Twam Asi: Thou Art That.

Third is that if worldly attractions do not lose all their appeal, then genuine dhyana has not been established.

> **In the event of an experience of anything pertaining to Supreme Reality or to the Self, one does not say: "Where have I been? I did not know anything for the time being." There can be no such thing as "not knowing."**

If there is a time when we seem to go to a higher plane and return to a lower plane or become unconscious and then become conscious, we can know that it is just part of the mirage of relative existence, just experience of the kind of dualities that only exist in the realm of basic illusion. We did NOT really go higher or experience real consciousness. For as Ma declares: There can be no such things as "not knowing" in the state that is itself Absolute Knowing. For that Knowing has no object: only experience of the eternal subject: the Self. Never is there entering or leaving, gaining or losing, knowing or not knowing. That is the essence of duality. That is why the Upanishad says: "He who tells knows it not. He who knows tells it not." It is beyond telling and knowing.

If it is possible to describe in words the bliss one has experienced, it is still enjoyment and therefore a hindrance.

Even saying, "I don't have any words for it" is not evidence of having had an experience of the Real, either. There is a silence that is ignorance and a silence that is knowing. How can we know the difference? More sadhana!

One must be fully conscious, wide awake.

If we think we have awakened, we have not. Only when we experience what we have always been are we awake. And we will not say we are awake because in our true essence we were never asleep. The essence of this sentence is the word BE. It is not "become."

I once read that at first we say: "I am that." Then "that" disappears. Then "I" disappears. Only "Am" remains. But that is just a hint–not even half the picture.

To fall into a stupor or into yogic sleep will not take one anywhere.

But if we do not want to get anywhere: what an opportunity!

After real meditation worldly pleasures become unalluring, dull, entirely savorless.

Naturally we will want to know how we can know the true nature of our experience, our present state of awareness, as sadhakas, is real. So Ma has just told us.

Now there is a pathological, ego-based imitation or illusion for every real, valid state or experience we can enter. So there are neurotics who just "have the blahs" and experience everything as false or unreal. They are always just passive and (to use outdated "hip" parlance) "bummed out." And there are psychotics who are so busy being intent on ego, their not-self, that they become depressed, hopeless, disillusioned, disgusted and repelled and aggressively passive in their response.

Rather than negative, what Ma has described is a very positive state. We are free from being allured by samsara, which we see as empty, valueless and unable to satisfy or even distract. In other words: We have awakened and are free of the dream illusions of this mirage we call the world. But that is only half the picture. We have now become awakened to the real nature of Reality. It is attracting, interesting and inspiring and utterly wonderful and enjoyable. And that is what Ma is points us to: the truth about the real perception of reality.

What does vairagya signify? When every single object or the world kindles, as it were, the fire of renunciation, so as to make one recoil as from a shock, then there is inward and outward awakening.

Vairagya is defined as: non-attachment; detachment; dispassion; absence of desire; disinterest or indifference–indifference towards and disgust for all worldly things and enjoyments.

Ma uses a very interesting definition of the reaction the sadhaka should have toward the world or its objects: recoiling as from a shock. Whether Ma means an emotion or the experience of an electrical shock, both are applicable here. I like the electrical shock simile because it implies an instant, willful though reflexive, separation from the objects of the world and the world itself because of the very experience of the world and its objects. It is a reflexive recoil from that which brings pain, and pain and suffering comprise the inherent nature and effect of the world on sentient beings. But the pain or aversion is only a means to a very desirable end: "then there is inward and outward awakening." That is, the sadhaka has seen through the world–seen it for what it is and is not. This is the arising of very practical and experiential jnana.

The sadhaka will not withdraw from the world because of painful experience, but because of insight and understanding. The wise sadhaka does not "hate" the world or have an emotional reaction to it, for being ego-based neither response can lead to liberation of the Self. Rather the sadhaka is employing intelligent reasoning instead of continuing a mere response to discomfort. Only insight and understanding can produce authentic vairagya.

Knowing or seeing through something or someone can be the opening of the path to freedom. I cannot but help remember Yogananda's account of a woman disciple who was married to a genuinely evil man whom Yogananda often told her to separate from and divorce. But because of moha–delusive attachment–she always made excuses such as that he was really a good man, that he could improve if she was patient, and other self-told fairy tales. One day, however, her husband lifted up a kitchen chair with the obvious intention of beating her with it. Suddenly she cried out: "Now I see you for what you really are!" He dropped the chair and ran from the house and she never saw or heard from him again.

Just having written the foregoing, I vividly remembered the time I asked a woman who had attended several classes and satsangs at our ashram: "How are you doing?" She smiled radiantly and joyfully answered: "Wonderful! I got rid of my husband!"

> **This, however; dues not mean that vairagya implies aversion or contempt for anything of the world, it simply is unacceptable, the body refuses it.**

When there is an emotional element involved in a decision there is a pretty sure chance that the decision will not last or be adhered to permanently. For aversion is just half of the magnetism that is also attraction. (We must consider duality seriously at all times in all things.) Ma therefore informs us that vairagya is not aversion or contempt, but simply realizing or finding that something is unacceptable intellectually and it is not loathed but is simply refused. This is the way of freedom and peace.

> **Neither dislike nor anger will arise.**

This is because intelligent reason and peaceful consideration has resulted in the refusal. The sadhaka is being realistic and practical because he is being calmly objective.

Now Ma is beginning a marvelous exposition describing the nature and effects of genuine vairagya.

> **When vairagya becomes a living inspiration, one begins to discriminate as to the true nature of the world, until finally, with the glowing certainty of direct perception the knowledge of its elusiveness arises.**

This is a happy result of arisen wisdom, not a sad or regretful and unwilling acknowledgement that is a reaction to disappointment or painful experience. Nor is it merely an intellectual insight or point of philosophy. As Ma says, it is living inspiration, a profound movement from within the awakening Self to withdraw from and end all delusive attachments and dependencies–addictions, actually. It is the beginning of freedom, of moksha itself.

Each and everything belonging to the world seems to burn; one cannot touch it. This also is a state that may ensue at a particular time.

This living vairagya is not just some noble ideal. Rather, Ma says that everything in and related to the world "burns" the sadhaka by its touch or even its very sight. Often we hear of people who were pained by the very sight of worldly entanglements and those who were entangled. Sri Ramakrishna is a prime example. The very presence or touch of materialistic people and the things to which they were addicted literally caused him pain like the sting of a scorpion. A very spiritually awakened American nun told me that at the final days of her senior year in high school quite a few of her classmates came in showing their engagement rings and rhapsodizing over their coming marriages. She told me: "Every time that happened I felt like I was suffocating inside, and I would inwardly pray in desperation: 'Please, Lord! Don't let that be me! Don't ever let that be me!'"

I knew a very dedicated yogi whose aspiration was to become a monk–which he did in time. He had a genuinely spiritual friend in a girl who was also a yogi and they often spent time together talking about spiritual matters. But one time seemingly out of the blue she asked him, "Are we going to get married?" He virtually shouted: "I would rather be dead first!"

There is a very old saying: "The burnt child fears the fire." And the wise sadhaka fears the contaminating touch of the world–and worldlings.

Note that Ma says about the awakened yogi: He cannot touch it. That is because the world violates and is antithetical to his very nature. Its touch is death–death to spiritual perceptions and death to spiritual aspirations.

Ma says that awakened state "may ensue at a particular time." And when it does he must hold to and guard and foster that state and make it the core condition of his life permanently. Someone asked Ma when a person should take to the life of renunciation. She replied: "The very day it arises in the mind." It must not be lost. For it is a matter of inner life and inner death. Naturally, I am not speaking about everyone, only those whose swabhava and swadharma is being described by Ma.

At present, what you enjoy does not impress you as being short-lived, rather does it appear to make you happy. But to the extent that the spirit of detachment is roused, the relish of such pleasures will die down, for are they not fleeting? In other words, death will die.

This is quite easily understood–even if not agreed with or liked. But it is the last sentence that must deeply affect us, for it is the implication that "life in this world" devoid of detachment from the world is itself death–death of our true inner being. The deadliest poison cannot harm us if it is not inside us, but the nature of the world is not to just enter us, but to arouse in us intense craving for it to such an extent that we think there is no life outside the world and its contact. This death-bearing illusion and addiction is fatal to life-bearing vairagya/detachment.

Now that you are advancing towards that which is beyond time, the semblance of happiness brought about by mundane things is being consumed. As a result, the question, "What actually is this world?" will arise. So long as the world seems enjoyable to you, such a query does not present itself.

Therefore the very questioning of the real nature of the world and what it really is in relation to us is evidence that the hypnosis of the world is lessening and in time may dissolve and complete vairagya prevail.

Ma says that the happiness of material existence and involvement is only a semblance, only an appearance. It is a mirage, not a reality. It is like hypnotic suggestion that vanishes when the subject awakens from the hypnotic state. When awakening begins we question the value of our prior condition and experience. If that continues unhindered, we come to realize that that condition and experience had no genuine value, but was false and itself a deception. But we cooperate with the deception for many lives, and blessed is that life in which its grip on us begins to loosen–and we begin to loosen our grip on it.

Since you are progressing towards that which transcends time, all that belongs to time will begin to appear to you in its true light.

Such progress and perspective only comes about in the consciousness of the dedicated yogi. Sadhana alone produces it or even makes it possible.

If after coming down from the state of contemplation you are capable of behaving as before, you have not been transformed.

This statement of bedrock truth is invaluable to the sadhaka. I cannot count the number of delusionals I have encountered over decades that had great revelations and cosmic experiences and were just the same after them as before them–except for the resulting inflation of their egos. In their childishness they fitted exactly the nursery rhyme:

Little Jack Horner
Sat in the corner,
Eating a Christmas pie;
He put in his thumb,
And pulled out a plum,
And said, "What a good boy am I!"

It is incredible how highly people can value complete folly and nonsense. But of course it is their ego they are reveling in and rejoicing over. I met a man who considered himself an enlightened master because once he dreamed he was eating a radish and when we woke up he belched radish!

When there is real meditation, which evokes indifference to the world, you will begin to pine keenly for the Divine, you will hunger for It and realize that nothing transient can appease this hunger or satisfy you.

These are results of real meditation:

1) Indifference to the world.
2) Pining keenly for the Divine.
3) Hungering for It.
4) Realizing that nothing transient can appease this hunger or satisfy you.

If these four traits are not strongly operative in your mind and heart, then you can be assured that your meditation is false and is deluding you. And observation of the increase or decrease will reveal whether you are progressing or regressing.

How am I to make it clear to you, Pitaji [Father]?

Words cannot. Only sadhana supported by the strict observance of Yama and Niyama, sometimes called The Ten Commandments Of Yoga:

Yama: 1) ahimsa–non-violence, non-injury, harmlessness; 2) satya–truthfulness, honesty; 3) asteya–non-stealing, honesty, non-misappropriativeness; 4) brahmacharya–continence; 5) aparigraha–non-possessiveness, non-greed, non-selfishness, non-acquisitiveness.

Niyama: 1) Shaucha: purity, cleanliness; 2) Santosha: contentment, peacefulness; 3) Tapas: austerity, practical (i.e., result-producing) spiritual discipline; 4) Swadhyaya: self-study, spiritual study; 5) Ishwarapranidhana: offering of one's life to God.

People come to this body and tell of their sons and daughters having got into a car and driven away, without even looking up to see whether their father and mother were weeping. They were quite unmoved by their parents' grief. You see, this is precisely what it is like at a certain stage on the Path; worldly enjoyment cannot possibly touch you. You feel: "Those whom I had believed to be my very own are merely related to me by flesh and blood–what is that to me?"

This seems quite severe because it is. In fact, drastic action is usually the most effective action–otherwise its effects may fade away after some time or be lost in the face of internal or external opposition. The sadhaka is engaged in a great civil war: the conflict of the positive and negative forces within. There can be no draw or peace treaty: only annihilation of one or the other. And here is a secret: the powers of the conquered are assimilated by the conqueror. So when the sadhaka engages in battle with inner negativity and conquers, he is not just a moral victor, he is markedly stronger than before. So: Press On!

> **Nobody deliberately puts his hands into fire or treads on a snake; in exactly the same manner, you just glance at the objects of sense and turn away.**

But we have to really consider that the objects of sense are truly fire or snakes that are deadly to us. Experience teaches us their true nature over and over from life to life, but our addiction to them both deceives us and make us deceitful in return through our continued indulgence.

Note that Ma does not say we will engage in some great inner struggle and wrestle with our attractions and addictions. No. She says: "You just glance at the objects of sense and turn away." This is a glorious state that can only be developed in us by a lot of sadhana and willful, unhesitating and determined turning away from the poisonous. And we do not just turn our back on them: we run away for our lives!

> **Then you will get into the current that takes you in the opposite direction, and later, when you have become detached even from detachment, there is no problem of detachment or non-detachment–what is, is THAT.**

There is an actual current or stream of vibrating energy that is essentially consciousness which takes us in the opposite direction from illusion and addiction. And that wondrous current is sadhana, an essential part of which is continual mantra japa.

God and His Name are One. This truth is to be realized by each sadhaka through his own experience and consequent divinization. When Ma was growing up there was a great sadhaka in her village whose body itself continually emanated the Name of Krishna. Every cell was a yogi engaged in Divine Name sadhana. If someone was himself a serious sadhaka the man's family would allow him to come into the man's bedroom when he was asleep. They would experience two things: first, his body would be glowing in the dark, and second, the Name of Krishna would be emanating from his entire body in a gentle, steady stream. A great tapaswin in Delhi once told me of another man known to her whose body emitted the divine Light and Name also.

The ego can turn anything into a mirror or extension of itself. Therefore there is an addiction to external manifestations of detachment by those who wish to be admired and thought supremely detached. Ma tells us that we must become detached from being considered detached–and therefore admirable and virtuous–by others and by ourselves. For no one can be detached from the true virtue of detachment since it becomes an ever-present condition of his consciousness rather than a mere attribute of his personality or mode of life.

Some say that by sustained effort one may attain to Enlightenment. But is it true that effort can bring about Enlightenment? Is Illumination dependent on action?

No. Illumination is not brought about, but revealed in the experiencing of the Self whose essence is enlightenment. Enlightenment is a state that cannot be produced, only revealed when the sadhaka's true Self is realized–and not as object but as Subject. Consciousness perceives Itself. And that is Enlightenment.

The veil [of illusion and ignorance] is destroyed, and when this has been accomplished, then THAT which IS stands revealed.

Sadhana is the revealer.

What is known as the fruit of effort is nothing but the illumination or the particular aspect towards which the effort has

> **been directed. Unveiled light (*niravaran prakasha*) is He Himself, the Eternal.**

Sadhana is the effort and manifests the Self as its fruit and lifts the veil to reveal the Light of the Self, the Eternal.

Someone asked Ma: At times we feel that sense objects really exist, at other times that they are merely ideas. Why does one and the same thing appear so different on different occasions?

> *Ma replied:* **Because you are in the grip of time. You have not yet reached the state where everything is perceived as the Self alone, have you? Herein lies the solution of the whole problem.**

We are in the grip of time–and therefore constant change–because we do not perceive the Self that is the Sole Existence, which is outside of time. That perception is the solution to everything. And sadhana is the sole producer of that perception-solution.

> **To feel as you do is good, since your feeling is related to the Supreme Quest; for nothing is ever wasted. What you have realized even for a second will, at some time or other, bear fruit.**
>
> **Thus, what water, air, the sky, etc. are, and hence what creation is, the knowledge of the real character of each element (tattwa) will flash into your consciousness one by one-just like buds bursting open.**

What produces that opening? Sadhana–constant, unbroken sadhana.

> **Flowers and fruit come into existence only because they are potentially contained in the tree. Therefore you should aim at realizing the One Supreme Element (Tattwa) that will throw light on all elements.**

Sadhana is the way.

> **You asked about sense objects. An object of sense, *vishaya*, (*vis:* sense object; *ha:* poison) is that which contains poison, is full of harm and drags man towards death. But freedom from the world of sense objects (*nirvishaya*)–where no trace of poison remains–means immortality.**

The poison of the senses is not the senses themselves, but the delusion/ illusion that arises from our belief and attachment to them as realities.

Inquirer: Still, is something of the burning pain of vairagya left over?

> **What is it that produces the sensation of burning?A sore surely! Because of it there is inflammation; but whose sore is it? Unless there is a sore, there can be no smarting. Therein lies the deception: so long as Reality is not revealed, the sore will persist. If the inflammation is a healing process, it is of course beneficent. A patient who becomes unconscious is not aware of his agony–you can see how man is drowned in pleasure, loss and affliction–this surely is not what is wanted! This is the way of the world with is never-ending uncertainties (*samsara*: world; *samsaya:* uncertainty).**

What we perceive as consciousness of various objects is really illusion that is ignorance of the real side, nature or character, of objects. And that illusion produces delusions without number–all of which we think are realities.

> **Can you tell why one feels anguish?**

Inquirer: One is pulled in two directions, towards God as well as towards sense enjoyment–this causes anguish.

> **You have a desire to give up, but you cannot let go–such is your problem. Let that desire awaken in your heart: its stirring**

signifies that the time is coming when you will be able to give up.

No comment needed. Just keep watching and wanting.

You obtain a coveted object, but still you are dissatisfied; and if you fail to get it, you are also disappointed.

The disillusionment you experience at the fulfillment of your wish is wholesome; but the torment of the unfulfilled hankering after the things you could not secure, drives you towards that which is of death, towards that misery.

Obviously, desire is the problem. What eliminates desire? Fulfillment–not of ordinary desire, but of the desire for That which eliminates desire. In the awakened human being the desire for realization of the Self will ultimately lead to finding the means of realization of the Self: sadhana. Those who do not find and engage in sadhana have no genuine desire for finding and knowing the Self. Otherwise the Self would come to them in the form of sadhana.

Inquirer: The hunger of the senses can never be appeased; the more one gets, the more one wants. The fulfillment of worldly desire only begets greater longing.

This world is itself but an embodiment of want, and hence the heartache due to the absence of fulfillment must needs endure. This is why it is said that there are two kinds of currents in human life: the one pertaining to the world, in which want follows upon want; the other of one's true Being. It is characteristic of the former that it can never end in fulfillment–on the contrary, the sense of want is perpetually stimulated anew. Whereas by entering the latter man will become established in his true nature and bring to completion the striving which is its expression. Thus, if he endeavors to fulfill himself by entering

this current, it will eventually bring him to the perfect poise of his own true Being.

Sadhana itself is the beginning of fulfillment because it increases and expands until it reveals the ultimate fulfillment. For sadhana is the seed, the essence, of Self-realization. Sadhana is the search of the Self for Itself. Sadhana and the Self are inseparable. But only persistent sadhana reveals that. You have to begin with what you wish to end up with.

Inquirer: And the anguish of not having found, the anguish of the absence of God? I have no wish for sense pleasures, but they come to me. I am compelled to experience them.

Ah, but the anguish of not having found God is salutary. What you have eaten will leave a taste in your mouth. You wear ornaments because you wish to, and so you have to bear their weight. Yet this weight is fated to fall off, for it is something that cannot last, can it?

Ma needs no help from me in the form of a comment.

Inquirer: Are there instances when an enlightened person may be in ignorance?

You call a person enlightened, and in the same breath say he may be subject to ignorance? Such a thing, Pitaji, is quite impossible.

There is, however, a state of attainment that is not maintained at all times, where what you suggest may apply; but never in a case of final Realization. In whatever way you may perceive an Enlightened Being, He remains what He is.

How can there be a possibility of ignorance in what is termed Knowledge Supreme? When you speak of ignorance with reference to a realized man, it is an example of Supreme Knowledge

being mistaken for ignorance. Therefore, you also talk of ascent and descent. Just as there is no question of a body for one who is liberated, so for Him there can be none of rising up and coming down.

Nevertheless, there is a state of achievement in which ascent and descent do exist, really and truly.

Thank you, Ma.

SEVEN

Solan, September 19, 1948.

Someone told Sri Ma about a man who, without stirring from his seat, would produce all sorts of articles, like flowers, garlands, sweets, etc. They just appeared in his hands. In this connection Sri Ma related an incident that had taken place in Dacca many years ago.

What an incredible number of similar incidents has this body not witnessed! As a rule this body makes no comments upon such things, but on a particular occasion somehow something rather strange took place. When a certain lady came, I felt like lying down across her lap. As I did so, I distinctly noticed that a bundle containing various articles was tied in the lady's sari in the region of her waist. Everyone began to request her to show them some objects that would come to her by supernatural means, since many had seen her do this before. People had heard it said that even the prasad from the Kali temple in Dakshineshwar would of its own accord appear in her hands.

This body said: "Even before it arrives from there I could disclose it; but would you like me to?"

The lady said: "Yes, of course!" The question was repeated several times, and every time she, as well as her devotees, replied: "Yes, please!" This is how it all came about. Even so, this body did not take anything out with its own hands–only what was fated to happen, happened spontaneously.

Afterwards one of the lady's devotees came to this body and inquired: "Ma, you never put anyone to shame, and certainly not in public. Why then did you do so in this case?"

She got the reply: "Yes, as you know, this body does not as a rule interfere with anyone's natural ways. Yet, whether it concerns the most ordinary or the most extraordinary event–call it as you please–what holds good for this body to this day and has until now been so always, is simply this: whatever is meant to come about just happens spontaneously. When that lady arrived, this body welcomed her with great respect, offering her its own asana and putting a garland round her neck. How very pleased everyone felt! Every form, every expression is He and He alone.

That day this body did not disclose anything.

But the lady of her own free will declared: "I shall come again tomorrow!' You all heard it, did you not? What occurred then was His way of revealing Himself. Tell me, what is there to do? By whatever method He may choose to teach anyone, at any time–as far as this body is concerned, it has no desire of its own–whatever comes to pass is all right.

When (in the early days) this body used to do pranam to every creature, whether an insect, a spider, a dog, or a cat, it did so with the full consciousness of the presence of the Supreme Being in everything.

"Whatever comes to pass is all right"–there is something else to be said in this connection. To take recourse to falsehood or deception can never be for one's good. He who deceives, will himself be deceived. On the other hand, falsehood may also be converted into truth. Someone may deliberately play false, yet through his disciple's sincerity the truth may actually be brought to light. As a result the disciple excels the guru. The resolve to find the truth will inevitably lead to its revelation.

I told that lady's devotee: "How many times did I not ask you all 'shall I disclose it?' And without exception you kept on begging me to do so. Therefore–what more can be said?" What a great variety of similar incidents occur!

Listen to the story of a young woman who, under the slightest provocation, would go into 'samadhi' so people believed. She

appeared to become lifeless, her hands and feet turning cold. When she came to this body, she also went into this strange state that people mistook for samadhi. The girl's mother was called 'grandmother' by this body, both of us being from the same village. She said to me: "Grand-daughter, please try and help this girl!" I quite understood what was the matter with the young woman, so I whispered into her ear: "You will very soon receive a letter from your husband;" whereupon she recovered in no time. The news of the cure spread far and wide. People felt greatly mystified, wondering at the powerful mantra Sri Ma had whispered into the girl's ear. Indeed, under the circumstances it was the appropriate mantra for her. The girl's condition was solely due to worrying about her husband's prolonged silence.

Then again there was a young man–into what supernormal states he used to pass, how many kinds of visions he had! He would, for example, do pranam and remain in that posture for hours together, without raising his head, tears streaming down his cheeks. He declared that he saw and heard Sri Krishna teaching Arjuna, as described in the Gita, and that he used to have many other visions and locutions of the kind.

This body told him that if a sadhaka could not maintain firm control over his mind, he would be liable to see and hear many things, both illusory and genuine, all mixed up. He might even be subjected to the influence of some "spirit" or power. Such occurrences, far from creating pure divine aspiration, would rather hinder than help. Moreover, to see someone in a vision or to hear him address you, may well become a source of self-satisfaction or egotistic enjoyment.To lose control over oneself is not desirable.

Any comment of mine would be an intrusion on perfection.

In the search after Truth one must not allow oneself to be overpowered by anything, but should watch carefully whatev-

er phenomena may supervene, keeping fully conscious, wide awake, in fact retaining complete mastery over oneself.

Loss of consciousness and of self-control are never right.

What explanation or comment is needed? Jai Ma!

In the course of the same conversation, Sri Ma said:

The Lord Buddha is Himself the essence of Enlightenment. All partial manifestations of wisdom that come in the course of sadhana culminate in Supreme Enlightenment (*Bodha Swarupa*). In a similar way, Supreme Knowledge (*Jnana Swarupa*) or Supreme Love (*Bhava Swarupa*) may be attained.

As there is a state of Supreme Self-knowledge, likewise is there a state of perfection at the zenith of the path of love. There one finds the nectar of Perfect Love identical with Supreme Knowledge. In this state there is no room for emotional excitement; indeed, that would make it impossible for Supreme Love (*Mahabhava*) to shine forth.

Perfect wisdom.

Be mindful of one thing: if, when following a particular line of approach, one does not attain to that which is the consummation of all sadhana, namely the final Goal, it means that one has not really entered that line.

The Real is One–and the one and only Goal. Ma is giving us a very simple instruction or precept that has unlimited application and should be kept in mind by the sadhaka at every moment: If any supposed devotee, yogi, or guru does not unerringly move toward the goal and manifest the symptoms of that progression, he has not been truly following a legitimate path at all, but only engaging in self-delusion. Consider the disciples of "Masters" who remain seekers all their lives and never become finders.

Now, there are two very important things to always be kept in mind: 1) There are those that never attain the Goal because the path they are on cannot, and therefore does not, lead to the Goal. 2) There are those that never attain the Goal because they are not really following any path–just deceiving others, and often themselves.

At the supreme summit of Love–which is Mahabhava–exuberance, excessive emotion and the like cannot possibly occur.

This is incredibly important and absolutely necessary to take seriously. It is almost universally believed in Bharat that Mahabhava manifests as loud weeping, crying out, shaking or falling on the ground, and other cataclysmic, hysterical manifestations–and thus is desirable and worthy of respect or even reverence, especially toward the person in which these things are occurring. But Ma tells us that not only is that erroneous, such things cannot even occur in true Mahabhava, with the implication that Mahavahava actually prevents such aberrations. I have seen this behavior myself, and Ma's vigorous and insistent suppressive response to it as spiritual insanity that could lead to psychological insanity.

Emotional excitement and Supreme Love are in no wise to be compared: they are totally different from one another.

Delusive, human carnal "love" is both emotional, sensual, aberative and can even be violent. But love for God is reflective of God and therefore above all egoic effusions, and even prevents such forms of ignorance and negativity from arising. Also, in Bharat many false "bhaktas" are sensual people and morally corrupt. This situation is not unknown even here in America. The so-called "Charismatic" and "Pentecostal" Christians are in the grip of their lower, carnal nature, and immorality is rife among them. This I know from having lived in the Bible Belt where they flourish, and I encountered them myself. Emotionality of any kind stimulates the lower, instinctual nature. As Swami Sivananda often said: "Devotion is not emotion."

> **While absorbed in meditation, whether one is conscious of the body or not, whether there be a sense of identification with the physical or not–under all circumstances, it is imperative to remain wide awake; unconsciousness must be strictly avoided.**

This is extremely important. Going into trances or sleeping and claiming it was samadhi or "astral travel" is harmful and delusional. Notice that Ma does not just say "awake," but "*wide* awake."

The truth is that a sadhaka, due to the effects of his sadhana, is more awake, alert or aware than others. Sadhana is the process of awakening and increases awareness and alertness. A diligent sadhaka is more alive than anyone else. He is more conscious than others, because his inner awakening produced by his sadhana broadens and deepens his awareness.

> **Some genuine perception must be retained, whether one contemplates the Self as such, or any particular form. What is the outcome of such meditation? It opens up one's being to the Light, to that which is eternal.**

In sum: genuine sadhana awakens, deepens and broadens the sadhaka's consciousness. Brahman is Sat, Chit and Ananda. The consciousness, the chitshakti, of the sadhaka, is continually broadened and deepened.

> **Suppose the body had been suffering from some pain or stiffness–and lo and behold, after meditation it feels perfectly hale and hearty, with not a trace of fatigue or debility. It is as if a long period of time had elapsed in between, as if there had never been a question of any discomfort. This would be a good sign.**

Sadhana is a most effective and direct form of healing because it corrects the mind which is reflected in the body which itself in turn reflects the mind. The healing of one produces the healing of the other. This must be experienced by a yogi for himself.

But if tempted at the first touch of Bliss to allow oneself to be drowned in it, and later to declare: "Where I was, I cannot say, I do not know"–this is not desirable.

Unconsciousness cannot result from consciousness. And consciousness is the essence of the very existence of the sadhaka–and of the Absolute Being as well. So to be godly or godlike is to be supremely awake and aware both inwardly and outwardly. Meditation is not a euphoric soporific but continual, progressive awakening.

As one becomes capable of real meditation, and to the extent that one contacts Reality, one discovers the ineffable joy that lies hidden even in all outer objects.

Two words in this first line are of supreme value and interest: "capable" and "real."

There is real and there is false meditation. Real meditation is only possible by the sadhaka who embodies the principles of yama and niyama. So let's repeat them here:

Yama: 1) ahimsa–non-violence, non-injury, harmlessness; 2) satya–truthfulness, honesty; 3) asteya–non-stealing, honesty, non-misappropriativeness; 4) brahmacharya–continence; 5) aparigraha–non-possessiveness, non-greed, non-selfishness, non-acquisitiveness.

Niyama: 1) Shaucha: purity, cleanliness; 2) Santosha: contentment, peacefulness; 3) Tapas: austerity, practical (i.e., result-producing) spiritual discipline; 4) Swadhyaya: self-study, spiritual study; 5) Ishwarapranidhana: offering of one's life to God.

Only real meditation produces a real yogi. By constantly and unswervingly observing, and thereby embodying, these ten elements the aspirant becomes capable of meditation. Without them, he has not even begun or is able to begin.

The purpose of all the elements of sadhana is contact with Reality, with Existence-Consciousness-Bliss: Satchidananda. And through effective meditation "one discovers the ineffable joy that lies hidden even in all outer objects." This is the fulness of life, not the mirages and distractions of the world.

> **If on the other hand one loses oneself as it were, lapsing into a kind of stupor while engaged in meditation, and afterwards claims to have been steeped in intense bliss, this sort of bliss is a hindrance.**

As a beginning yogi I met several people who thought blanking out and becoming basically unconscious was samadhi. Well, it was a good sleep! And also through it they avoided contact with God to Whom they really had an aversion. (A lot of people are allergic to God.)

But Yoga is something just the opposite: Deep Awakening.

Unfortunately the opposite is addicting to the ignorant and an impassible blockage to authentic yoga and realization. We have to choose between being "happy as ducks" paddling in the waters of samsara or eagles soaring into limitless consciousness through liberating sadhana.

> **If the life-force seems to have been in abeyance–just as one has a sense of great happiness after sound sleep–it indicates stagnation.**

In other words, their samadhi is only the tamasic state of deep sleep.

> **It is a sign of attachment, and this attachment stands in the way of true meditation, since one will be apt to revert to this state again and again; although from the standpoint of the world, which is altogether different, it would seem a source of profound inward joy and therefore certainly an indication of spiritual progress.**

Self-delusion finds many ways to keep itself intact as Ma describes here.

Long ago I saw on television a very interesting movie, "Lady From Lisbon." The plot was that during World War Two someone stole the Mona

Lisa from the Louvre and brought it to Lisbon to sell to someone fleeing to America. But forgers had produced many fake Mona Lisas, and everyone bought the fakes and rejected the real one, saying that it looked fake!

This is the situation in the spiritual world: the fake seekers only accept and follow the fake teachers and the fake yogas. And since they are in the vast majority, the fakes are extremely successful and considered authentic–as are the fake seekers. I have seen fake seekers from the West react with complete indifference to Ma even though they had travelled thousands of miles to India supposedly seeking spiritual wisdom. Some of them had even came to India to specifically meet with Ma! But they were blind to Her.

There is an interesting aspect to the foregoing. Once someone asked Ma: "When we think of You, do You think of us?" Ma replied: "How could you think of this body if there was no kheyala?" Her meaning was that unless She willed it (had the kheyala) no one could even think of Her, much less see Her. Many times I have sat in front of Ma and rejoiced, knowing that She wanted me there to see Her. To even think of Ma now is an indication of Her grace. So is your reading of this book. And so is my writing of it. Jai Ma!

To be held up at any stage is an obstacle to further progress–it simply means one has stopped advancing.

The problem is: How does an aspirant break through that barrier? Surely diligent and unswerving sadhana is the way.

While engaging in meditation, one should think of oneself as a purely spiritual being (chinmayi), as Self-luminous, poised in the Bliss of the Self (atmarama).

The sadhaka must realize that illumined consciousness is his essential nature–is his Self.

The young man previously mentioned (the one who used to have visions) was intelligent, and therefore able to understand

> **this sort of reasoning. As a result, the spectacular experiences ceased, and he now attends to his meditation and other spiritual exercises in a very quiet, unobtrusive manner.**

This is of prime importance. The carnival sideshow of phenomena must cease, and the steady and sure practice of sadhana must continue until it ends in moksha. And for that practice to be effective and successful it must be continual and carried on "in a very quiet, unobtrusive manner."

Later, when the conversation again reverted to dhyana and asana, Sri Ma said:

> **Look, if you spend hour after hour sitting in a certain posture, if you become absorbed while in that pose and are unable to meditate in any other, it shows that you are deriving enjoyment from the posture; this also constitutes an obstacle.**

That is, it is bhoga–enjoyment–not yoga. Such absorption is a mind-drug and a comforting escape from true Self-realization through Self-experience.

> **When one first starts practicing japa and meditation, it is of course right to try and continue in the same position for as long as possible. But as one approaches perfection in these practices, the question as to how long one has remained in one posture does not arise; at any time and in any position–lying, sitting, standing, or leaning over to one side, as the case may be–one can no longer be deterred by anything from the contemplation of one's Ideal or the Beloved.**

Profound inner awareness must become akhanda–unbroken–and not affected or diminished by any external situation or condition. Akhanda sadhana ensures this.

> **The first sign of progress comes when one feels ill at ease in anything but a meditative pose. Nothing external interests one; the only thing that seems attractive, is to be seated in one's favorite posture as long as possible and to contemplate the Supreme Object of one's worship, plunged in a deep inner joy. This marks the beginning of single-mindedness, and hence is a step in the right direction. Yet, here great prominence is given to posture.**

Self-delusion can produce false versions of wisdom, and this description given by Ma is easily and readily falsified by the self-deluded. The externals of this description can be both hypocritical and even a state of psychosis.

How can it be determined as to whether what Ma describes is true or false? The resulting mental state and behavior of the person engaged in these things reveal whether this behavior is false/delusional or real and indicative of progress.

The wise sadhaka engages in close and continual scrutiny of both his inner and outer activities to determine their actual character: true or false.

> **If one stays in that position as long as the inclination lasts–confident that the Beloved can never do one harm–and if one is able to remain fixed in it, then the posture becomes of overwhelming importance. This only shows that one is nearing perfection in the practice of asana. Standing, sitting, walking in fact, any gesture taken up by the body is called an asana. It corresponds to the rhythm and the vibration of body and mind at any particular moment. Some aspirants can meditate only if seated in the pose indicated by the guru or formulated in the shastras, and not otherwise.**
>
> **This is the way to proficiency in meditation.**

But asana–meditation posture–is not dhyana–meditation. Only preparation for meditation. So undue importance should not be attributed to it, because:

> **On the other hand, someone may begin his practice while sitting in any ordinary position; nevertheless, as soon as the state of japa or dhyana has been reached, the body will spontaneously take up the most appropriate position, after the manner that a hiccup happens involuntarily. As one's meditation grows more and more intense, the postures will of themselves correspondingly gain in perfection.**

If this happens it should be accepted. But if it does not happen, we should not try to fool ourselves and pretend that the meditation postures we adopt are spontaneous. In genuine meditation practice what is beneficial will occur and what is not beneficial will not occur. But that is a condition that rarely is the case with a beginner. Some practice and experience may be needed. And we should not deceive ourselves and pretend something is spontaneous when it is not. Lying to oneself is not an aid to sadhana. Ever.

> **When a little air is pumped into a tire, the tire will be flabby; but when it is filled to capacity, it remains completely stable in its own natural shape. Likewise, when real meditation has been attained, the body feels light and free, and on rising after meditation there is no fatigue of any kind, no pain, numbness or stiffness in one's limbs.**

This should really be heeded as bedrock truth. And we should honestly observe what is occurring spontaneously. Self-honesty is an absolute necessity for the sadhaka, since we have been lying to ourselves for countless lifetimes and it has become a habit we need to consciously and actively break and banish.

See how practically and sensibly Ma speaks regarding sadhana. She was the embodiment of truth and therefore of practical good sense.

> **In true meditation Reality is contacted, and just as the touch of fire leaves an impression, this contact also leaves its mark.**

This is a primary principle we must keep in mind and scrutinize our mind and conduct to see if our meditation is resulting in truth or in vain imagination. The ability for complete self-honesty is a fundamental trait of a worthy sadhaka.

> **What happens as a result?**
> **Impediments fall away–they are either consumed by vairagya, or "melted" by devotion to the Divine.**

How simple–as truth always is. So by observing ourselves we can know if were are on the path to Reality. For vairagya and devotion are actually traits of the emerging Self that is on the path to liberation.

> **Worldly things seem dull and insipid, quite foreign to oneself; worldly talk loses all its appeal, becomes devoid of interest, and at a further stage even painful.**

We must sincerely observe ourselves and see if this condition is arising and becoming established in us. For it is the indication of the dawning of inner wisdom–even life itself.

> **When a person's earthly possessions are lost or damaged, the victim feels disturbed, which gives evidence of the stranglehold that sense objects exercise over men's minds. This is what is called granthi–the knots constituting the I-ness.**

I was privileged to see and observe a great yogi-devotee of Ma, Professor Pannalal. He was a very intense and rather eccentric individual, but pure of heart and firmly set on the path to Self-realization. At one time he was governor of Benares (Varanasi/Kashi). He lived in the governor's palace, but had constructed a small, simple hut for meditation behind the palace. Once when he was meditating someone came in panic and told him the palace was on fire. "I am meditating!" he replied. "Look to it yourself!" This was repeated a few times. When he finally emerged from the hut he saw that the palace was now only a heap of ashes. Everyone was standing around, anxious as to how he would react. He studied it a moment then said to them. "It looks like we will have to build a new one." And that was that. Ma loved him very much, and his guru had once told him, "God is incarnate right now on the earth. I will not meet the Incarnation, but you will in time." And so it was. And so it was with us, too. Jai Ma!

> **By meditation, japa and other spiritual practices, which vary according to each one's individual line of approach, these knots become loosened, discrimination is developed, and one comes to discern the true nature of the world of sense perception.**
>
> **In the beginning, one was enmeshed in it, struggling helplessly in its net. As one becomes disentangled from it, and gradually passes through various stages of opening oneself more and more to the Light, one comes to see that everything is contained in everything, that there is only One Self, the Lord of all, or that all are but the servants of the One Master.**
>
> **The form this realization takes depends upon one's orientation.**
>
> **One knows by direct perception that as one exists, so everyone else exists. Then again, that here is the One and nothing but the One, that nothing comes and goes, yet also does come and go–there is no way of expressing all this in words.**

Nothing need be said. This must be our living, personal insight.

> **To the extent that one becomes estranged from the world of the senses, one draws nearer to God.**

So if we wish to draw nearer to God we will distance, even divorce, ourselves from the world. One time someone asked Ma if they should become a sannyasi. She simply replied: "He who does sadhana automatically becomes a sadhu." One time in Ranchi Dr. Ghosh, a devotee of Ma, brought some Catholic nuns to meet Ma. Ma said to him: "Tell them that this body also is a nun."

"He that hath ears to hear, let him hear," (Matthew 11:15; Revelation 2:7).

> **When attaining to true meditation, one's chosen posture no longer represents either an obstacle or a source of enjoyment; in other words, it is quite immaterial in what particular pose one happens to be. Whether one sits straight or crooked, the right posture will form of itself, pulling the body into the proper position.**
>
> **Again, there are occasions when one becomes entirely independent of the physical pose; in whatever attitude the body may happen to be, meditation just comes about effortlessly.**
>
> **Though, without a doubt, there is also a state in which, if one takes up a special pose, such as for instance, padmasana (the lotus pose) or siddhasana (the perfect pose), no interruption of one's union with the Supreme Being can ever occur.**

This needs no comment, just understanding through one's own sadhana which potentially is the source of all knowledge and will lead to the realization Ma is describing.

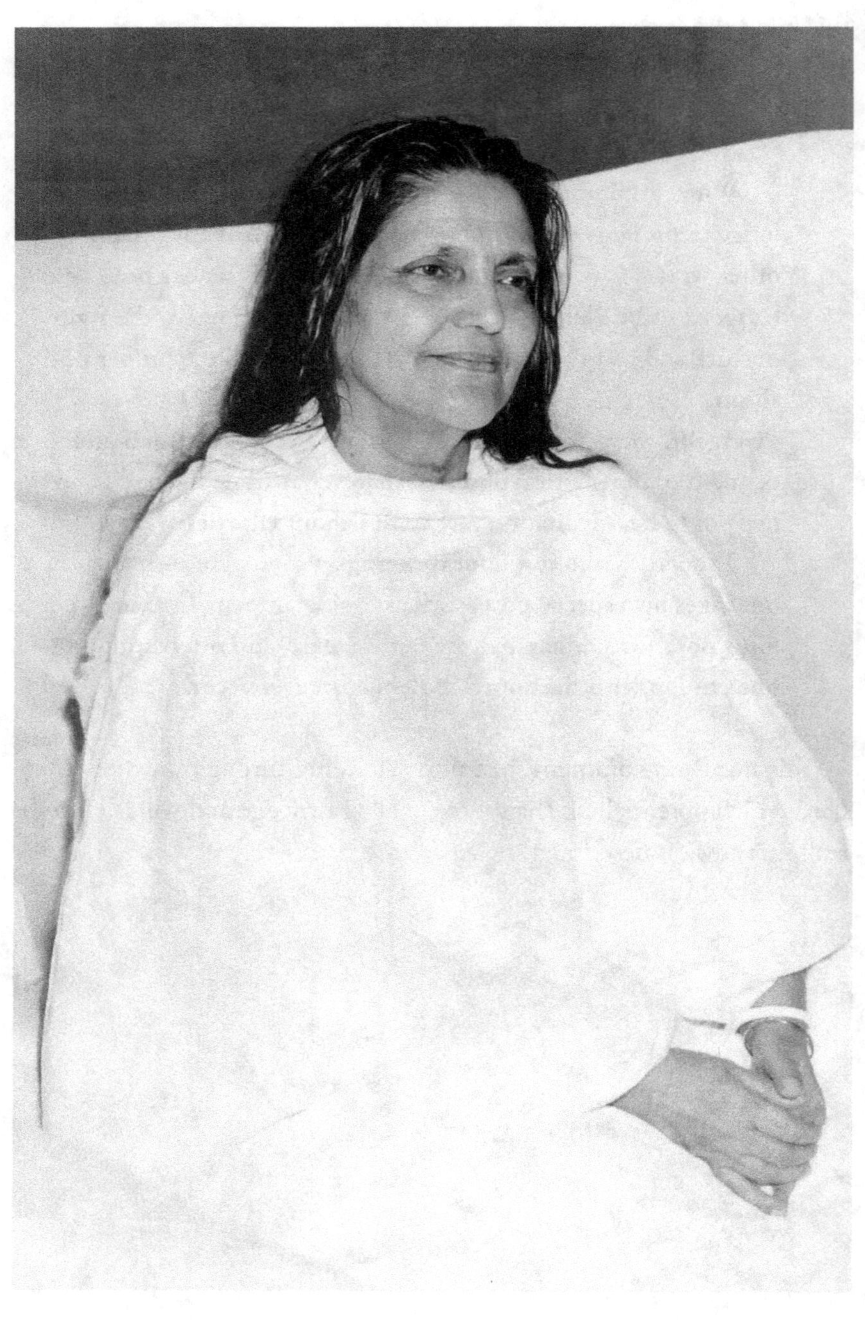

EIGHT

Benares. August 11, 1948.

Inquirer: The other day, when speaking about visions and similar experiences that one has during meditation, you said these were not real visions but mere "touches."

> **Yes, viewed from the level where one can speak of "touch," this is so; that is to say, you have not been changed by the experience. Yet it is attractive to you, and you can express the feeling in words, which implies that you still take delight in sense objects. Therefore it is a mere touch. If transformation had ensued, you would be unable to feel worldly enjoyment in this way. How can there be enjoyment or relish in a transformed state of being?**

People continually have "experiences" of various sorts which assure them that they are special and on the right course. But Ma goes right to the heart of the matter: what is the result of visions and other "experiences"? If the person is not changed significantly for the better or made wiser, the experience is either negligible or completely false. But they boost our egos and we like to think of ourselves as budding mystics. This is actually dangerous. Many seemingly exalted experiences are found to be baseless, without substance, and actually pathological–symptomatic of instability and delusion.

Ma tells us that the result of a genuine spiritual experience is the arising of vairagya through spiritual insight, true jnana and viveka. Real transformation does not make us pleased with ourselves or give us an emotional or experiential "high." It changes us profoundly and is the advent of Self-awareness leading to Self-realization. Sadhana is the surest and safest approach to spiritual unfoldment and experience.

Inquirer: Atman and Brahman are different only by way of posited limitation. The vision that comes by constant meditation on "I am Satchitananda" is Atmadarshana [the vision of the Self]. Since there can be no vision of the Brahman [Which is beyond all conception or sense-perception], it must therefore be a partial, that is a limited vision of the Brahman. Is this correct?

> **If you think there are parts in the Brahman, you may say "partial." But can there be parts in the Absolute? As you think and feel in parts, you speak of "touch"–but He is whole, THAT which IS.**

Brahman is one in every sense of the term–absolute Unity. Therefore, can you experience a "touch" of Brahman? Of course not! Because Brahman is not outside us, is not separate from us. What is needed is the experiencing of Reality arising from our own depths which are rooted in and inseparable from Brahman. That is why God-realization and Self-realization are the same thing. They are God-experience and Self-experience. They are not two, but the same in the ultimate sense.

Advaita, for example, is not a viewpoint but an experience beyond all relativity, the experience of the ever-non-dual Self. Can we "experience" Brahman when That is the essence of our own Self? Realization of the Self is the realization of Brahman and contrariwise. For there is only the One of which we have been told by the realized sages of all ages: Thou Art That. And conversely: That Art Thou. For only Unity is the truth of all existence.

We cannot "know" God/Brahman as an object because it is essentially one with us–is the Self of our Self. We cannot understand that, but we must come to know it within our own essential being which is Brahman. It is erroneous to speak of Brahman and our Atman as one. They are beyond even Unity. They are THAT which transcends both duality and unity. That is why the sages are munis–silent ones. Whom will they speak to or tell it to if they see all as the One?

Inquirer: Are there grades [krama] in knowledge [jnana]?

No. Where knowledge is of the Self (Swarupa Jnana), how can there be various kinds or grades? Knowledge of the Self is one. "Proceeding step by step" refers to the stage where one has turned away from the pursuit of sense objects and one's gaze is entirely directed towards the Eternal. God has not yet been realized, but the treading of this path has become attractive [to him].

Experiencing attraction to knowing the Real and attraction to sadhana is a manifestation of the dawning of Reality in the aspirant's mind.

Along this line there are dharana, dhyana and samadhi. The experiences at each of these stages are also infinite.

But experience is not insight or understanding!

Where the mind is, there is experience.

And the mind is not the Self, therefore experience may lead to the Self, but it is not the Self, nor does it guarantee eventual realization of the Self.

The experiences at different stages are due to various forms of desire for Supreme Knowledge.

And this implies immersion in intellectual concepts of Reality rather than Atmadarshan which is direct knowing beyond the intellect. And we must realize that experience itself is not knowledge, only the possibility of reaching true knowledge, true knowing.

The mind that has formerly been engrossed in material things, and arguing that one cannot know whether God exists or not, and had come to deny Him, is now turned the other way.

But turning is not seeing and knowing. It is only the possibility of seeing and knowing.

> **Therefore, is it not natural that light should dawn upon it in accordance with the state it has reached?**

Which indicates that a "state" cannot be knowledge of The Real, for That is beyond conditioning or limitation–beyond any "state" that has been "reached." It is a continuation of duality though it may be a hint of the possibility that knowledge of the Real is becoming possible to some degree. We must not either underestimate or overestimate what we find in our mind. It is a matter of waiting and seeing.

> **These states are known under various names.**

But if they can be named they are not That which transcends name and concept. There is an adage: Talk does not cook the rice. But neither is talk the rice or the fire that cooks it.

> **When do the visions that one gets in meditation cease? When the Self stands Self-revealed (Swayam Prakasha).**

When the Unseen is revealed, seeing stops and knowing begins.

Inquirer: Does the body survive when the ego-mind has been dissolved?

> **At times the question is asked: "How does the World-teacher give instruction? From the state of ajnana?" If this were so, the mind would not have been dissolved, the threefold differentiation (triputi) of the knower, the knowing and the known, could not have been merged. So what would He be able to give you? Where could He lead you?**

This answer does not mean the teacher would be ignorant if he considered there was the duality of the teacher and the taught or if he catered to the present ignorance of the seeker in order to be able to communicate with him and yet by his teaching imply the reality of the division-separation of teacher, teaching and the taught.

Basically the question is whether a teacher can impart anything of value to the unknowing person rather than more unknown words to one who is already an "unknower." Unknowing would seem to prevail, whatever the intention or desire of the teacher and the taught. Could learning be the result?

Ma gives the necessary perspective:

But there is a stage where this question does not arise.

So as long as there is a question there is no jnana. And the Question Game can be used a substitute for genuine inquiry–even a way to avoid the necessary questions by piling up useless ones.

> **Is it the body that is the obstacle to Supreme Knowledge? Is there even a question of whether the body exists or not? At a certain level this question is simply not there.**

In Atmajnana the Self is realized as the sole reality. This can be taken in two ways: 1) Nothing is real but the Self. 2) Everything is the Self, at least in extension or reflection. Therefore we do not seek the Self, we *realize* It. And since "Seek, and ye shall find" (Matthew 7:7) is true, the actual character and value of a supposed seeker and his sadhana is revealed: The finder truly has been seeking; the non-finder has truly not been seeking. As Jesus also said: "By their fruits ye shall know them" (Matthew 7:20).

> **On the plane where this question arises, one is not in the state of Pure Being, and one thinks this question can be raised and also replied to. But the answer lies where there is no such thing as questioning and answering where there are no "others," no division. And so, how can one possibly approach the Supreme Teacher and receive instruction? Similarly, the teachings**

of the shastras and other scriptures have then become quite useless. This is one aspect of the matter.

And it is the most important and beneficial aspect of the matter. As in all things, the seeker chooses if he will be successful in his search, and further he is the one who decides exactly what he will or will not find.

To speak of grades (krama) in knowledge, as if one were studying for a university degree, is presenting the matter from the point of view of sadhana. Where the Self stands revealed, there can be no question of this. Yet, where there is personal effort, like the practice of meditation or contemplation, it will certainly bear fruit.

Obviously true.

But in the state of Self-illumination, there can be no such thing as attainment or non-attainment: though being there, it is not; and though it is not, yet it is–just like that.

It is not a matter of attaining, but of simply realizing/seeing the Self–as when we are looking for something and find it. Recognition is realization. Seeing or not seeing is the essence of the whole thing. It is not a question of being or not being.

Some say a last vestige of the mind remains. At a certain level this is so; however, there is a stage beyond, where the question of whether a trace of the mind remains or not, does not exist. If everything can be burnt up, cannot this last vestige be consumed too?

We must note and take quite seriously Ma's insistence that in time no question at all of any kind can exist because realization of the Whole ends all quests. Also, there is nothing (or no thing) to seek and therefore no seeker since the sought has been found.

There is no question of either "yes" or "no": what is, IS.

This is a comment on the previous question: "If everything can be burnt up, cannot this last vestige be consumed too?" Yes and No are dualities, but where there is unity they do not apply. So when the mind is consumed or dissolved there is no impression of either duality or unity. There is just IS–Pure Being about Which nothing can be said, it being beyond the dualities of Is/Is Not and Yes/No.

> **Meditation and contemplation are necessary because one is on the level of acceptance and rejection, and the aim is in fact to go beyond acceptance and rejection.**

What is necessary is to awaken into the state of such perfect unity that acceptance/rejection cannot exist since only the eternal Subject remains and there is no object to accept or reject–or even the duality in the observing mind that can accept or reject.

> **You want a support, do you not? The support that can take you beyond, to where the question of support or supportlessness no longer exists: that is the supportless support.**

This supportless support is a state of consciousness–not a state of mind or an external object that can be either accepted or rejected.

> **What is expressible in words can certainly be attained. But It is THAT which is beyond words.**

This is because Brahman, Absolute Being, is beyond either perception or attainment since It is not an object but the eternal Subject, Satchidananda: Reality-Consciousness-Bliss. It is Self-existent Existence Itself.

Inquirer: I have read in books that some say they have to descend in order to act in the world. This seems to imply that although they are established in Pure Being, they have to take the help of the mind when doing action. Just as a king, when acting the role of a sweeper, has for the time being to imagine he is a sweeper.

> **In assuming a part, surely, there is no question of ascending or descending. Abiding in His own Essential Being (Svara) He Himself plays various parts. But when you speak of ascending and descending–where is the state of Pure Being? Can there be duality in that state? Brahman is One without a second. Though from your angle of vision, I grant, it does appear as you put it.**

So all we can say about Brahman is that we cannot say anything about It since It is beyond the perceptions of the mind which is the realm of thoughts and words. And since Ma was, as She Herself said, Purna Brahma Narayana, the only thing we can truthfully say about Her is that we can say nothing about Her. She is beyond all words, thoughts or conceptions. As previously mentioned, that is why in some English praises of Her I wrote: "Thou art All and Thou art Nothing. To Thy mystery we bow."

There is no way to convey or to describe either Her or to describe what it was like to be in Her presence. In a sense it was not an experience but an entering into Being Itself. The fact that it is beyond words is the proof of the truth, the reality, of what I am saying. It is summed up in the words Yogananda even set to music: "He who knows, knows. None else knows." There is a knowing beyond knowing because it actually is BEING. Ma embodied that and conveyed that to us.

Inquirer: You have explained this from the level of ajnana (ignorance). Now be pleased to speak from the level of the enlightened (jnani)!

> **What you say now, I also accept. Here, [pointing to herself] nothing is rejected. Whether it is the state of enlightenment or of ignorance–everything is all right. The fact is that you are in doubt. But here there is no question of doubt. Whatever you may say, and from whatever level–is He, and He, and only He.**

Our mentality is based on our relative experience which is experience of duality. Neither the Absolute nor Ma are/were dual. But we are. So Ma is beyond our conception or description. She is That which the scriptures of India has described as: "That from Which the mind and the senses turn back." Non-perception of Her was a profound perception on our part granted to us by Her. It makes no sense to our limited minds, but it was real and unforgettable even if undefinable.

Jai Ma!

Inquirer: If this is so, is it of any use to ask you further questions?

> **What is, IS. That doubts should arise is natural. But the wonder is, where THAT is, there is not even room for different stands to be taken. Problems are discussed, surely, for the purpose of dissolving doubts. Therefore it is useful to discuss. Who can tell when the veil will be lifted from your eyes?**
>
> **The purpose of discussion is to remove this ordinary sight. This vision is no vision at all, for it is only temporary.**
>
> **Real vision is that vision where there is no such thing as the seer and the seen. It is eyeless–not to be beheld with these ordinary eyes, but with the eyes of wisdom. In that vision without eyes there is no room for division. Here, (pointing to herself) there is no question of giving and taking, neither of serving. On your level they exist, from there these topics arise.**

These words of Ma are comprehensible to a yogi. But he only comprehends them, he cannot explain them since they are beyond words. That is why the upanishad says: "He who knows tells it not. He who tells knows it not." We could paraphrase it as: "He who knows does not speak. He who speaks does not know." There is only one solution to this: "Become a yogi" (Bhagavad Gita 6:46).

This evening the following statement was made "Through the observance of silence one attains to Supreme Knowledge (Jnana)."

When speech is suppressed, the activity of the mind still continues.

That is why Ma said that silence is not mere refraining from speaking, for the mind can keep on chattering though the mouth is silent. Silence is from within, a state of consciousness and being. That is why a person can appear silent but inwardly be speaking, and an adept yogi can be speaking but inwardly be silent.

All the same, such silence helps to control the mind.

So the wise sadhaka values silence and observes it.

As the mind dives deeper, its activity slackens off, and then one comes to feel that He who provides for everything, will arrange matters.

This means that the truly silent one is keenly aware of the dynamic, living presence of God and its possibilities. It is not emptiness, but fullness–full potential.

When the mind is agitated by thoughts of worldly things, the benefit that should be gained by abstaining from speech is lost.

Therefore control of the mind must accompany silence, otherwise it is empty and valueless. Writing this I am vividly remembering how when I lived next door to the Hollywood Self-Realization Fellowship center often people would come into the cafe with a piece of paper pinned to their clothes that said: "Today is my day of silence." Some silence–outer but not inner.

By the way, Ma adamantly said that a person keeping silence never engages in gestures or any kind of communication–and especially not accompanied by making noises through closed lips. People did it anyway. I was there.

> **One may, for instance, keep silent at the moment of anger, but some time or other it is bound to burst forth.**

For the mind has been mulling over and jabbering to itself and immersing itself in the anger. Then the dam breaks and the volcano erupts. There has been no true silence whatsoever.

> **When the mind is centered in God, it keeps on advancing steadily, and along with this emerges purity of body as well as mind.**

Authentic sadhana is described here. Constant japa and regular meditation produces the advancement of the mind and centers it in both God and the sadhaka's Self. Progress is inevitable and sure. Even the body will reflect the purification of mind and heart.

> **To let thought dwell on the objects of the senses is a waste of energy.**

Since it is not a physical activity, people do not realize that simply thinking itself expends energy. That is the basis of the term "brain fatigue." The brain is physical but the mind is a field of subtle psychic energy which also can be depleted. So what Ma says is quite literally true. And being intent on the objects of the senses is the door to even more depletion. Further, it becomes a psychological addiction, even enslavement. The mind and the body are interdependent and usually function as a unit. That is why thought is action and creates karma as much as physical activity. Even in our outer makeup unity is the fundamental condition.

When the mind is thus occupied and silence is not observed, it finds release in speech. Otherwise, this kind of silence might put undue strain on the senses and possibly result in ill-health.

But when the mind is turned inward, not only can there be no injury to health, but more than that, by constantly dwelling on the thought of God, all the knots (granthi) that make up the ego are unravelled, and thereby that which has to be realized will be realized.

Only in Sanatana Dharma are the body and mind fully understood and utilized for their intended functions which ultimately lead to Self-realization. Outside of Sanatana Dharma the aim of our very existence is impossible to attain.

To observe silence means to keep the mind fixed on Him.

For God is Consciousness and in the silence of the lesser consciousness of the mind the way to higher and ultimate Consciousness is revealed and accomplished. Yoga sadhana is the path to the revelation-realization of the divine Self which is inseparable from the Absolute Consciousness: Brahman.

But Ma is also pointing out that the purpose of observing silence is to be intent on japa and meditation. There are a lot of "munis" who are just intent on their mind chatter which endlessly fascinates them since they consider themselves the center of all that matters. A lot of people just brood and sink further into their ego-involving thoughts and impulses. A great deal of self [ego] worship goes on in the minds of such silent ones.

At first one feels the impulse to talk, later all inclination and disinclination vanish.

When the mind is fixed on genuine interior sadhana–mantra japa, not just ruminations of the wandering mind–the sadhaka begins to understand that he is becoming more and more interiorly aware–and therefore more alive in the true sense. He is literally increasingly himself in the highest sense. Since this is his eternal, natural condition, like the bee on the flower savoring the honey he becomes disinterested in all that disturbs his inner delight and remains intent on the Real. Satisfied in this condition, his interest is one-pointed, and ideas of talking or not talking do not arise. As the Gita (5:24) says, his "joy is inward, inward his peace, and his vision inward."

> **It is also like this: just as the bee collects honey, so all that one needs is gathered together naturally. What is necessary becomes available of its own accord–presents itself, as it were–when there is ever closer union with Him.**

This is true Self-sufficiency which is attained through the complete and unbroken Self-awareness that is "ever closer union with Him." As the Bhagavad Gita (5:24) says: "He whose happiness is within, whose delight is within, whose illumination is within: that yogi, identical in being with Brahman, attains Brahmanirvana."

> **When one entirely refrains from speaking and even from communicating by signs or gestures (*kasta maunam*), how is the body kept alive? Everything dovetails, and the silent person just watches as a kind of spectator.**

This is the perfection of what is called by sadhakas "witness consciousness," that consciousness which itself is the essence of the yogi, his very Self. It is experiential knowledge of the eternal Subject–the Self.

> **In the measure that one progresses towards union, one will notice that obstacles disappear, and whatever is necessary provides itself.**

The unaware person believes that all obstacles to his realization are external, and if they are eliminated then his path will be clear. But the practice of authentic sadhana gives him not just clear sight, but clear *insight*.

It is one thing if everything happens by itself, and quite another to make arrangements by one's own effort.

Authentic realization comes from the Self alone. Genuine sadhana clears the way to realization which arises naturally. There is no need to produce, it for that is the sadhaka's essential Self. The yogi only needs to remove the inner hindrances, and that Self which is ever-present becomes perceived.

Real silence means there is actually nowhere else for the mind to go.

This is remarkably profound. True silence is Self-awareness that is Self-knowledge. It is not attainment it is realization: Atmajnana.

In the end, whether the mind exists or not, whether one speaks or not, makes no difference.

For Reality is beyond the mind and therefore beyond thought or speech. The perfected yogi has entered into the reality of his own Self–which is ultimately the Supreme Self.

To say "through silence He is realized" is not correct, because Supreme Knowledge does not come "through" anything–Supreme Knowledge reveals Itself.

Sadhana does not produce realization: it removes the blockages, the elements, that prevent our awakening into the experience/awareness that is Self-realization. So involvement in the gimmickry that is commonly thought to be yoga sadhana only compounds the problem and permatizes it through the sadhaka's mistaken involvement and satisfaction in it.

For destroying the "veil," there are suitable spiritual disciplines and practices.

Japa Yoga (Mantra Yoga) was the only yogic discipline/practice that Ma recommended for Self-realization. But there were many things that supported or ensured the successful practice of japa yoga.

Because I had become involved with various false practices presented as yoga before I came in contact with Her, Ma explained to me the erroneous and harmful nature/effect of those practices and insisted on japa as the sole way to spiritual realization. This was because I had asked Her what I should be doing for sadhana. Throughout Her explanation of the erroneous nature of these methods She kept saying to me: "Because you asked me I am telling you these things." In this way She indicated that I must always ask Her regarding my spiritual discipline and not assume that what I was doing was correct or assume that Ma would of Herself tell me if my practice was not legitimate or correct. At the end of this session, Sri K. Bose, the General Secretary of the Anandamayi Sangha and administrator of all the Anandamayi Ashrams, said to me: "Sitting here with you today I have heard from Mataji's lips what I have never heard before."

Inquirer: What about the silent sadhu at Navadvip?*

[Many years ago, when Sri Ma went to Navadvip with Bholanath, a sadhu there attracted very wide attention. He used to sit all day long in the lotus pose, so perfectly still that it was difficult to find out whether he was a living man or a statue. Everyone felt awed and took it for granted that he was a great saint in a state of deep samadhi. Sri Ma, however, made no comment on the matter. Staying next door to the man, she soon made sure that he bathed, ate and slept secretly during the night. By and by the sadhu confided to Sri Ma that he was made to assume that pose in order to get money. Through Sri Ma's benign influence he gave up this life of deception.]

By practice he had made the body still, but his mind had not been transformed at all; it was a case of mere physical control. If

his mind had been stilled, that kind of worldly behavior would have been impossible. However, even such practice is not altogether useless, it does lead to some result. But That, which is the real need, is not found.

Fortunately, Ma told us what was the real need and the way to find it.

NINE

Benares, September 27, 1948

Inquirer: When the mind is immersed in samadhi, does one or does one not experience the supernormal (chamatkara–inner vision)? If so, does this imply that one has deviated from the object of one's contemplation? And what is the real cause of this?

Samadhi means samadhana (solution, completion).

There are different forms or types of samadhi. One is even called "jada samadhi" when means going unconscious and basically being in a dreamless state that has nothing supernormal about it, but is a tamasic condition that is at best without effect or has a deadening and delusive effect. A lot of people claim to be in samadhi when they are asleep. A friend of mine was in a group meditation and one man was asleep and leaning further and further forward. So my friend gently woke him up. When the meditation was over and they were outside, the man berated my friend vigorously and said: "I was in samadhi and you brought me out of it!" There really is such a thing as "invincible ignorance."

Anyhow, Ma is saying that true samadhi brings about the completion, the ending of ignorance and samsara. So "Ye shall know them by their fruits" (Matthew 7:16-23). Unless Self-realization is furthered or fully attained, such samadhi is no real samadhi at all. We should understand the truth about such delusionals' "samadhi" even if they do not.

Inquirer: Solution involves a question, whereas samadhi is a state in itself.

This person knows better than Ma! How amazing. But Ma is having none of it.

So She says:

> **This body does not use the language of the shastras; it refers to ordinary things, such as water, earth, air, and so forth, when it speaks. Those who have understanding are able to comprehend this kind of broken and incomplete language. Samadhana signifies the perfect resolution of form, formlessness, manifested being, and non-being–of everything. The solution of a problem is one thing; yet there is another kind of resolution where the possibility of problems and their solutions cannot occur; this is called samadhi.**

As Ma says: "Those who have understanding are able to comprehend this kind of broken and incomplete language." Apparently "Inquirer" could not.

Ma said consistently that She did not have a mind. All her words were the result of a movement, a manifestation, of consciousness itself. She spoke in a manner she herself calls "broken and incomplete." Ma spoke in a kind of verbal shorthand. For example, her version of this sentence of mine would be something like: "Ma verbal shorthand." So when we read Ma's words in a book or article, we are reading a speculative reconstruction of her words. For example if Ma had said the preceding sentence it might be: "We Ma words speculative." Swami Bhaskarananda told me that he had met three people who had known Sri Ramakrishna and they all three said that he spoke exactly like Ma did. And he, too, was considered an incarnation of God.

It was not unknown for people to try and set Ma straight if they did not like (or understand?) her words. So most of the things we will find an "Inquirer" saying is of negligible–if any–value or accuracy. More is to come. Let's just get through it.

Inquirer: Quite so; thus there are two kinds of samadhi, namely savikalpa and nirvikalpa.

The first signifies the resolution of cosmic existence into the One Pure Existence (Satta), and as for the second–there, there is even no such thing as 'Existence'.

Inquirer: No such thing as 'Existence'? What then is it?

So long as thoughts and ideas (sankalpa and vikalpa) persist, not even Savikalpa samadhi can occur. Savikalpa samadhi signifies Awareness of Existence. But when there is no question of Existence–when there is no possibility of differentiating 'what is' from 'what is not'–can anything be expressed in words, however little? This is nirvikalpa samadhi. Where is there room for the supernormal here?

Inquirer: The supernormal, in other words, matters that are beyond this world (aloukik), are not within the reach of ordinary intelligence; yet they can most certainly be grasped by the mind. If one accepts the mind as a fact, its own creations are themselves the subjects about which it thinks. There is of course something apart from the mind–Chit [Consciousness], which is said to be complete in itself. Anything before the vision of the mind in contemplation, other than THAT, is what is usually called chamatkara [inner vision].

Who perceives the chamatkara [inner vision]?

Inquirer: The mind.

So then, if there is no mind, the super-normal cannot be perceived. Consequently, how can visions be seen in nirvikalpa samadhi?

Inquirer: My reason tells me that in both types of samadhi the mind must be present. According to the shastras, in Nirvikalpa Samadhi the mind ceases to be. Of course, the gross mind does not persist, yet it will have to be admitted that the subtle mind remains in a state of latency. Otherwise, how could the experience be known afterwards? In other words, is it or is it not remembered when it is over? If it is, then it will no doubt have to be conceded that the subtle mind still exists.

> **Some say that a tiny particle [the technical term is 'avidya lesa'–a small residue of ignorance] of the mind remains; for if it did not, how could there be the manifestation of the body? But this body declares also this: If by the fire of illumination everything can be consumed, should not this tiny fragment be burnt up as well? Where experience occurs, the mind must of course exist; there can be no chamatkara [inner vision] without the mind.**

Inquirer: If that small portion of the mind ceases to exist, how can the body continue? In which condition does the last trace of the mind disappear? While the prarabdha is still active, or after it has been exhausted?

> **What is your opinion, Pitaji? Of course, some maintain that in samadhi the ego-mind does not exist. However, this body says that, if by Supreme Knowledge everything is burnt up, should it not have the power to consume the praradbdha as well?**

Inquirer: If the prarabdha has been effaced, how can the body possibly persist?

> **Do you mean by this that so long as the body endures, there must of necessity be some prarabdha left over, and therefore the mind must also have survived? Well, yes, if you accept as a reality the body in the usually accepted sense of the word, you will undoubtedly have to admit the existence of prarabdha and, from your point of view, the existence of the mind too. 'Body' [Sharira–body, *sora*–to move away] means perpetual change, that which is ever moving away. But in the state where death may be said to be dead, can there still be any question of a body?**

Inquirer: When one has visions of the supernormal, does it indicate that one has turned aside from the Supreme state, or not?

When the Ultimate Reality has been attained, there can be no question of either the state of deviating or not deviating from Reality.

What is meant by videha-mukti?

Inquirer: Not to be obligated to assume another body after this one has been left, is called videhamukti.

Very well; is the body then an obstacle, and does it therefore fall away?

Inquirer: No, the objective of nirvikalpa samadhi is to attain to the power of imparting true knowledge to seekers (and for this a body is required).

Samadhi also has to be called a state. Everything is possible according to the particular stage of a person's development. Everyone will assuredly gain the knowledge pertaining to the state he has reached.

Inquirer: This being so, it is obvious that experience of the supernormal indicates a deviation from one's object of contemplation.

When one's object of contemplation has become Self-revealed, that is to say, when there is the revelation of THAT in the form of one's object of contemplation, how can one deviate from it?

Inquirer: Has the experience of the supernormal not its root in desire?

That only becomes manifest, of which the seed is sown; otherwise, how could it come into being?

Inquirer: Take the waves of a lake; they do not constitute the nature of the water, they are created by the wind; how is it possible to become desireless?

> **So long as the seed has not been sterilized, it is bound to germinate. Now then, what is your opinion: does the body survive or not, when true knowledge of the Self supervenes?**

Inquirer: I should think it would survive.

> **Yes–as some say, supported by the tiny portion of the mind that has been preserved!**

Inquirer: Does a spiritual teacher instruct from the state of Self-realization or is he still in the state of ignorance?

> **It would certainly not be right to presume the state of ignorance of Reality when the aim of the instruction is Self-realization.**

Inquirer: This is why I feel that the karma cannot have been completely exhausted.

> **Just as an electric fan continues to revolve for a little while after the current has been switched off?**

Inquirer: In this example, the electric current has been cut off completely. Does this then imply that, in a similar way, ignorance has been entirely destroyed?

> **The connection is broken. What had already begun and is taking effect is called prarabdha.**

Inquirer: If this be the case, can prarabdha bear fruit or not? I think that its destruction is not in keeping with the facts.

Does the teaching of the Enlightened Sage (Jnani) refer to truth as it reveals itself before His prarabdha is exhausted, or does it refer to the truth beyond?

Inquirer: No, not to the Truth beyond. Instruction on pure Truth, untouched by prarabdha, is given by an Avatara. The Jnani's teaching is limited by his prarabdha.

Where Knowledge is Self-revealed, does its Self-revelation depend upon karma?

Inquirer: There are two kinds of knowledge: Svarupa Jnana (Knowledge of Self) and vritti jnana (acquired mental knowledge). The second kind of knowledge, which pertains to the jnani, enables him to reap the fruits of his prarabdha.

Do you mean to suggest that, just as a child gradually increases his knowledge by continuous study, here also there is progressive accumulation of knowledge? But this can not be called the state of a Jnani!

Inquirer: Swarupa Jnana is Self-revealed, whereas vritti jnana is knowledge of objects. Swarupa Jnana does not make a jnani, He, who posses vritti jnana is called jnani, for knowledge of the Self is common to all.

Does 'Knowledge of the Self' mean that one is established in any particular state?

Inquirer: One is established in the Self.

Quite right, Pitaji. As you say, every-one without exception is rooted in Knowledge of the Self; yes indeed, this is so.

Inquirer: Nevertheless, not all are aware of this Knowledge. Those who have gained vritti jnana may alone be styled jnanis, for they will be able to guide an aspirant in keeping with his mental make-up.

> **Yes, but what has this to do with the state where the Self in its Glory stands ever Self revealed?**
>
> **He who by gradual development has acquired knowledge and been progressively enlightened, he, as you say, is established in vritti jnana.**

We have finally gotten through Inquier's muddled and worthless thinking. Now let's consider Ma's wisdom.

> **Words, arguments, language, and the like, are of the mind; whereas in the state that has just been referred to, there, language has no place.**

Naturally there must be "words, arguments, language, and the like" where the lower mind is functioning, but there is indeed a level where language is not needed, where communication takes place in the higher bodies, in the buddhi and beyond in the intuitive reaches of the mind which are unknown to most people, even in theory. But the yogi continually opens himself to those levels by his sadhana and becomes more and more consciously functional on those levels. This is what a "complete person" really is: one who functions fully in the physical, pranic, sensory, intellectual, and intuitional bodies–the annamaya, pranamaya, manomaya, jnanamaya and anandamaya bodies.

> **This body respects whatever anyone may say, because each person's point of view depends on the particular stairway by which he ascends. Whatever idea may be held–be it on a high or low level–it is all the same, so far as this body is concerned.**

It would be good if those who fancy themselves philosophers and savants would adopt this viewpoint when relating to others and their opinions and philosophies. There is a level when a sadhaka understands that all words are true and at the same time untrue, owing to the limitations of language itself and the human mind.

Those who can communicate in silence are the best and most reliable teachers, and those who can comprehend such communications are the best or most worthy students. I once read the account of a man who went to see Sri Ramana Maharshi with several questions no one had been able to answer to his satisfaction. When he learned Sri Ramana usually was silent, he was disappointed but went into the hall and sat there. Sri Ramana at one point began to scan the gathering, momentarily looking into the eyes of each person. The man knew the answers to all his questions simultaneously the instant Sri Ramana looked into his eyes.

Self-realization is the answer to all questions.

> **For this reason, whether anyone is of the opinion that the body can or cannot exist without or advances a theory from whatever point of view, everything is right on its own plane. Yet, beyond words and all expression, where there is manifestation and non-manifestation, duration and non-duration, space and space-lessness–there, nothing holds good.**

Eventually the questing intelligence comes to the point Ma is speaking about: That everything is true–if we accept the reality of relativity. And that nothing (no-thing) is true–if we accept that the Absolute alone ever is and alone is real. But still it is talk, and Brahman is beyond words and therefore beyond concepts. So it is not a matter of statements being true or false, but the fact that they are both true and false simultaneously–that the Real yet incomprehensibly both includes and transcends both Thing and No Thing.

I once heard someone say that in the phrase: "I Am That" we can eliminate "I" and "That" so only AM remains. And that is incomprehensible and indefinable and therefore inexpressible. So the true jnani is a muni. Silence alone suffices.

Considering what I have written I could not help but remember a Zen story of some men who decided to have a silent meditation retreat.

After many hours one them said: "Do you realize we have not spoken for several hours?" "Well you just DID" barked one of the men. So silence prevailed for a long time until the third man said: "Do you realize that I am the only one who hasn't spoken?"

We do the best we can.

Even the essence of the things of this world cannot be spoken about; but the essence of Transcendental Being is something far more remote. Then, there is also what is known as 'merging.' But from that into which one is said to have merged, a yogi may be able to extricate one again; this also is a possibility mentioned by you people, is it not? Yet in the state of which this body tells, there it is not so–and 'not so' does not express it either. By reasoning and discrimination, one may arrive at the conclusion that a small portion of the mind remains so long as physical existence continues. But this body speaks of a state where there is not even the possibility of a trace of the mind.

How can this be commented on?

Inquirer: Does the body then continue to exist or not?

In this particular state, if the body were an obstacle this state could simply not be. In this condition, the question whether the body is being retained or not, cannot arise.

Inquirer: Can there be inquiry and response in that state?

Yes, there can be–if the idea of the body is there. For those who think there are disciples and Gurus, for them there are questions and answers.

Inquirer: But then to speak of Gurus, disciples and so forth, is quite meaningless.

The progress of the disciple continues up to where the position of a teacher is held. If the teacher is in the state of ajnana, and the question is asked by one also in ignorance, how can there be even an expectation of the revelation of real Knowledge? All the same, a discussion that aims at elucidating Self-realization will naturally be helpful and beneficial.

So we are not completely hopeless.

Very well, Pitaji, tell me, in the case of a preceptor who is a World-teacher, is it not natural that there should be questions and answers with a view to the attainment of Self-realization? It is and will ever be so–surely is this an untruth?Something else has to be considered: Say, who replies to whom?

That questions are being put and replied to, is merely the idea of the inquirer at his stage. Can you call him who gives answers an individual, just because he responds? To whom does he reply? Who replies, and what is the reply? Who is who in that state of Pure Being? The place of vritti jnana is where Self-revelation is not. This is difficult to accept, while it is still a matter for acceptance or rejection. On the level where the question of acceptance or rejection cannot possibly arise, how can there be talk and conversation?

Pitaji, when you asked: "Tell me your experience," it would imply that the experiencer has still remained. This cannot be so here; furthermore, the question of transmission of power by the guru to the disciple is equally non-existent. If there is no body, this question cannot be there either. There is no question of a physical or any other body. What is beyond even that, cannot be put into words in any language.

Whatever can be expressed in words or speech, is a creation of the mind.

Pitaji, as to the saying "There is only one Brahman, without a second"–in the Self there is no possibility at all of a "second."

The notion of the "two" has come about through the operating of reason.

Just as you say: "Without feet He walks and without eyes He sees."

This body maintains that whatever anyone may say from the plane of reason–with the idea that the body exists, from the standpoint of the disciple–can be supported on the level of reasoning.

For one's vision is conditioned by the spectacles one uses. This body declares that, whatever theory anyone may hold is based on reasoning, which presupposes the existence of a residue of the mind and of prarabdha. But where THAT stands revealed, it is quite otherwise: there, to discriminate or speculate is impossible. Beyond reason, beyond points of view, there is a state where none of these can be.

Pitaji, in very truth, in THAT there is no room for words, language, or discrimination of any kind. Whether one says "there is not" or "there is"–these are also merely words, words *floating* on the surface [Bhasa–means language and also–spelt differently–"to *float*."] Therefore it said that here words, language, utterances of any type, have no place. This is the truth, Pitaji, do you understand?

You will not have received precise replies to your queries. From what has been said, you will have to take what can be grasped by the intellect.

How do you explain the Unexplainable or any discussion about the Undiscussible?

Silence is wisdom.

Ten

Benares, August 12, 1948.

Inquirer: What are the benefits to be derived from hatha yoga, and what are its drawbacks?

> **What does 'hatha' mean? To do something by force. 'Being' is one thing, and 'doing' quite another. When there is 'being', there will be the spontaneous manifestation of what is due to be manifested, owing to the prana functioning in a particular centre of the body.**

"Spontaneous" is the operative word here.

> **On the other hand, if one practices hatha yoga merely as a physical exercise, the mind will not be transformed in the very least. By physical exercise bodily fitness is developed. One hears quite often of cases where the giving up of the practice of yogic postures and the like, has resulted in physical disorders.**
>
> **Just as the body grows weak from lack of adequate nourishment, so the mind has need of suitable food. When the mind receives proper sustenance, man moves towards God, whereas by catering to the body, he only increases his worldliness. Mere gymnastics is nutrition for the body.**

What is the food and exercise the sadhaka requires? Japa, meditation and the observance of Yama and Niyama.

> **Now, as to 'doing': Sustained effort ends in effortless being; in other words, what has been attained by constant practice is finally transcended.**

Transcended by that which IS in which there is no need or possibility of further effort.

Then comes spontaneity. Not until this happens can the utility of hatha yoga be understood.

In Ma's sadhana lila nothing was intentional. Everything simply took place. And Ma is saying that hatha yoga is not at all a practice, but is actually a spontaneous expression of what already is. That we find this incomprehensible is not a problem but a symptom pointing to the necessity for entering into That which is beyond comprehension and beyond Being and Non-being: AM.

When the physical fitness resulting from hatha yoga is used as an aid to spiritual endeavor, it is not wasted. Otherwise, it is not yoga, but bhoga (enjoyment).

No comment needed.

In effortless being lies the path to the Infinite.

Hatha yoga cannot lead to effortless being which is only revealed through sadhana.

Unless hatha yoga aims at the Eternal, it is nothing more than gymnastics. If in the normal course of the practice His touch is not felt, the yoga has been fruitless.

It has not even been yoga but bhoga, as Ma has said.

One comes across people who, by engaging in all sorts of yogic exercises, like neti, dhauti, and others of the kind, have become seriously ill. At Nainital I recently met a young man who had ruined his health completely by practicing hatha yoga. He

was suffering from persistent diarrhoea, which simply would not stop. He and some of his friends had decided to become experts in hatha yoga, and to start a college, where union with God would be attained through this discipline. But they, one and all, fell ill.

The conclusion to be made is evident.

A competent teacher, who understands every change in the movement of the disciple's prana, will accordingly either speed up the process or slow it down just as a helmsman steers a boat with the rudder held firmly all the time. Without such direction hatha yoga is not beneficial. He who would guide must have first-hand knowledge of everything that may occur at any stage, must see it with the perfect sharpness of direct perception.

For is he not the physician of those on the Path? Without the help of such a doctor, there is danger of injury.

And with such a teacher of hatha yoga nothing will be attained but avoidance of illness.

Everything becomes smooth once the blessing of His touch has been felt. It is just as, when bathing in a river, one at first swims by one's own strength; but once caught in the current, whether a good swimmer or not, one is simply carried away. Therefore it is detrimental if this 'touch' is not experienced.

No one but the sadhaka is even reaching out for that Touch.

One must enter into the rhythm of one's true nature. Its revelation, acting as a flash of lightning, will attract one to it instantaneously, irresistibly; there comes a point where no further action is needed.

Sadhana and its inevitable results are indicated here.

What sadhana did Ma advocate? Japa and meditation of the Divine Name.

> **So long as this contact has not been established, dedicate to God whatever inclinations or disinclinations you may have, and devote yourself to service, meditation, contemplation–to anything of this kind.**

This is colossal, however short and simple it may appear to be. For it calls for a total rearranging of thought and deeds. It is a grave error to think that Ma's instructions are easy. It is calling for a profound reorientation of mind and life. If someone thinks Ma is outlining a simple and easy way: just go ahead a try it. In the meantime I will analyze it in detail.

So long as this contact has not been established.

Ma defined this contact when she just previously said: "One must enter into the rhythm of one's true nature." In a sense, one must *become* one's Self through direct knowledge and practical manifestation of It, with the entire being unified in perfect alignment with the Self. This can only be accomplished and maintained through constant sadhana.

Dedicate to God whatever inclinations or disinclinations you may have.

Whatever the impulses that arise into the mind, they must be submitted to the perspective of divine experience. Only the yogi can do this, for only the yogi is engaging in continual and thorough centering of his consciousness in the Self. And that process is: yoga. All the philosophy in the world means nothing if wisdom is not evoked from within and maintained by the external life. Again: "Become a yogi" (Bhagavad Gita 6:46). This is the only path to life. For life is within us, and is the Self.

And devote yourself to service, meditation, contemplation–to anything of this kind.

These three elements have many aspects and many levels on which they can be engaged in. Ma is declaring that external conduct must be accompanied by sadhana! For it is sadhana that empowers and illuminates our external actions. Those actions should be extensions of our sadhana. That is why we have the term karma yoga: yoga that IS action.

Generally you perform your daily worship in the accustomed manner.

Ritualistic worship produces many benefits, both inwardly and outwardly. The very practice of putting our attention on symbols of the Divine Reality draws our minds toward the subtle realms and at the same time draws the subtle vibrations of higher consciousness into the level of our usual life. It is both an ascent and a descent that are divine in character. And continual interchange of consciousness is the purpose of what is mistakenly called "external, material" action. For nothing is merely physical or metaphysical. There is a simultaneous movement in both the material and psychic realms, though it may not be perceived.

During my first pilgrimage to India a friend of mine told me about a man who was very devoted to Sri Krishna in the form of Balkrishna, the Child Krishna. He had an image of Krishna and spent a great deal of time in ritualistic worship of that image. His family were not pleased with this and often admonished him to stop spending so much of his time in worship. He paid no attention to them, so they went to a local saint and asked him to come and straighten the matter out. He agreed and went to the man's home and observed his very long worship. When he came out of the puja room he told the family: "You are only seeing him worshipping Krishna, but I tell you that Krishna is worshipping him in return."

I also met a simple elderly woman who did not have room in her tiny apartment for a worship area. So every day she went to her son's house where she had been allotted a tiny area in a storage room and did worship. One day I was wandering around, and I went there out of curiosity. The moment I stepped in that area I felt an intense divine presence. That woman's family may not have respected her worship, but God certainly did!

If you feel the desire to practice some extra japa or meditation, it shows that you have caught a glimpse, however faint, and there is then hope that gradually the rhythm of your true nature may emerge.

The ultimate purpose of external worship is to purify and train the mind to look within and perceive the all-pervading Reality. Therefore it is natural that the external worship will awaken in the sadhaka the desire to give more time to japa and meditation when the worship is complete. For japa and meditation are interior processes, though to some degree external actions. The worshipper is experiencing the inner call of the Self through his external activity. This is proof of its legitimate and worthy character. And hopefully that call of the worshipper's true Self will prevail and be fully answered. For the inner urge to perform outer ritualistic worship comes from the person's Self which desires to be revealed through that worship. And it will be so. There are no such things as "mere externals" as spiritual slackers like to say. For nothing can be done if there is not an inner impulse toward it.

In this condition, the sense of I' (aham) still persists, but this I is turned towards the Eternal, intent on union with Him.

And that "I" is the Self, not the ego, that is being drawn to fix the mind on the inner reality. When its impulses are followed it can increasingly become perceived by the sadhaka until the spirit-essence stands revealed.

Whereas, actions done with a view to fame or distinction are of the ego (ahamkara), and therefore obstacles, impediments.

This is simple truth.

Whether you practice hatha yoga or raja yoga, or any other yoga, it can be harmful only if pure spiritual aspiration is lacking.

There is a lot of noise about how yoga can be "dangerous" for various reasons, especially hatha and raja yoga since they involve physical discipline and effort. Anything can be detrimental if it is done in a foolish way. And there are fools who deliberately act in a manner that will harm them–for that is their intention. Through the years I have heard such spiritually dishonest people defensively say: "Well, I gave it a chance." But they deliberately did "it" in the wrong way so it would be either useless or harmful.

Figures do not lie, but liars figure–and so do evil and evil-intentioned people who pretend to spiritual life when their real aim is to excuse themselves and defame the philosophy or disciplines by wrongly applying them–or sometimes by overdoing them. I have known such people and watched them exercising their "exit strategies." But Ma says that if there is pure spiritual aspiration in the practice, then the aspirant will not do things incorrectly or will realize any error and correct it. The higher Self of the yogi is a trustworthy guide. But the ego and the lower mind, the not-self, of the unworthy non-aspirant, will work very real havoc. Intentionally.

> **When doing asanas and the like, if you have found access to nature's own rhythm, you will see that everything proceeds smoothly and spontaneously.**

But if not, troubles will develop or the results will be nil. This is all a matter of the aspirant's personal intuition.

> **By what signs is this to be recognized? There is a sense of play, a deep delight, and the constant remembrance of the One.**

Ease, happiness and satisfaction arise, but most importantly the continual awareness of the inmost Being, the Self, will prevail.

> **Indeed, this is not the outcome of the practice of worldly [merely external] observances. What has been referred to here is that which can only become revealed spontaneously–of its own accord. This is why there is constant remembrance of the One: man's true nature flows towards God alone.**

But how does our nature flow toward God? First, by the nature of our very Self, which is divine in essence. And what is "constant remembrance of the One?" Japa and meditation–constant japa and daily meditation for a reasonable and therefore effective amount of time.

> **Again, sometimes when sitting in meditation you will find that rechaka [exhalation], puraka [inhalation], or kumbhaka [pause in breathing] have come about without effort.**

This is so. There will be neither effort nor intention. You may not even be aware it is occurring because your attention is fixed on a higher level.

By the way, it is not mentioned in any of these sayings of Ma, but She was adamant that sadhakas in general should never do pranayama of any kind. (There were exceptions.) Rather, the breath should be effortless and spontaneous, and these elements of pranayama should occur only spontaneously.

> **When the movement of your true nature sets in, then, because it is directed solely towards God, the knots of the heart will be unravelled.**

All obstacles and "glitches" will in time disappear effortlessly.

> **If during meditation you find perfectly correct asanas forming of themselves–the spine becoming erect of its own accord–then you should know that the current of your prana is turned towards the Eternal.**

This needs no comment. Whatever is natural, effortless and spontaneous is beneficial. And it will occur to the persistant sadhaka in time.

> **Otherwise, when you are engaged in japa, the right flow will not come, and your back may begin to ache. Still; even this kind of japa is not without its effect, although its specific action is not**

experienced. In other words, the mind is willing but the body does not respond, and therefore you do not get the exhilaration that comes with the aroma of the Divine Presence.

I find it interesting that Ma gives no advice as to what the sadhaka should do at such times. However, She does say to keep on with the japa and meditation as it will in time produce the good and right effect–if we are doing it correctly.

To let the mind dwell on sense objects, still further increases one's attachment to them. When intense interest in the Supreme Quest awakens, ever more time and attention will be given to religious thought, religious philosophy, the remembrance of God as immanent in all creation, until thereby every single knot is untwisted.

Well, Ma certainly does not ascribe to the "spiritual but not religious" cant that negative people in the West love to spout. The sadhaka can know that his practice and life are correct when he is increasingly involved in religion, both theoretical and practical (action). Yes. He listens to religious/spiritual discourses and discussions, he reads religious/spiritual books and articles, he participates in the activities of "organized" religion, and he strives to be aware of the Divine Presence in the world around him. And "thereby every single knot is untwisted."

One is stirred by a deep yearning: "How can I find Him?" As a result of this, the rhythm of body and mind will grow steady, calm, serene.

This is the awakening of the inmost reality, the sadhaka's Self. This is not merely intellectual and is not at all emotional. It is the arising of true Reason and Understanding that are attributes of the awakening Self.

Note that Ma says something I have not found anywhere else but in Her teachings: "As a result of this, the rhythm of body and mind will grow steady, calm, serene." The sadhaka's external, material life and existence will reflect the inner state of the awakening Self. Actually, if this does not happen, then the person is not on the right path. The inner life of the sadhaka pervades and transforms his external life until the two are one. The sadhaka's life becomes as transformed as his inner life and reflects it completely. This is the beginning, the foreshadowing, of eventual Divine Union.

> **Some of you naturally conceive a desire to do asanas and the like as spiritual exercises. If in this no wish to show off is present, it will be easy to enter into the rhythm of your true nature.**
>
> **But if the mind is held captive by the body, these exercises become mere gymnastics.**

We determine this ourselves, and clear-sighted self-examination is needed.

> **It happens that aspirants are driven in the direction they are meant to go, although at first they are not conscious of this, or even if they be, they are unable to resist.**

I once read a book on inner life that spoke of the aspirant being "driven into the Divine Presence." Of course, the aspirant is the "drawn" and his higher Self is the "drawer." If they are in genuine synchronization, it is the Atmabala, the Power of the Self, that is manifesting. Saint John Vianney described the true spiritual life as "a shot from a cannon." It is irresistible and inevitable. And permanent.

> **Suppose some people go to bathe in the sea and make up their minds to swim ahead of everyone else; consequently they will have to look back. But for him, whose one and only goal is the Ocean Itself, no one has remained for whose sake he looks back or is concerned; and then, what is to be, will be.**

This is stunning in its simplicity and absoluteness. For the seeker who is determined to be a finder looks only to the Infinite. He does not look back because he knows those "back there" are part of unreality. For him they no longer exist in the practical sense. When that is the genuine mentality of the sadhaka that prevails and continues, then there is no question: he reaches the Goal. That journey truly is The Flight Of The Alone To The ALONE. There are only two on the path to the One: the seeker and the Sought.

> **Give yourself up to the wave, and you will be absorbed by the current; having dived into the sea, you do not return anymore.**

To dive into the sea, the whole person, body and mind and soul have to go in together. So then our entire being is given "up to the wave" and carried onward to the Goal because we have become one with it–and we have no other destiny or desire. We will not return to the restless (because it is so shallow) sea of samsara.

> **The Eternal Himself is the wave that floods the shore, so that you may be carried away. Those who can surrender themselves to this aim will be accepted by Him.**

It will be even better if we can actively move forward on this "wave" through continual sadhana. Then we cannot fail to reach the Goal. Ma is implying that our very purpose for existing is to merge ourselves with the wave that carries us into the Infinite Being. To succeed in this is the only true success, and to fail is the ultimate failure. Sadhana is the very being of the sadhaka. It is his only purpose. That is why he exists at all. We entered relative existence as an atom of hydrogen with that sole purpose: Liberation through Self-realization. Sadhana alone can keep us from being failures–cosmic failures!

> **But if your attention remains directed towards the shore, you cannot proceed–after bathing you will return home.**

If our attention is toward the finite we will remain in the finite. But if it is toward the Infinite we will turn from the finite and merge with the Infinite. That is the simple truth. We choose. Swami Vijayananda, a Frenchman who lived in the Anandamayi Asham in Dehra Dun, as a young man visited an esoteric community in France and asked what their purpose was. One of them simply answered: "To make sure our past does not become our future." We must realize the direction we are truly moving in and ensure it is toward the Infinite that is our true Self.

If your aim is the Supreme, the Ultimate, you will be led on by the movement of your true nature.

Two things are needed: that our aim is the Supreme and our true nature is operative within us and therefore can take us there. Then in the most glorious sense nature will take its course and bear us onward to our Self.

There are waves that carry away, and waves that pull back. Those who can give themselves up will be taken by Him. In the guise of the wave He holds out His Hand and calls you: Come, *Come*, COME!

This giving up is not passive, but the highest endeavor, for it manifests as sadhana which is the total alignment of ourselves with the Godward Current–no small accomplishment, and one that must be absolutely made permanent and irreversible. Within and without the Absolute is calling and reaching toward us. And the call is urgent, as Ma's words indicate. What is needed is our calling to the Infinite and our urgency of will and aspiration. When our will to the Infinite equals Its will toward us then success is assured and inevitable.

Inquirer: How can we benefit spiritually by action?

By doing action for its own sake, engaging in karma yoga. As long as a desire to distinguish oneself is lurking, it is karma

bhoga–acting for one's own satisfaction. One does the action and enjoys its fruit, because of the sense of prestige it brings. Whereas, by relinquishing the fruit, it becomes karma yoga.

Inaction–the will to inaction–is also action. So both action and inaction can be a karmic force.

How does a sadhaka engage in action without desire or ego-involvement? By engaging in effective sadhana which by its nature eliminates both desire and egotism from the sadhaka's inner makeup. Simple. But not easy. Yet possible: inevitable. See *Soham Yoga. The Yoga of the Self.*

Inquirer: How is it possible to act without desire?

By doing service with the feeling that one is serving the Supreme Being in everyone. The desire for God-realization is obviously not a desire in the ordinary sense. "I am Thy instrument; deign to act through this, Thine instrument...."

By regarding all manifestation as the Supreme Being, one attains to communion that leads to liberation. Whatever action is undertaken, let it be done with one's whole being and in the spirit: "Thou alone acteth," so that there may be no opportunity for affliction, distress or sorrow to creep in.

Only the yogi can accomplish this. And only by action empowered with aspiration to perfect Self-realization.

To consider that God alone is the Doer is not a mindset or inner willing. It is an experience, the experience of Self-realization wherein the sadhaka KNOWS "Soham Asmi"–I Am That.

Another point: If the attitude "through my shortcoming the action has not been done well enough, I should have taken still greater pains over this service," is not persisted in, the action must be considered to have been done carelessly. Therefore, as far as it lies in your power there should be no neglect. Beyond

> **that, feel that whatever happens is in His hands; you are but the tool. Because of this, put your body, mind and heart into any service you may do, and for the rest take it that what comes about was destined to be: "Thou has manifested Thyself in this way as was ordained, and so has it been wrought."**

Again: only the yogi can do this because it involves thinking in a wholistic manner that seems to be self-contradictory, even seems to be moving in two opposing directions at the same time. But actually it is transcending linear thought and encompassing the non-duality that is the only Truth. It is not thinking at all, but KNOWING and BEING.

Inquirer: Even when there is spontaneous action, it is still action. Hence, if there is no other guru, how can our doubts be cleared?

> **There are two kinds of action you may say, and an infinite number of kinds. However, this requires explanation.**
>
> **When an asana begins to form, it speaks just as you–"I do." In what manner? When the purpose for which the asana is done becomes disclosed, when that which can be attained through any particular yogic posture, is accomplished, this may be called as "its language."**
>
> **When a sick man moves about too much, he overstrains himself and becomes breathless. Naturally everyone's breathing changes its rhythm constantly according to the way one sits or moves, only one is not aware of it. One who has control over his breath can transfer it at will to any level. In the beginning, those of you who practice yogic postures do not know which leg to cross first and which after, and whether to inhale or exhale while doing so. Consequently, what you do is in part incorrect. Why?**
>
> **When you want to open something and you do not know how it is done, damage may ensue. When an asana forms spontaneously, you will notice that your legs fold and unfold in the correct manner and in harmony with the breath. It is a sign that**

the guru is at work, when the asana and the breath are in perfect concord. While before one had no knowledge of the posture, it is now clearly understood. In terms of the mind: one watches oneself as a witness, like a child as it were; one feels that someone is causing everything to be done, and that at the same time the movement of the mind is being stilled.

This needs no comment. It is practical observation. However, Ma would not have said these things if they were not necessary for those to whom She was speaking. Therefore not a single word from Ma's lips can be left unheeded. But their relevancy will be according to the individual's mentality and involvement.

When the vibrations of your body and prana have reached a stage where there is great skill in everything relevant to the Supreme Quest, you will find yourself voicing spiritual truths–this is the spontaneous action at that stage.

And when you become established at the level of a Rishi to whom mantras are revealed, that is to say, when the vibrations of your body and prana have become centered there, words corresponding to this level will issue from your lips.

These are remarkable words, especially Ma's implications that these conditions and states will occur to everyone at some time in the future. To fully comprehend them intellectually at present is unlikely. So we should keep focused on our present sadhana without which these conditions and states cannot occur. Though it is a certainty that there are those who will try to act as those these states are manifesting in them and even fake them according to their understanding as to what they would appear to be.

There is a state in which you may have neither knowledge nor understanding of what is taking place, as for instance, when a yogic posture of which you are ignorant forms unawares. Who has brought it about? The inner guru.

In a similar way, when a mantra bursts forth, the solution to your problem and the inner significance (tattwa) of the mantra in its supramental form (pratyaksha murti) appear directly before you. In other words, together with its essence its subtle form stands revealed. At that moment you come to understand the real nature of the inner guru: He dwells within and acts from there.

Not only have your doubts been dispelled, you have also gained understanding of the mantra's esoteric meaning. This is real darshana.

Here you receive a response without being aware of how it has come about. In another 'variety of experience,' the hidden process of what is taking place is uncovered. Here the mantra, the tattwa, the guru and the Ishta are revealed simultaneously. This is an example of receiving revelation with the full knowledge of all its phases and aspects. Suppose one is engaged in japa or meditation. A question arises in the mind. In a flash the reply is there. One realizes: "The guru has told me this; what has come to me is the guru's own teaching."

This, too, we should be wary of applying to ourselves. Ma has told us these things because we should keep them in mind for the future where these things may occur. They certainly have relevance, otherwise Ma would not have spoken them.

There is a line of approach through action, and another through the mind: or to be more precise, in the first case action predominates, in the second the mind, although concentration of the mind is necessary for both. They act together, only there is predominance of the one over the other: when asanas are done, that means action prevails, but when mantras are used, the mind. Again, who is it that guides me from outside? It is also He, for verily, there is no other.

This must in time be relevant for all sadhakas, but caution must be observed lest we attribute these states to ourselves erroneously.

> **What has just been said are fragments from here and there. They have been given, so that each one may get what is helpful to him, and as much as he is able to grasp.**

This should be kept in mind. I learned from a devotee that had travelled with Ma that occasionally one of Ma's attendants would say: "Call Gopinath Kaviraj! Ma is speaking, and none of us can understand what She is talking about!" Gopinathji was perhaps the greatest scholar in India at that time, and he often had to explain to those around Ma Her meaning when She began to speak spontaneously and in great detail about very high spiritual matters.

ELEVEN

Benares, August 13, 1948.

Pitaji, what do you call "niskama karma" (action that is free from desire)?

Inquirer: Well, it does not seem possible to perform action without desire, that is to say, devoid of attachment for either the action or its fruit, but solely from a sense of duty. According to the shastras, only the man who has achieved perfect fulfillment is capable of such action. So long as one is linked to sense objects, it is impossible. Yet, what is taken up in a spirit of dedication to God may well develop into action done without any desire.

Whether with or without desire–it is still action. One cannot possibly remain without action until the state of Pure Being comes.

The sense of "I do" is inherent in all action of the ordinary person. But when the Self is realized and is the director of all subsequent actions, the sadhaka truly knows that all doing is done by God in the ultimate sense. For without the Power, the Shakti, of God nothing even exists to be done. So "doing" is completely Divine Action. This cannot be comprehended or even acted upon until one's Divine Self is perfectly realized as Pure Being.

Therefore, let this aspect of the matter also be understood. When you surrender yourself to the guru, you have to obey his orders unconditionally. In this, your sole motive is to carry out the guru's will. Consequently, when going about the task you grow eager to do your utmost, can you call this also a desire in the ordinary sense of the word? To set your heart on being effi-

cient, with the one object of fulfilling the guru's will, is certainly a good desire. If for any reason there should arise even the least feeling of resentment, the action can no longer be described as being without attachment.

No comment needed.

Suppose for example, after having accomplished by far the greater part of some work, you have to abandon it, and towards the end someone else takes it up, completes it, and gets the credit for having achieved the whole of the task. If you mind this even in the slightest degree, how can the work have really been done disinterestedly? Obviously it was not quite without a desire for recognition.

No comment needed.

When you have surrendered yourself to the guru, he may do anything, subject you to no matter what trials, yet you still regard yourself as a tool in His hands. You will then have reached a stage, where in spite of all difficulties, you persist with the work, knowing it to be the guru's order. Keep in mind that by this attitude you will grow steadfast in endurance, patience and perseverance, and your energy and capacity will be enhanced.

But this is not passive "surrender." It is very dynamic action. When the yogi understands that everything is a manifestation of the Infinite he is able to enter into and experience Infinite Life as far as he is capable. And that capacity will continue to expand and deepen as time goes on in that state.

In action there is bound to be conflict. When can there be freedom from this conflict? When there is no question of feeling hurt. Even in the midst of work, at all times and under all circumstances, one must be prepared to obey any kind of order.

Imagine you are hungry, and just as you are raising your hand to put food into your mouth, you are asked to go elsewhere. At that very instant, you should gladly let fall the food you were about to eat, and obey the call. Such an attitude is an indication of one's becoming established in a happiness that is not of this world.

When it is possible to feel that we are living and moving (acting) in God, then all goes well. We experience our action as rising from God and therefore essentially divine. But the moment another human being is involved, we become inwardly territorial and defensive. And "feeling hurt" is a primary activity of the ego. But Ma tells us we must become so at one, so identified with our true Self, that in dealing with others we experience that we are dealing with the Divine Self in them–and therefore with our own Self. Truly, "such an attitude is an indication of one's becoming established in a happiness that is not of this world." This must be our aspiration.

When one is nearing effortless being ("Sustained effort ends in effortless being–in other words, what has been attained by constant practice is finally transcended. Then comes spontaneity"), whether one is blamed or not for some shortcoming in one's work, leaves one quite indifferent. Then only does one become an instrument in His hands.

The body moves like a tool, and one watches it in the nature of a spectator. Then one observes what a great variety of work gets done by such a body, and in how very smooth and efficient a manner.

Egoless work is full of beauty, for it is not prompted by a desire for self-gratification. So long as the knots that constitute the ego are not unravelled, even though you intend to act impersonally, you will get hurt, and this will produce a change in the expression of your eyes and face, and be apparent in your whole manner.

To long: "let my heart be free from craving for results," is still a desire for a result. Nevertheless, by thus aspiring after selfless action there is hope of its coming to pass. A knot means resistance. Hence, so long as the ego persists, there will be clashes at times, even when impersonal work is attempted, because one is bound and therefore pulled in a certain direction.

I cannot deny that as I read this and the previous section I am inwardly seeing the people that Ma usually travelled with. And I know these words of Hers were necessary, but I have a pretty good idea that they had little effect. I speak from experience and observation.

Anyway: Ma tried. And with some people She did succeed.

Inquirer: So, until one has attained to perfect fulfillment, acting without a motive is an impossibility?

When impersonal work is being carried out and watched as by a spectator, a deep joy surges up from within. If at that time the body gets injured, even this becomes a source of happiness. Nevertheless, this welling-up of joy is not identical with Self-realization. The thrill of delight brought about by impersonal work is His delight become one's own. His gladness felt as one's own indicates a stage has been reached where happiness is bound up with Him. In this condition, since one has lost interest in worldly pleasures, a great deal of work can be done in a perfect way; and even if despite one's utmost efforts some task has not succeeded fully, one does not feel disturbed. For everything has its place–here also His Will prevails.

Do you not see what an exquisite path this is!

Yes. Now let's do it.

But the aforesaid holds good only when action is not tainted by a sense of possessiveness. However, even this state is by no

means Self-realization. Why not? Whether with or without desire, it is work that is referred to here. Although done impersonally, the action still remains separate from the doer. Whereas, where the Self is and nothing but the Self, there the guru, his instructions, the work, cannot each exist separately. So long as the duality of precept and action persists, one cannot possibly speak of Self-realization. The Lila of one who has attained to final Consummation is entirely different from the work that has become selfless by effort. This has been explained here in reply to your question.

But it will not be understood until one's own perfect Self-realization occurs. This is why sadhana is essential at all times in all matters and in all situations.

Even when the state of samadhi has been reached, during which one seems to be wholly absorbed within, this also is still a state. Yet, when by this spontaneous inner process (antarkriya) the veil is lifted, then the Vision of Reality may come about. It can never come through outer activity, such as the attempt to efface desire.

This reminds me of a man once telling me: "I have really been working lately on being more spontaneous." What could be less spontaneous? I did not say anything. That *was* spontaneous.

Another thing, Pitaji: There was a time when this body tried to carry out to the very letter anything Bholanath asked for. But when he saw that this body became rigid, that it was incapable of performing certain types of worldly actions, unable to bear them, he himself mostly and gladly took back his request. This is how, notwithstanding that some tasks could not be attended to, strict obedience was being observed in one sense.

However, one day the husband of Bholanath's sister, Kushari Mahaya, came on a visit. When he saw that this body obeyed

Bholanath in all matters, he felt annoyed and exclaimed: "Have you no opinion of your own? Have you to consult your husband about every little detail? What a state of affairs! Suppose he asked you to do something wrong, would you obey then also?"

He got the reply: "Let such an occasion arise and, on setting out to put the order into practice, see what would come to pass." This answer left him dumbfounded. Thenceforth he changed his mode of life and remained ever devoted to the Supreme Quest.

There is a state in the spiritual life where unconditioned, self-sprung action is possible, because there are no ties. And where no ties exist, there is no danger and no wrong path–one cannot take a false step.

This is perfect and beyond comment by me.

Inquirer: Was it not after Self-Realization that you were in that condition?

Leave this body out of it!

I have told people that the only thing that could be said about Ma was that nothing could be said about Ma. That sounds like cute, "Zen" word-juggling, but it is not. Ma was simply outside the world in which we were rooted and absorbed. The need was to pass over into Ma's world. And She could/would not bring that about. We had to pass over by our own will and resolve. And Ma knew who really wanted that passing-over and its subsequent results. So She opened the way. But we had to desire it first and then pass over into Her Reality. A lot had to be left behind in that passing, so very few really passed over. We could sit next to Ma's body, but really be worlds away from her. And that is true right now. It is our choice.

If you say that this condition only comes after Self-realization, you will have to understand that then it is possible to play anywhere, in any way, Oneself playing all the parts of Oneself,

> **of course, which is quite a different matter from what has just been mentioned.**
>
> **It is a state of Oneness.**
>
> **Even while remaining in division one is undivided, and remains in Oneness though appearing divided: this is THATness Itself (Tat Sva). Here, to obey and to disobey–both are THAT.**

And it is all up to us. We do or we do not. Words mean nothing. Sadhana does. For genuine sadhana yields genuine results. "Surrender" will not do it. That is just a specious and despicable attempt to avoid both responsibility and attainment.

One time Ma said: "He who does sadhana automatically becomes a sadhu." So that is how we can know who is doing genuine sadhana and who is not.

I vividly recall the Western men who observed that the power figures in India were the sannyasis. So being at the top as Westerners there was only one course for them: they would ask Ma if they could take sannyas. Ma always said: "Let us see what happens." They would go back home and a month or so later the letter would come: "Please ask Ma to bless my marriage." Sri Ramakrishna called this "monkey renunciation." There are a lot of monkeys about.

> **There are signs by which actions done as an instrument before Self-realization can be recognized. At this stage, the stream of action is directed towards the fulfillment of actual needs. Whereas, in the state of Pure Being it is totally different: to do or not to do, call it what you will, all is THAT. Within this sphere everything is possible: not to eat while eating, and to eat though not eating; to walk without feet, to see without eyes, and much more of the kind, as you would put it.**

This is obviously and vastly beyond the usual human condition. But it is open to us through sadhana.

When established in the Self, who obeys whose bidding? There are no "others," none are separate. No longer does one talk to another–how can there still be the relationship, that is based on the sense of separateness?

This being so, observation of the sadhaka will reveal whether he is genuine, or a sham, or just self-deluded.

The level of selfless action is quite different from the state of Self-realization. So long as the guru, the love of Him; the work, the "I," are perceived separately, there is no question of Self-realization. Yet, it must be said that action dedicated to God is not of the same order as work prompted by desire. The one is for the sake of union, which leads to Enlightenment, the other for the sake of enjoyment which leads to further worldly experience.

Now we come to the heart, the crux of the matter:

What alone is worthy to be called "action" is that action by which man's eternal union with God becomes revealed; all the rest is useless, unworthy of the name of action, no action at all.

Sadhana alone is "worthy to be called 'action.'" So who is a "karma yogi"? Only he who is acting in union with God: the diligent and constant sadhaka. For only sadhana "is that action by which man's eternal union with God becomes revealed." And again the words of Ma: "He who does sadhana automatically becomes a sadhu." As Jesus said: "By their fruits ye shall know them" (Matthew 7:20). Look and see.

It is not a new kind of union, which has to be established, but rather the union that exists throughout eternity is to be realized.

It is truly Self-realization in the absolute sense. It has always been our real state. We have not even "fallen" from it, we have only forgotten it. We have never been otherwise than united with, one with, the Self that is part of the Absolute Being. That is why Self-realization is also called Self-awakening.

> **Very well, now listen to something else. There is a stage where working is very delightful and gives intense happiness. Here one is quite unconcerned with what may or may not result from one's action; the work is done entirely for its own sake, for the love of it. Neither is there an external guru in this, nor the love of Him. A state of being of this kind does exist.**

It is called Atmabhava: the state that is the experience of the Self.

> **There is great diversity in the realm of action.**

And often it is a jungle, moving through which requires both exterior and interior illumination. For within the many there is always The One. The many exist in and by The One. Therefore realization of The One is the supremely realistic endeavor. And for anyone awakened to any degree it is the solely realistic endeavor.

> **The sense of contentment experienced at the fulfillment of some worldly desire is relative happiness. This desire may be for one's wife, son, a relation, or any other person, and accordingly the fruit inherent in each particular action will be reaped. This is working for the sake of self-satisfaction (bhoga), not for the sake of union (yoga); it brings sorrow along with joy.**

The truth is, sorrow is inherent in joy, for only the Absolute is beyond and free from the dualities, the dwandwas. Indeed, to seek for anything within relativity is to seek equally for its opposite–which in time will be found. When this kind of seeking is over, then the ultimate Finding is possible. But only possible. Actualization requires immeasurable resources and their perpetual, unbroken application. Only the dedicated sadhaka even approaches success.

To every man there openeth
A Way, and Ways, and a Way.
And the High Soul climbs the High way,
And the Low Soul gropes the Low,
And in between, on the misty flats,
The rest drift to and fro.
But to every man there openeth
A High Way, and a Low.
And every man decideth
The Way his soul shall go.
(John Oxenham)

Now to come back to what has just been said about work done for the love of it, not for anybody. Imagine how much at times gets accomplished even while walking in the street, not for anyone's sake, work for the sake of work, work itself being one's only God.

This also is one of the states. But if one goes on performing action of this kind, there comes a day when one is liberated from action.

Right Action by its inherent nature leads beyond ordinary action.

There is such a thing as laboring for the welfare of the world, but here even this purpose is absent.

This is because such action arises from the reality of the individual which always transcends this world. There is a time when embracing the world frees the individual from the world. This is the true Karma Yoga. And it is so rare as to be virtually non-existent.

It is a type of work not actuated by desire or craving, one just cannot help doing it. Well then, why is it done? One simply is in love with the work. When God manifests Himself in the

form of some work, which therefore exercises intense attraction on a particular person, then, by engaging in this work again and again, one is finally liberated from all action.

To heed is to act and become free.

Inquirer: Work only begets more work; how can it come to an end?

Do you not know this? If you can become so completely concentrated in any one direction that you cannot help acting along that line, wrong action becomes impossible. In consequence, action is losing its hold on you and is bound to come to an end.

How many states and stages there are! This is one of them. Here one has certainly not yet attained to Knowledge of the Self; but one cannot act wrongly.

Neither is there an opportunity for considering whether one should act in accordance with the shastras or against them. Nevertheless, in such a state of one-pointedness, wrong action that violates the laws set forth in the shastras cannot occur.

The human body–the vehicle through which the work is being done–has entered a current of purity, and as a result satkarma, action in harmony with the Divine Will, is performed.

Only the yogi is able to even grasp the implications of these words. And frankly, only the yogi really wants to. So only the yogi ever will understand and attain.

It is only on the level of the individual that pleasure and pain exist. In spite of attachment to wife, husband, son or daughter, during spells of severe pain, when one tosses about in burning agony, is there room left for the thought of these loved ones? Does one not groan in a frenzy of self-pity? At that moment the delusion of family ties loses its hold, while the delusion of identifying oneself with the body reigns supreme.

It all comes back to ego.

> **Everything exists in one's Self, that is why everything exists. From here, on this basis arises the alleged coming and going of the individual, its round of births and deaths.**

Remember: there is the Self–and there is the Self of the Self: Parabrahman, the Absolute Satchidananda. Still, these words are so absolutely and fundamentally true and evident that for maya-blinded minds they are inexplicable, incomprehensible.

Sadhana is the only path to comprehension resulting from direct experience.

> **Now you should understand that one who loves God is but out to destroy identification with the body.**

For identification with the body blinds the individual completely on every level, misperception being the most virulent element. Now in the beginning the devotee many not realize that his love for God, or his striving to attain it, must come to fruition in total annihilation of everything but the direct experience and comprehension of his identity with God. That he is as bodiless as God is bodiless. That he has/is nothing but God–not as an object but as eternal Subject. Once he has attained the I-AM Consciousness, the whole matter is ended.

> **When this has come about, there is destruction (nasa) of delusion, of bondage, in other words, of desire (vasana), of 'not-Self' (na Sva). Your dwelling place (vasa) at present is where the Self manifests as 'not-Self' (na Sva); when that is destroyed; it is only destruction that is destroyed.**
>
> **Furthermore, what is known as worldly craving may also be characterized as the activity that takes place because the action of Self-revelation is absent.**
>
> **HE is not there, this is the crux of the matter, is it not?**

One of Ma's traits was Her absolutely practical good sense. The chapter on Her in *Autobiography of a Yoga* presents Her as a kind of transcendental I-will-go-along-with-anything halfwit. Not so. Ma's clarity of expression was as constant as was Her practicality and ability to communicate. When Ma spoke to someone, it was their Self speaking to them. For Ma was the Universal Self in manifestation.

> **This body tells of yet another aspect; can you guess what it is? Just as the Beloved (Ishta) is the Self (Swayam), so destruction is also He Himself, and likewise is that which is destroyed.**

In the beginning there was One. Then that One by internal self-will became Two, functionally speaking, while yet remaining One essentially. Then a countless series of dualities manifested as relative existences/manifestations while the unity remained intact. Thus was made possible both actuality and appearance–essence and attributes. And always there was never anything but The One.

This One manifested as creation/manifestation and dissolution/unity while remaining perpetually unchanged. It created a creation that was really itself in manifestation and then uncreated itself and "became" unmanifested unity. But there never was an actual, external change. Rather, there was the ideation, the conceptualization of alternation/manifestation. So the Absolute Reality created and destroyed Itself while remaining unchanged. In other words: Maya came into existence–yet only as appearance; never Actuality.

Therefore to the sadhaka nothing ever really happens, but change is constant in/to his mind until unchangeability prevails and the original state of being results. And all along nothing ever really happened or changed. Only an adept yogi can accept this. Note that I do not say "experience" or "perceive," but "accept." For those are mayic processes, mere appearances. Yet the False is the Real since it arises from the Real and resolves into the Real.

So Ishwara creates and dissolves/destroys Himself. (Ishwara being of positive polarity is "He," whereas His Maya being of negative polarity is "She.") Please understand that "positive" and "negative" are modes of polarization/manifestation and should not be taken in the sense of moral character–that takes place very far down the line of manifestation–almost at the end.

Ma is not expressing how She "saw" what She describes, but what She WAS: Unity appearing as duality. Often when Ma spoke of differing views or modes of existence/being that intellectually seemed opposites, she would say: "But there is a state in which the question/conception cannot arise." This was Her constant state. And it is ours, but we do not know it. Yoga sadhana is the only path to that knowing/knowledge.

> **This is so where the Self is and nothing but the Self. Hence with whom can one associate? Therefore it is said that He is without another, existing alone.**
>
> **When speaking of Him as appearing in disguise, what is the disguise? He Himself, of course.**
>
> **You speak of the world. Jagat (world) means movement and what is bound is jiva (the individual). As the saying goes: "Wherever a man is, there is Shiva; and wherever a woman, there is Gauri."**

This is perfect. To comment would be to cloud our understanding. Inwardly we all know this as truth. But it remains in our journey through samsara to emerge into the realization that is essentially ourselves. Simply reading Ma's words carefully and with focussed attention can open our atmic eye and get a glimpse of Her meaning. But the moment we decide to "understand" it that inner opening is prevented. If spontaneous being and spontaneous perception and spontaneous action were practical attributes of Ma, then they are our attributes as well. She allowed them; we do not.

> **Where no question of birth and rebirth exists, no question of being bound, this surely, is called eternal.**

Do not try to understand this. Just carefully read it. "Be still, and know" (Psalms 46:10). The Hebrew words more accurately mean: "Let go and see."

> **Now grasp this thoroughly; how can that, which is perpetual motion be bound [made static/unmoving]? Does it remain in one place? Just as it does not remain confined to any place, so it cannot be bound when the mind is dissolved. Therefore, since it never stays bound in any particular spot, can one not call it free?**

Ponder this carefully by simply reading it and then quietly sitting and looking at the words without any deliberate thinking or deliberate non-thinking. Just look. If insight comes virtually spontaneously, instantly, then note it. If not, that, too is right, and continue reading the following.

> **Well then, what goes and what comes? Behold, it is movement as that of the ocean (samudra), He expressing Himself (Sva mudra). The waves are but the rising and the falling, the undulation of the water, and it is water that forms into waves (taranga), limbs of His own body (Tar anga)–water in essence.**

This is not hard to understand, and do not make a mind-game of it or an intellectual exercise/torment. Again: as just previously, sit and look.

> **What is it that makes the same substance appear in different forms, as water, ice, waves? This again, is asked from a particular plane of consciousness. Reflect, and see how much of it you can grasp!**

Examine and question your own mind. Literally explain it to yourself. There was a time in my sadhana when I would simply put a question or concept before my mind and then answer it–usually speaking aloud (sometimes walking back and forth as I did so) and paying close attention, for I was instructing myself. Since I was a diligent, practicing yogi, my mind had plenty to say because I had opened its inner doors and could still my mind to perceive its response. If this does not work for you, there is no problem. It is not your natural way. Each sadhaka is increasingly unique. That is why true sadhana is, as said before, the flight of the alone to the Alone.

> **No simile is ever perfect; yet has it not helped you to view the problem with reference to the world? What actually have you realized?**
>
> **Find out!**

For strange as it may seem, you know far more than you presently think you do. Within you is stored knowledge accumulated in countless past lives. Let it come forth by its own self-impulse. If it does not come forth immediately then wait and try again. In the meantime: japa and meditation are the two keys that unlock all the inner doors in time. Just keep on keeping on.

> **Very well, you call transient that which never stays fixed anywhere, do you not?**
>
> **But what does not stay?**
>
> **Who does not stay?**
>
> **Who comes?**
>
> **Who goes?**
>
> **Change, transformation–what are they?**
>
> **WHO?**

For It is a Who–not a what. A consciousness–not an object. It is you; your Self.

> **Grasp the root of all this!**

The root is simple; the principle: Tat Twam Asi. YOU ARE THAT. But to get to that inner essence sadhana is the only way.

> **Everything passes away, that is to say, death passes away–death dies.**
>
> **Who goes and whither?**
> **Who comes and' whence?**
> **This ceaseless coming and going–what in essence is it?**
> **WHO?**

Again Ma reminds us: we are looking for a Who, not a what. And that is the Self which reveals itself in yoga sadhana.

This reminds me of a spiritual slacker that had taken a course in meditation I taught at a university, and sometimes hung around to be entertained or at least distracted from his willful spiritual emptiness. On occasion when someone would ask me a question he would bray like a donkey: "Why ask him anything? He'll just tell you to meditate!"

He was right. I had learned from Ma. Meditation is not the answer, but it reveals The Answer: The Self.

> **Again, there is no question of action, no question of coming and going; where is birth in me? Where death? Ponder over this!**

Atmajnana–knowledge of the Self through Atmadarshana, the experience of the Self–is the only permanent answer to anything.

But the mind of the non-yogi who does not observe Yama and Niyama is "like the troubled sea, when it cannot rest, whose waters cast up mire [mud] and dirt [clay]. (Isaiah (57:20).

> **Look, this universe, you will say is nothing but the One Self.**
>
> **As such, every form is He in His very own Form (Sva akara); that is, the Self (Sva), the Eternal, revealed as Form (akara). What does this imply? Non-action (akriya). In what sense non-action?**
>
> **"Action dedicated to God is alone true action; all the rest is useless and therefore no action at all." This is your idea from the point of view of the world. But here, this kind of action does not exist. What then does exist here?**

> **Self-Action (Sva-Kriya)–He Himself As Action; He Himself As Form–for this reason He is called Sakara (With-Form; He Himself As Qualities (guna)–therefore, He is called Saguna (With-Qualities). Where the Lord (Isvara) or anything pertaining to His Divine Splendor is manifested, He Himself (Swayam) appears in action, yet ever remaining the non-doer. He, as such, is the Essence of Absolute Truth.**
>
> **Non-action (akriya), yet form (akara)! Form means embodiment (murti), in which there is neither action nor one who acts. Of what can He become the doer, and who is to be the doer, and where? In what you see as bondage by action, He is not revealed. He Himself is action (kriya), He, the Eternal that can never be destroyed. Destroyed (nasta) means 'not-the Beloved' (na-Ishta), not He, who can never be undesired (anista); for He is the one and only thing desired by all creation, the All-Beloved.**

Since Parabrahman is Existence Itself, then nothing exists but Parabrahman. There are no objects separate from That, there is no experience separate from That, there is no being-existence separate from That, there are no objects or "things" separate from that. Yet in the face of that Unity we can speak dualistically because that is the basic character of our entire existence. Without that duality do "we" exist?

Is this an insoluble problem? Not really. The problem is language itself, the assumption of object/observation/observer: dualistic expressions in talking about That Which is ONE. When we speak we establish the consciousness, the assumption, of speaker, the spoken and the spoken-to. And that is real, for is a conception not real, at least momentarily? Ma continually tried to enable people to realize that all concepts fail ultimately in expressing the full truth of anything. Also, we glibly speak of "real" and "unreal" while unable to completely define those terms in an absolute, unquestionable manner.

What is the solution? To stop playing with talk of duality and non-duality and enter into direct experience of That Which is appearing as both one and two and yet is always beyond them–and always has been: the

Transcendental Reality that is also our only real Self. It cannot be conceptualized; it cannot be truly spoken about; and it cannot be known, since it transcends knowing, knower and known. We cannot say it exists or does not exist.

What is the solution? To drop it all and engage in yoga sadhana that reveals the inmost reality which is beyond all words and therefore beyond all definition or statement.

"Be still, and know" (Psalms 46:10) is the divine counsel. The word *raphah*, translated "still," means that, but in the sense of to abate, to cease, to forsake (abandon), to leave, to let alone. *Yada*, translated "know," means to know, be aware of, ascertain, recognize, comprehend, be sure of and understand.

Objective awareness and insight-understanding are the prerequisite of true Knowing. This objectivity was being spoken of by Saint Paul when he said: "Wherefore come out from among them, and be ye separate, saith the Lord, and touch not the unclean thing; and I will receive you" (II Corinthians 6:17). Perfect separation from materialistic and ego-based consciousness is necessary to attain the knowledge of Reality that as spiritual alchemy turns us into The Real Itself. This is possible because we are That eternally. Involvement in Maya produces the spiritual amnesia that we mistakenly think is normal, but sadhana restores to us the knowledge of our true Self. The simplicity is drastic but actual. Just wake up.

When Ma speaks of this Absolute Reality She speaks of it as though She knows it, which She does, because She IS It. But She implies that we, too are That–we have just forgotten that, lost sight of it. There can be no greater loss than that, nor greater gain than its recovery since it is ours, our eternal nature–and which we have as surely as ever we did. But we have lost the awareness of That which we can never really lose, since we are That ourselves. We do not need to become anything: only awaken to what we have always been.

We are like the drunk in a joke I heard many long years ago. A drunk was walking along with one foot on the street and the other up on the curb, bobbing up and down with great effort. Someone stopped him and asked, "Why are you walking with one foot down on the street and the other up on the curb?" The drunk burst into tears and exclaimed: "Thank God! I thought I was a cripple!" We just need someone to point out our absurdity, our misperception–and therefore our erroneous conclusion about ourselves and the world around us. We all need to Wake Up and Stop It. Yoga sadhana is the way–uninterrupted sadhana supported by the empowering safeguards of yama and niyama. Let's repeat them here:

Yama: 1) ahimsa–non-violence, non-injury, harmlessness; 2) satya–truthfulness, honesty; 3) asteya–non-stealing, honesty, non-misappropriativeness; 4) brahmacharya–continence; 5) aparigraha–non-possessiveness, non-greed, non-selfishness, non-acquisitiveness.

Niyama: 1) Shaucha: purity, cleanliness; 2) Santosha: contentment, peacefulness; 3) Tapas: austerity, practical (i.e., result-producing) spiritual discipline; 4) Swadhyaya: self-study, spiritual study; 5) Ishwarapranidhana: offering of one's life to God.

Please understand that these ten factors must become the very fabric of our lives. They awaken us and keep us awake.

Therefore you should grasp that the One who is "Without Form" (Nirakara), "Without Qualities" (Nirguna), is also "With Form" and "With Qualities."

It should also be understood that Brahman is not just with and without form or qualities: Brahman is also *beyond* form and qualities. Brahman–Reality Itself–has all these aspects. It is necessary for us to also understand that we are an inseparable and eternal part of Brahman, and therefore what is said of Brahman is also true of ourselves, if even in a finite degree. As two mirrors facing each other reflect one another in a series of countless forms, so it is with both Brahman and ourselves. Since we are one, neither Brahman and ourselves are independent of one another. If either one of us would cease to exist, so would the other!

We have to keep coming back to the understanding that Unity is the truth of everything and duality a mere appearance. And everything is a manifestation of that One which is also at the same time and to an equal degree: No Thing. Remember: Advaita does not at all mean One. It means

Not Two, which is far from the simplistic view that our limited minds naturally lead us to. We also need to comprehend that what we call existence is beyond our comprehension. Until we attain Self-realization we should mostly remain silent in the face of these seeming contradictions which arise simply because our minds are immersed in a duality which itself is only an appearance, a misperception. Again, this is why the wise are called munis, silent ones. Nothing definitive can be said about these seemingly eternal dualities. Further, the Unity we talk about is just a concept in our minds. We do not see the actuality of the matter.

There is only one solution: "Become a yogi" (Bhagavad Gita 6:46).

> **Water and ice–what in essence is the difference between the two? Can you tell? Hence He alone IS, and nothing but He. The One who is Pure Consciousness and Pure Intelligence has many shapes and forms, and at the same time He is formless.**

It takes a mind of deep clarity to even grasp these ideas–a mind purified by yoga sadhana so it can reach beyond appearance, reason and even conceptualization into the realm of pure Being which is our original and essential nature. Liberation and Self-realization are simply a matter of direct Knowing and therefore Being.

> **For this reason, call it worldly action or the action of the seeker, both are THAT.**

What distinguishes them from each other is difference in seeing and interpretation–for "understanding" is not possible here. We usually think if we can put a label, a name or definition, on something we understand it and know it. This is a fantasy. Only the knowing that is beyond the mind and intellect is true knowledge. And it cannot be put into words. Words hide it and delude us as to what it is–and what we are.

When we come to a summation, the only real action possible is sadhana. A true teacher and guide always brings the student back to this.

> **Every action is free, in other words, there is no question at all of action. That is why, you know, it is like this: There is only One Eternal Reality (Nitya Vastu), but since you are limited by your diverse angles of vision, you speak of the non-eternal and hold to the idea that the result of action cannot endure, that change is its very nature.**
>
> **Where does ceaseless change of the ever-changing world lead to? Action in which there is no possibility of bondage is indeed 'being'.**

Why juggle words? Become a yogi.

> **'Jagat' (world) signifies the movement which is a constant dying, in other words, perpetual change is its innate character. On the plane of the individual and therefore of bondage, all change pertains exclusively to movement of this kind.**

Here we see that death is not a static condition, but one of constant action, of whirling around in the mirage. Remember how as children we were so entertained by sitting in water and splashing in it? That is what life in this world is for the non-yogi: going nowhere–nowhere being the state of embodiment in the world. And that is death: the non-perception, the non-experience, of the reality that is our own Self. The mirage of the world is only secondary; it is itself blindness. Why aspire to grasp or perceive a Reality that is "beyond the world," when the Reality is manifesting as the world?

Maya does not exist as an external, objective entity. Maya is the illusion of the mind, created by the mind. Therefore the mind must be taken in hand and directed to its own truth. And since it is "our" mind, we are the only one who can do that. All the poetry about a sage or a guru dispelling our misperceptions and ignorance is just that: mind chatter. You and I alone can take away the veil and See and Be. And the only means for that is sadhana. Presently we are self-deluded, but in time we shall be Self-realized. It is our doing alone.

Ma says all these profound things to us because She knows that we can liberate ourselves–that no one can do it for us. Tat Twam Asi is Guru's Grace, but Soham–I Am That–is our grace, our only liberation.

> **Facing towards THAT (Tat mukti), many are striving, each in his own particular way; effort of this kind is certainly everyone's duty. In order to divert the course of his life into this direction, the average person must occupy himself with actions aiming at THAT (Tat karma).**

We like to think of God reaching down and lifting us up or of God's messengers coming and turning us about and leading us onward, but all that is only what makes the beginning of our journey possible. Those who turn within and enter into the reality of the Self are their own divine messengers and saviors. Only the yogi can and will realistically and effectively "occupy himself with actions aiming at THAT."

> **But now, think carefully and realize you are eternally free, because action is ever free, it cannot remain bound.**

If we were not already free we could not realize that. Our sadhana itself is the dawning of Self-realization. The moment we start we are at the goal.

> **Do you not know that the rope with which you tie anything in this world must rot or wear out? And though you use iron chains, or even golden, whatever binds will one day break or be shattered.**

Therefore our liberation is absolutely guaranteed. But we choose whether we get there sooner or later.

> **Do any worldly fetters exist that can never be broken, never destroyed? It is solely the cry of lament over temporary ties that alone fashions the bondage of the mind–the mind that can not be confined to any place.**

"My wife/husband, my children, my work, my obligations (often self-willed and imaginary), my health…" are a whole string of iron chains that do not even really exist outside the world-addict's misdirected will and orientation toward the death-bearing world. Death will break them all in time, but how desperately they cling to them, already dead in delusion.

> **Like a restless child, unconcerned with good or bad, it [the mind] seeks Supreme Bliss, never satisfied with momentary happiness and therefore ever wandering.**

This is proof that the mind itself arises from the Self and the impulses of the Self toward realization of and union with the Supreme Self are inherent even in that which can became a major block or distraction from Self-realization. In relative existence there is nothing that cannot either help or hinder the impulse to higher consciousness, according to its polarization and focus. But at their root everything is oriented toward Self-realization, even if that orientation is highly convoluted and contains impulses both supporting and hindering the movement toward that realization. The result: confusion and inconsistency that distract us from the way to clear (in)sight.

It is said that this wandering is inherent in the mind, but that is only true of the upper, objective layers of the mind. The inner mind has always been attracted to the Real, but those upper, objective layers of the mind suppress awareness of the inner, subjective layers of the inmost mind that always move toward the realization of the Self.

The basic polarity/polarization of the antahkarana, the inner consciousness, must be oriented steadily toward its expansion and deepening. This orientation is accomplished and established by deliberate purification of body, impulses, thoughts and will. Purity of diet is an indispensable foundation of this along with purity of environment. For we live both inwardly and outwardly–and all actions (which include thought) create karma and samskara. So it is crucial that we ensure they are always of a positive, enlightening character. Sadhana is the main foundation, japa is next in importance/necessity and uninterrupted observance of yama and niyama along with association with those of like-mind and mode of life. Yogananda often said: Company is greater than will power.

The path to the revelation of the divine Self is a path of inner and outer purification and cultivation. Wherever we go we take our entire makeup along with us. Therefore we must actively strengthen, purify and direct it. It is a matter of literal self-salvation. Who else can do it for us?

> **But how can it possibly be at rest until it has discovered a way to the Supreme Reality, until it has become wholly absorbed in its source, reposing in its own Self?**

Until the questing mind has discovered sadhana and the disciplines that facilitate and strengthen it, there is no possibility of either attraction toward higher life or success in its pursuit. For this alone allows the sadhaka's awareness to be polarized to the Self so intensely that his entire being, inner and outer, moves onward to the goal of its own nature and impulse. The aspiration to the Supreme which has always been its inmost impulse becomes its continuous, conscious and deliberate way of life. Not only is the mind one-pointed in meditation, the sadhaka's life and will become one-pointed in every facet so that the path to the Absolute becomes constant in mind and deed. This alone is the way of peace and fulfillment.

> **In your innermost heart you know that you are free; that is why it is your nature to yearn for freedom.**

Ignore the negative and foolish mind and any negative and foolish people that would hinder your intense and forward-moving path to Self-realization through scrupulous discipline and self-purification. If they cannot or will not come along with you on the Journey To The Light, then forget them and speed on toward the Goal. I have already quoted Yogananda's statement that company is greater than will power. So do not endanger yourself and risk falling-away and failure.

I well remember as a child hearing a song that said:

> On the Jericho road there is room for just two,
> No more and no less, just Jesus and you.

Only two people journey together on the way to God: God and you.

> **Likewise, when by some good fortune He becomes revealed as action, action will stop of itself.**

That is, when God is revealed as both the impulse to divine realization and as the search for Self-realization itself–God acting in and through you as your true Self–then your action, your sadhana, will cease to be mere activity, however sacred, and become Consciousness revealed.

> **Stagnation is death; solely to give up this blocking of the movement, man resorts to countless devices.**

We are often actively but unconsciously blocking the movement toward Self-realization. Therefore the wise engage in many forms of sadhana and supports of sadhana in order to remove all blocking or even slowing of our inner evolution. To not do so is to invite stagnation and death.

> **Only what falls away of its own accord is to be given up.**

A lot of spiritual slackers would love to get hold of this and claim that Ma said we must only do what is "natural to" and "comes easy" for us, otherwise we will be hypocrites. "But if I don't feel like meditating, why should I meditate?" a friend of mind used to say–until she quit meditating and ended her inner, real life.

What Ma is saying here is that the yogi that is practicing correctly will find Godward action increasing and ego-serving negative action decreasing automatically. There will be no need to "force it." The spiritually positive life will become not just "second nature" but the only nature. But she is also indicating that what the yogi sees is no longer attracting his mind is what must then be intentionally "given up" and consciously sent away by banishment from his life-sphere.

> **You go on insisting that the mind must be dissolved. But do not forget, it is this very mind which is the mahayogi [great yogi], yes indeed, the sublime yogi.**

There is no way to know what word(s) Ma is using for mind. Two terms are very important and mean utterly different things. *Manas(a)* is always translated "mind," and means the sensory mind, the percepting mind–and that is all. It is passive and limited to awareness of the senses. *Buddhi*, on the other hand, means the intellect, the thinking-reasoning mind The manas sees a tree–and that is all. The buddhi says: "That is a tree."

Because the senses cause so much trouble to sadhakas, it is in this context that the dissolution of the manasa-mind seems desirable, even necessary. But who wishes to be blind, deaf, and numb? So the idea of dissolving the mind is absurd and reveals both lack of understanding and control. What is needed is dominance of the buddhi, the intelligence, for that is what makes human beings superior to animals. And not just control is needed: the intellect must be expanded, strengthened and trained. The mahayogi is one whose buddhi is in total control and comprehension. This also means that to become a mahayogi the yogi must have potential ability for practice of sadhana. The intellect-mind of the adept yogi is a transmuted and empowered instrument that makes Self-realization possible. But it is just an instrument. It is the Self of the yogi, the Atman, that dominates every aspect of the yogi's existence and function.

Ignorant and weak religion insists on suppression and even elimination of the mind and faculties, and rigorous domination of the body as well. But the body is completely controlled by the mind, so development of the yogi's mind and intellect is the means to mastery of his entire being. Of course, it is not academic cultivation of the intellect, but the freeing of the inmost reality, the Self, of the yogi through sadhana that brings about this mastery.

Your scriptures describe such a yogi as behaving like a mischievous child, or as being oblivious of cleanliness, decency, and propriety; also as a lunatic, or again as one seeming inert and unfeeling. That which resembles complete indifference and inactivity, you regard as very exalted, and moreover you say: "What is contained in this microcosm is in the macrocosm."

And Ma implies that this is foolishness. Note that She says "*Your* scriptures," meaning that they have nothing to do with Ma. The description of "a yogi as behaving like a mischievous child, or as being oblivious of cleanliness, decency, and propriety; also as a lunatic, or again as one seeming inert and unfeeling" comes from the tantric tradition.

As the most ancient religion in the world Hinduism has the vastest number of scriptures which expound every possible viewpoint. Therefore in India there is found every shade of belief and dogma. The only intelligent atheism in the world, the Charvaka philosophy, is part of Indian philosophy. I have always enjoyed reading the Charvaka texts. I do not share their conclusions but I admire their intellectual calibre.

Ma said emphatically that every statement the human being can make has both a true and an erroneous (mistaken) side. Therefore She rejected no genuinely philosophical statement, and always reminded Her hearers that there is a state beyond all statements which is the true Wisdom and Knowing. And that must be our ideal and practical goal.

The statement: "What is contained in this microcosm is in the macrocosm" is not correct when by "this microcosm" is meant the body and mind. The body and mind reflect the macrocosm, but it is only a reflection, and that is not the whole of the microcosm. A mirror reflects anything put in from of it, but the reflected object is not actually in the mirror. This is why Ma avoided most blanket statements. Because of the inherent limitations of the human intellect it cannot possibly embrace the totality of anything–even as a concept however wise or exalted it might appear.

A Divine Incarnation (Avatara) playing as a child–how lovely it is, how enchanting!

The very idea of avatara is wondrous in many ways, but perhaps the most delighting is the image of the divine incarnation manifesting as a divine child. We especially see this in the childhood lila of Sri Krishna, which has an enchantment beyond calculation. The Biblical expression "God With Us" is awesome beyond comprehension. Obviously an Omnipotent Being can do anything except will Itself out of existence. But it is the will to be with human beings as one of them that moves us the most. For God to submit to the human condition, including mortality, demonstrates to us immeasurable love. As a hymn I heard as a child said:

> O the love that drew salvation's plan!
> O the grace that brought it down to man!
> O the mighty gulf that God did span at Calvary.

But not just in Bethlehem and Calvary–also in Ayodhya, in Brindaban and Kheora (Ma's birthplace): the inconceivable fact of the Eternal Unborn being born in human form as God With Us.

Emily Dickinson wrote: "Because I could not stop for Death–He kindly stopped for me...." But how much more wondrous is the truth that since we could not go to God, God came to us. And not just once, but many times. This is the mystery of avatara, the descent of the Divine into this world and that Divinity moving and living with human beings, usually being mistaken for an ordinary human being.

In the Bhagavad Gita Arjuna says to Sri Krishna: "Carelessly I called you 'Krishna' and 'my comrade, took undying God for friend and fellow-mortal, overbold with love, unconscious of your greatness. Often I would jest, familiar, as we feasted midst the throng, or walked, or lay at rest together: did my words offend? Forgive me, Lord Eternal" (Bhagavad Gita 11:41-42). It is said that often when Sri Krishna and Arjuna were lying together at rest, Arjuna would push Krishna with his foot and tell him to move over and give him more room. Remembering this, Arjuna was chagrined at his conduct.

But God agrees to undergo this every time he wills to incarnate in human form. Love and condescension beyond expression or comprehension! This is the wonder of God With Us. And even more: the suffering the avatar undergoes in human form. Think of the incredible grief and struggles experienced by both Sri Rama and Sri Krishna. Think of the persecutions, slanders and even attempts on Her life that Ma Anandamayi endured to the end of Her life just to be with us. Let me give you some background.

Once a devotee of Ma was in a hospital, so She went to visit that devotee. When She left the devotee's room She went over to a stairway and started going up. When those with her asked what She was doing, She replied: "I am going to see a friend." She got off at an upper floor and walked down the hallway to a room with a sign saying: No Admittance. She opened the door and went in. There was an unconscious man lying there. Some of the hospital staff objected, but Ma said: "I will just stand here for a while." Ma put Her hand on the bed next to the man and stood there in silence for some minutes. Then She turned and left. That man was Jawaharlal Nehru, the future Prime Minister of India. His appendix had burst and he was in a coma and not expected to live. But he did, and though he was not at all religious, his wife was–and she became a fervent devotee of Ma and practiced her Hindu faith with real dedication and fervor, often going to spend time with Ma.

Since Ma had saved his life, Nehru had tremendous gratitude and respect for Her and always came to see Her when She came to the New Delhi ashram. Sometimes he brought dozens of rudraksha malas for Ma to bless, and he would give them out to various government officials. And his daughter Indira, who also became Prime Minister, did the same. In fact, Ma gave her a rudraksha mala, and the rumors went out that as long as Indira wore that mala she could not be defeated by her political opponents. During one of my pilgrimages to India I saw a political cartoon in a newspaper which showed Indira hopping from tiny island to tiny island as she held on to that rudraksha mala.

Opponents of Indira Gandhi believed that Ma was keeping her in power, so they decided to assassinate Ma! They did not dare doing anything overt, so they hired very real and very powerful evil magicians to kill Ma with their magic. Ma told the devotees about this, saying that people that appeared to be fervent devotees were actually the ones hiring the magicians to kill Her. Ma accepted anything that happened, and so the devotees were afraid that She would not resist the negative occult bombardment and so would be harmed or killed. One time when She was at the Kankhal Ashram Ma was talking alone with Brahmacharini Udas. Suddenly She opened her hand and showed Udas a deep cut clear across the palm of that hand. Naturally Udas was horrified, but Ma closed then opened Her hand again and the cut was gone. But Udas and the devotees got the message: Ma was speaking the truth about the occult attempts to kill Her.

A few years afterward when I was with Ma in Brindaban, I noticed a peculiar-looking man sitting there staring at Ma in a very strange manner. I saw instantly that he hated Ma. Later that day one of the brahmacharinis who travelled with Ma came and told me that an hour or so before that man was found sitting in Ma's room intoning curse mantras to take Ma's life. Ma was sitting watching him with real interest. Since Ma did not reject anything, the curse mantras worked and two days later Ma was brought to the Hardwar train station on a stretcher looking absolutely dead. Our ashram members that were with me and I went along to Western India where there was a tiny ashram in an isolated place. There we kept vigil and prayed. Fortunately I had brought with me to India several sacred amulets that were powerful shields against negative entities and energies. (I have written about them in *Psychic Defense For Yogis.*) I gave some to those who were staying with Ma constantly and they put them near Ma. By Her own divine will Ma survived the hateful attacks and became Her usual active self.

But Ma was always bombarded with hate from evil sources. Sri K. Bose (Panuda), the General Secretary of the Anandmayi Sangha, told me that every week somewhere in India at least one defamatory article about Ma was printed in a major newspaper. "If Ma let us sue them all, we would become the richest spiritual organization in India," he said. I, too, heard over the years outrageous lies about Ma when I was in India. Of course we knew that Ma could take care of Herself–otherwise who would look after and protect us? Jai Ma.

But back to avataras.

> **When ordinary people read or hear about the childhood of Sri Krishna or see it enacted, they interpret it in the light of the behavior of their own children, for this is what they are familiar with.**

So their interpretation and response is just one of hearing about a really special child.

> **From where would they get the capacity to grasp its inner significance?**

Only from the avatara himself. That is why in India they say: "When someone chooses God it is because God has chosen them first." As I have said previously, Ma said that no one could even see Her if it was not her will (kheyala). So I would sit and look at Ma and revel in the knowledge that She wanted me there looking at Her. "O the love!" indeed.

> **When you witness a dramatic representation of the love play for Radha and Krishna in the Rasalila, or a performance of the Ramalila, you do not see the real Lila, which is entirely spiritual, supernatural (aprakrita), transcendental.**

God is the Inner Controller, the Inner Guide, of creation, so every moment of an avatar's life and actions is of divine origin. Veiled in Maya this is not seen by us unless, sitting in our hearts, He reveals it to us. That is why it was inspired wisdom to name Bhaiji's book about Ma's grace toward him: *Mother As Revealed To Me*. Countless times I have told myself in wonder and awe: "I am part of Ma's Lila in this world."

> **Where there is actual experience of it, it is due to the functioning of spiritual vision.**

I have experienced moments in the Rasa Lila, the dramas about Sri Krishna, when the wonder of God With Us was absolutely revealed and imparted to us. How many times the devotees have called out in praise and love when special moments of the avatara's life were performed. To those whose souls are awake and alive the lilas of Krishna and all avatars are seen as wonders of love and life.

Inquirer: When there is spiritual experience, how is it interpreted in terms of worldly occurrence?

As one is released from bondage, the destructible destroyed and the Beloved alone shines forth–say, what can one behold?

What is "spiritual experience"? Experience of "spiritual" things or events, or experience of Spirit Itself. The first, the experience of "spiritual" things or events, is the usual interpretation, mostly because of the shallowness and inexperience of the individual. But that shallowness and inexperience is exactly what is destroyed, and non-objective consciousness as the Self is being revealed! Since God (Ishwara) is fundamentally the Self of our Self, the enlightened person is seeing his own Self and nothing else. So there is no "other" or "second" person to behold. Dual experience is no longer possible since it is illusory. Only the truth of Unity is experienced. This is why Ma said: "I neither come nor go."

When ties are being broken, it is the breakable only that breaks.

Only the destructible can be destroyed. All ties, all bonds and bondage, are broken and dissolved when pure Jnana, pure Consciousness, arises in the form of Self-experience.

But the bond of the love of God is not that kind of bond–it is an 'unbinding.'

Swami Sivananda often said: "Bhakti begins with two and ends with one." For love by its very nature is a movement toward unity, therefore the lover of God is more and more approaching the union with the Divine which is expressed as Soham: I am That. The subject has awakened into the consciousness of its eternal identity with and as The One. The illusion of duality has disappeared just as darkness vanishes at the advent of day. For the light alone is real; the darkness was just a negation, an absence, of the light. What is love? It is the magnetic attraction that Sivanandaji meant when he said that bhakti begins with two and ends with one. For it is not just a matter of like attracting like, but of the fundamental unity manifesting itself. Ma embodied that Unity.

Further, where the Knowledge of the Absolute (Brahmajnana) is, there the ordinary function of understanding no longer exists. For to understand means to throw off one load, only to stand under a new one; whereas the Knowledge of the Supreme Reality is beyond thought and speech.

Where the Knowledge of the Absolute (Brahmajnana) is, there the ordinary function of understanding no longer exists. This is because the Absolute is not an ordinary object for us to perceive or understand. Rather, the Absolute is Unitary Consciousness whose function is bring into union with itself all that approaches or touches It. The ideal is not to know the Absolute, but to become the Absolute through perfect union with It–the duality becoming unity. The mind, the manas itself, becomes absorbed or transmuted into the buddhi which is an extension of the consciousness that is the Self. The finite becomes the absolute–which has always been the real situation. Therefore nothing has really happened except the revealing of the ever-existing unity. Maya has vanished and Reality is revealed. Self-realization is not an experience, but a state of being which is not abstract but fully functional within relativity.

When the average person sees a performance of the Rasalila or Ramalila; what can he possibly grasp of its significance that will not be colored by his worldliness?

Naturally a person will view anything through his own personal perspective, including projecting his personal ideas as to their nature, meaning and value. My cousin, Kevin, when he was seven years old was taken by his mother to a shoe store. Another boy, younger than Kevin, was crying hysterically as a salesman was trying shoes on him. Kevin said to his mother: "That boy must think that man is a doctor," revealing that Kevin was afraid of doctors. In this way even adults will project their viewpoint or experience on sacred events. Ma is saying that the exalted, divine meaning of the lives of Krishna and Rama cannot be grasped by minds conditioned by worldly perspectives. Let me tell you an illustrative joke.

A man went to a psychiatrist who as a preliminary showed him ink blots. Every time he asked the prospective patient, "What does that suggest to you?" he would answer: "Sex." "Well, I have an idea as to what we will be investigating," said the doctor and had the man make an appointment. When the man came for his session, he brought another man along with him. "I'm sorry," said the psychiatrist, "but therapy is deeply personal and cannot involve another person." Oh, said the man, "He just wants to see the dirty pictures."

In the same way, morally corrupt people project their defiled minds on to the divine lilas of Krishna and Rama. Here are examples. Once after a terrible war which He won, Sri Krishna married over fifteen thousand women whose husbands had died in the war, and He built an entire city to house them. I have seen propaganda where this compassionate act of Krishna is cited to prove that He made those women his harem because He was so immoral. Because Sri Rama had the chastity of Sri Sita publicly tested and proved genuine because of defiled-minded people defaming her, He is denounced as cruelly doubting her purity and embarrassing her.

Some people project their own degraded minds on to others. Ma Herself was constantly defamed in various ways. Arthur Koestler wrote a book called *The Lotus and the Robot* whose purpose was defamation and mockery of India and Sanatana Dharma. In one chapter he calls Ma "a weatherbeaten old sex kitten." A few years after he wrote this I was at a satsang in San Francisco. One of the men told me that he was preparing to travel to India, particularly to meet Ma, because he had read Koestler's book and realized that Koestler was just angry because no one in India was impressed with him, and obviously Ma was a great spiritual figure. So Ma could call anyone through any means!

> **Where is the capacity to experience anything beyond it? Nevertheless, since it is God's Divine Lila that he is taking in through his ears and eyes, there is hope that the capacity may come.**

We have heard the maxim, "Thoughts are things," but it goes the other way: Things are thoughts manifested in matter. And in the subtle levels there are what are called "thought forms," subtle energies that convey both intellectual comprehension and intuitive insight. The dramatic presentations of the lives of avatars and holy teachers open the intuition of the spectators and enable them to comprehend the divine manifestations that occur(ed) through them. Avatars do not have karma, so every moment of their life is a revelation of their divine will, purpose and power. And it is much the same with liberated masters. That is why there is a book about the disciples of Sri Ramakrishna called *They Lived With God.* Those whose lives were touched by Anandamayi Ma were touched by God, for Ma was the Absolute appearing in human form. When I was preparing to go back to India for my second pilgrimage I wondered if I would still see Ma as divinity Itself. In the evening when I stood outside the small house where Ma was staying I heard Ma's greatest devotee, Sri Gurupriya Devi, whom we all called Didi (Elder Sister), speaking with Ma's mother, Sri Swami Muktananda Giri. I felt so grateful that I knew their voices! And then I went into the house and into Ma's room. She had become so frail in those few years, and yet I stood there in awe, asking myself: "How did I miss so much before?" For Ma's divinity was many times more evident than it had been during my first pilgrimage. And believe me, it had been apparent, then. Ma was always awesome. And at the same time She was profoundly ours. Which is reasonable, because She was That which is seated in the hearts of all beings, in the heart of every atom. Someone once asked me,

"Why do you believe in Anandamayi Ma?" I simply told them: "Because She wants me to." And She gave me the capacity to see and hear Her divine presence. One time Ma said to me: "Every day say to yourself: 'Ma has been with me in all the past. Ma is always with me now. And Ma will always be with me in all the future.'" Awesome words and awesome experience.

> **It is the nature of the mind to accept the many. All that is needed is to focus this acceptance on one particular thing, with or without form, which, when accepted, leaves no further choice between acceptance and non-acceptance. This One Thing altogether excludes the possibility of duality. This is why one becomes one-pointed. The mind points to the many. Amidst the cross-currents of the divergent mind, one has to become firmly concentrated on one goal.**

By Ma's grace these words can become realization and reality.

> **Think of a tree. The boughs and branches that spread out from every side yield the same kind of seed as that from which the tree originated. This is how one single seed potentially contains innumerable trees, innumerable boughs, branches, leaves and so on.**
>
> **There is infinite becoming and infinite being, infinite manifestation and infinite potentiality–the seed grows into a tree, the tree brings forth seed. Therefore when one becomes wholly concentrated on any one thing, why should not the One be revealed?**

From the One comes the All–which therefore is at all times the One, for duality is never real. This is the mayic power, the bewitchment of the One, the Mahamaya which is none other than Parabrahman Itself.

> **There is endlessness in the One, and end in the Endless; but where the Infinite ONE is, there the question of finiteness and infinity cannot arise.**

Again, silence is often the most eloquent wisdom. Shankara wrote in his hymn on the guru that the guru remains silent but the questions of the disciples are all answered in that silence. This was true of Ma. More than once people came to Ma with a bundle of questions, but the moment they entered Her presence they were answered in an instant or were seen as unnecessary or irrelevant. Ma was The Answer.

> **What is, IS–this is what is wanted.**

But that is not to be merely believed, it must be actualized in the sadhaka's consciousness and life.

> **Where you perceive an end, there is actually no end; for verily, He is infinite. In all forms and in the formless is He, and He alone. This much about attachment to work (karma).**

Attachment to action is not ended by indifference, but by the living experience/insight of the presence of the Divine Reality that is in all and transcends all–which is also the truth of our own Self.

> **Again, there is attachment to bhava.**

[Bhava means inner disposition; it reveals itself as karma. Bhava is latent karma, whereas karma is bhava actualized.]

> **Bhava also belongs to the realm of action, only there is predominance, sometimes of action, at other times of bhava. This is all very difficult to understand.**
>
> **Someone has asked the question: "What is attachment to bhava?" Here is one example: When one practices yogic postures and breathing exercises, ritual worship, the repetition of God's Name, meditation, contemplation–any of these–for the sake of getting into a particular bhava, and having reached one wishes to remain in this state all the time. So long as it lasts, or**

rather, so long as this condition predominates, one is steeped in bliss. But in this one has not yet attained to Enlightenment, one is only on the way to it. This is a pure kind of attachment and therefore one may progress beyond it.

Indeed, one must progress beyond it, for enjoyment is of the ego, whereas ananda is the state of the Self.

Since one delights in lingering on the level of this bhava, one could possibly indulge in it day after day or even for the rest of one's life. Although remaining in this state for a great length of time does induce transformation to a certain degree, yet there can be no special progress. But if by some ineffable touch this bhava could find its consummation, one would be able to proceed further.

So there is safety in cultivating indifference toward bhava, and a healthy mistrust of it. For enjoyment of this lesser sort is only of the ego and therefore a mode of samsara.

There are states where one soars up and glides down again. But to become established in perfect poise, where ascent and descent are out of the question–surely this is what is wanted.

Simple truth!

Not until both karma and bhava are brought to completion can one go beyond them.

How are karma and bhava brought to completion? It is not a matter of perfecting or fulfilling, but of ending. This is accomplished by entering in the state that is *bhavatitam trigunarahitam*–beyond bhava and the three gunas which are the field in which karmas are sown for future reaping. It is a matter of transcendence which exists only in the transcendent Self. The only solution to the riddles of life is the Self-realization that is attained only through yoga sadhana.

In reply to a question, Sri Ma said:

> **Give in charity, engage yourself in service, do obeisance pranam ["To do pranam means to pour oneself out at His Feet, to become closely bound to Them and thereby united to Him, to become His who alone Is."], and you will yourself come to understand in what spirit these acts are being performed by you.**

It is necessary for the sadhaka to ruthlessly and ceaselessly inquire at the rise of any action or propensity to action: "Where, or what, does this arise from?" This is an essential part of the *swadhyaya*, the self-study, that is declared an essential element for enlightenment/liberation.

> **Feel convinced that, no matter what the state or condition you may be in, out of that very state Enlightenment may come.**

For all states arise essentially from our own Self or its adjuncts–such as mind, intellect, emotions and even the body. And they are all elements or steps on the journey to enlightenment. Indeed, if enlightenment was not inherent in them, it could not arise in or emerge from them. There are many applications and insights to be gained from the understanding that enlightenment is in the essence, the core, of all external and internal experiences and states of being.

> **Never harbor the idea that you are involved in sin and evil deeds, and can therefore not get anywhere.**

Please do not pervert these divine words of Ma into the meaning that no actions are sin or evil and they need not be ended. What Ma is saying is that you must never think you cannot progress beyond your present state and therefore stagnate in that condition. Ma means that there is no one that cannot turn about and repolarize the entire direction of his life and begin the ascent to perfect Realization. We are only hopeless when we refuse to be like the Prodigal Son (Luke 15:18) and resolve: "I shall arise and go" out of the shadow into the light. As John the Beloved Disciple wrote: "Every man that hath this hope in him [God] purifieth himself, even as he [God] is pure" (I John 3:3).

No one is hopeless if he ends all involvement with "sin and evil deeds." If he does so, he can therefore attain the highest states of Realization. For that Realization is his nature, as it is with all human beings whatever their present situation or condition.

> **At all times and under all circumstances you must keep yourself in readiness to tread the path to the Supreme.**

Every positive thought and action is a step on the path to the Infinite. And Ma says that we must be ready at all times and under all circumstances to begin walking on that path that ends in our perfect union with "the Supreme." And since the path is primarily interior we can tread it at all times through sadhana, especially continuous japa.

> **Who can tell at what moment your giving, serving, or obeisance will become an act of consecration to the One?**

Therefore we must at every moment be engaged in giving, serving, and obeisance. In that way our entire life "will become an act of consecration to the One."

> **Everything is possible.**

No aspiration is too high or impossible for us to achieve. Ma is confident of this and assures us of this.

Many years ago I sometimes sang in church:

Got any rivers you think are uncrossable?
Got any mountains you can't tunnel through?
God specializes in things thought impossible,
And He will do what no other power can do.

And at every moment He is seated in the heart of each one of us and empowering us with Divine Power from which we are inseparable. The Divine Manifestation that was Ma Anandamayi has given us that assurance.

TWELVE

When one has acquired the necessary capacity (adhikara), that which could not be understood formerly, is completely grasped.

This is a matter of both ordinary intellect and intuition–a matter of intelligence and intuitive insight. Both are developed through meditation, through diligent yoga sadhana. I have seen very ordinary people become intelligent and creative through practicing meditation. I say "become," but they were already intelligent and creative in their inner mind, and sadhana released-revealed that intelligence and creativity. Yoga sadhana is itself a divine wonder.

With age and wisdom, understanding comes in its fullness.

Insight, understanding and, ultimately, enlightenment arise from within the yogi because they are inherent in his very makeup. Every human being is a potential yoga siddha.

In the field of sadhana everything is infinite.

This is an amazing statement in which Ma is saying that the potentials and the effects of sadhana are infinite. Sadhana is the path to the Infinite, and itself is the action of the Infinite within which brings about both the sadhaka's practice of sadhana and his ultimate Self-realization. We can therefore say that the dedicated sadhaka's enlightenment and realization are guaranteed. All that is needed is persistence and regularity in practice.

As one goes on practicing japa–at some moment or other, the fire will be set ablaze.

Here we have Ma's assurance that japa itself kindles the inner fire of Self-realization.

The great master yogi Kabir sent his son to the great master Tulsidas, who was living on an island in the Ganges, with a brief note that said: "Try to teach this fool something." So Tulsidas worked some tremendous miracles in his presence, including healing a huge number of lepers by dipping a tulsi leaf in Ganges water and sprinkling it on them. When he was to return to his father, Tulsidas wrote the Name of Rama on a tulsi leaf, tied it in the end of his dhoti and said it would enable him to walk on water. So he stepped out and to his amazement he could walk on the water as though it were land. So he began walking over the water, but when he was almost to the other side he decided to see what magical object was enabling him to do so. When he untied the knot he found the tulsi leaf, looked at it and said: "What is this? Just the Name of Rama!" And he immediately sank in the water and had to fight his way to the riverbank–barely managing it.

So there are those who sneer at japa and even say that it is for "babies" and not for real yogis. Such reactions–both faith and disbelief–are all a matter of samskara. I remember vividly the first time I read the words: "God and His Name are one." I felt like a trumpet blast had sounded in my soul and I knew it was true: the Divine Name IS the Divine Itself, an embodiment–and therefore the power–of Divine Consciousness and Self-realization. Saints through the ages have proved this through their own Self-realization. In these words we have Ma's guarantee, but you can prove their truth by your own japa.

> **Fire exists everywhere, only one does not know at what instant the friction will suffice to kindle a flame. Therefore, be ever prepared!**

In Sanatana Dharma it is held that the element of fire is inherent in everything, but only the right conditions will bring it forth. Friction is one sure condition. So we rub or strike two flammable things together to create a spark which the ignites them and we have fire. It is said in yogic texts that the body and mind of the yogi is one fire-stick (arani) and the Divine Name is another. By the "friction" of japa the inherent enlightenment in the Divine Name and in the inner being of the yogi "flame on" and produce total enlightenment eventually if the japa is maintained. Therefore the wise yogi always keeps aware of his mental japa throughout every waking moment. That way he is "ever prepared" for the moment that will come.

Once someone complained to Ma that he could not believe that enlightenment would come from something as easy as japa. Ma simply replied: "Try it."

> **Persevere in the practice of japa. It will be carefully stored for you, as if kept safely by your mother.**

This tells us that the power of japa is cumulative, especially when done without a break through every waking hour. Furthermore, the divine shakti and consciousness inherent in the mantra will continually increase and remain as in the charging of a battery. But it is the Divine Mother that will keep that power and consciousness safely within us so that when "critical mass" is reached the divinizing power will be released in the transformation of our consciousness which is our Self. So Ma assures us.

> **The moment may come at any time, when you will realize the many in the One and the One in the many.**

Ma emphasized that the sadhaka must though constant japa be alert and watchful inwardly at all times for the advent of what Ma called The Great Moment in which the Consciousness that is the One will be revealed in and to the sadhaka as his own consciousness, his own Self.

> **The Name and the One whose Name it is are indivisible; thus, what you have offered will come back to you.**

It will come back to you in the form of your own Self-realization. For Tat Twam Asi: you are yourself that One Whose Life and Consciousness is in His Name. This is an incomprehensible mystery, but it will be known by you in direct and immediate experience. Do not try to intellectually figure it out. Practice and experience it. That is why Yogananda sometimes sang over and over: "He who knows, knows. None else knows." Be A Knower.

If japa has been practiced continuously, it is bound to bear fruit some day.

Even in the highest metaphysical realms the law For Every Action There Is An Opposite And Equal Reaction holds true.

Just do it and see for yourself.

THIRTEEN

Raipur, Dehradun, December 3rd, 1948

One meets some very keen seekers after Truth. The union of the individual with the All eternally exists.

I well remember how in my first pilgrimage to India a yogi I met more than once said to me: "When someone has chosen God, you can know that God has first chosen him." Some metaphysicians refer to human beings as reflections of God, and this is true. Our search for God is an extension-reflection of God's search for us. Since we are one with God, the search takes place on both sides, but it is the same search as we reflect the divine outreach. Therefore our search will eventually succeed, for it is really only a revealing of what is a part of universal being.

Actually, we do not end duality and establish unity, we end the delusion of duality and reveal the eternal truth of unity within our own selves. We speak of searching for God, but that search is really the search for our Self of which God is the ultimate, inmost Self. It truly is a matter of realization, not of any change at all except in our awareness.

Is not the eagerness to become aware of this union due to the fact that the One will reveal Himself?

So in the inner impulse to reach and unite with the Absolute is itself the assurance, the guarantee, that in time the One will reveal Himself as our ultimate Self. It is the Inner Call of the Self. So the sadhaka should be calmly assured that success is inevitable because it already is a fact awaiting our realization. There is no seeking or finding, there is only awakening and realizing. This vividly underscores the counsel of Krishna to Arjuna: "Therefore become a yogi" (Bhagavad Gita 6:46). "Where Lord Krishna is, and Arjuna, great among archers, there, I know, is goodness and peace, and triumph and glory" (Bhagavad Gita 18:78). Where there is the realization of Brahman, the Paramatman, in the consciousness of the awakened self-realized yogi, there is revealed the eternal goodness and peace, and triumph and glory that is the Self.

None can foretell at what particular time circumstances will co-operate to bring about that Great Moment for anyone.

The hermetic principle: "As below so above; as above so below" is true. There is nothing only external, only internal, nothing without, only within. The dualities are fundamental facts. Therefore, on both the inner and outer levels of the yogi there are factors which coalesce to bring about the Great Moment. This is the law and applies to all.

Since Ma says, "None can foretell at what particular time circumstances will co-operate to bring about that Great Moment for anyone," it is our duty as sadhakas to just keep on maintaining our sadhana and the disciplines that support and empower it. The Great Moment must come. So we must keep awake and alert for its inevitable coming.

There may be failure to begin with, but what counts is final success.

One time a man who was obviously mentally flawed brought his also obviously mentally flawed daughter to stay with Ma. ("Stay" meant constant travel with Ma to various spiritual centers and ashrams, etc.) He was also obviously simply getting rid of her as a nuisance and potential liability. When Ma left with her usual entourage he was at the train station and said to Ma: "I see my daughter is leaving with you. Does that mean she has passed the test?" Ma replied, "Baba, the only test that matters is the final test." In a few days the ashram contacted him and said he should come and take his daughter home. Ma always gave people a chance to reveal themselves.

Many people seemingly succeed spiritually for years, even decades, and then one day the karmas and samskaras arise and strike and devastation results. So no matter how well the sadhaka feels he is doing, he must be at all times aware of potential failure and guard himself against it by diligent sadhana and observance of yama and niyama. Success may be our goal, but awareness of possible failure must never be out of our minds.

A perfect example of this principle can be found in the account I once read of a man who was applying to the local school board for a position as driver of a school bus. One of the board members asked him: "If you were driving a busload of children in winter over a bridge that had no railings and was coated with ice, how close do you think you could drive to the edge and feel safe?" The man answered: "I would drive right in the middle as far from each edge as I could be. And even then I would be afraid every second until I reached the other side." The board member replied: "Then we hire you! We don't want anyone driving our children who could be confident taking chances with their safety."

There is no value in beginning well if we do not end well. So the worthy sadhaka is aware of possible failure at all times and diligently guards against it.

You might be interested to know that the renowned Gita Press in Gorakhpur, whose magazine "Kalyana Kalpataru" is read throughout India, has the strict rule to never print the photograph of, or an article about, any living spiritual figure in that magazine. This is because through the years many respected figures in spiritual circles have fallen away and become a disgrace and scandal.

An aspirant cannot be judged by preliminary results.

Again, the only test that matters is the final test. Often people have a kind of meteoric rise in spiritual matters and then have a meteoric fall. So how a beginner begins does not indicate how he will end. Many who seem losers in the beginning become winners in the end, and many who seem winners in the beginning become losers in the end. As Jesus said: "He that endureth to the end shall be saved" (Matthew 10:22). Some of the world's biggest failures seemed in the beginning to be the biggest successes.

Now the important thing is for each one of us to take Ma's statement to heart about ourselves and not think that because at the moment everything seems the best with us, it will always be that way. For, again, karmas and samskaras are there like seeds awaiting germination and growth. Many decades ago I never missed "The Shadow" radio program. In every broadcast the main figure, the Shadow, would say: "What evil lurks in the hearts of men? The Shadow knows!" and would laugh ominously. The wise sadhaka knows that negativity can lie hidden like deadly seeds within our conscious and unconscious minds, waiting to sprout, grow and flourish. At the same time there are equally positive and life-supporting seeds. So we must watch our mind and heart at all times and honestly examine and classify the workings of our mind and heart.

A lot of inwardly corrupt people are very bullying about being "positive" so they can badger people into not looking at them and seeing their evil. They also hate the laws of action and reaction. But Saint Paul rightly and wisely said: "Be not deceived; God is not mocked: for whatsoever a man soweth, that shall he also reap. For he that soweth to his flesh shall of the flesh reap corruption; but he that soweth to the Spirit shall of the Spirit reap life everlasting" (Gal. 6:7-8).

The sum of this is that we should not judge either others or ourselves by initial conditions or successes, but wait till "it all comes out in the wash." As Ma said: The only test that matters is the final test. And consider this maxim well: In the beginning is the end. So from the first we must ensure our success by a determined will and heart.

In the spiritual field, final success means success right from the beginning .

Previously I have remarked: "In the beginning is the end." This is because time and space are illusions. Therefore there is a point where all time and space are present in their totality. That point is also infinite–infinity itself. Therefore according to the intention of the individual person his entire past and future is determined, and is present in seed form which as his future unfolds is revealed as time moves onward.

There is another aspect to this. According to the fundamental orientation or intention of the individual–especially the sadhaka–the end of the matter is determined at the very beginning, and in that sense is present right from the first. So as the sadhaka begins, so should he end. And although there is an illusory aspect to relative existence, in the realm of intent and will the end is already a present fact. In over half a century as a yogi, I have seen numberless people who began sadhana (or the appearance of sadhana) with the full inner–even if subliminal–intention of failing. And I have seen a few who began with the intention to succeed–and they did. So an experienced or intuitive observer knows how the whole matter is going to end.

Back to the school bus example. The applicant for the driver's position not only wanted to be the bus driver, he wanted with his whole heart to do it right and well. Therefore he would have done so in actual life.

Bringing it all home to us as sadhakas. We are all psychic with intuitional knowledge of every item and point in our life. Those who are out of touch with their inner nature and inner mind are wandering in the dark. But the real yogi knows right from the start where he intends to end up, and intuits the possibility of his success. And that perspective produces intelligent and diligent endeavor–not in fits of stop and start, but as a continuous, steady movement onward.

Please realize that each person has to make it completely on his own. Just as helping a bird hatch from the egg deprives it of the necessary effort and employment of force it needs to develop its strength for life after the hatching, so also coddling, cajoling and cutting corners for a beginning sadhaka dooms him to failure. We all need to go through "hard" and "tough" times as we move onward through life. Nietzsche was right when he said: "What does not destroy me makes me stronger." That implies that we have to meet, cope with and overcome difficulties in all aspects of life, and that includes spiritual life. Those who fall down–or apart–at any difficulty, opposition or snag will FAIL. And willingly.

For the hermetic principle As Above So Below implies that what is in our inmost, subconscious and superconscious minds is exactly–and only–what will manifest in our external life. Therefore there are two essential things to do. The first is to ruthlessly examine our mind and motivations and squelch or eliminate any tendencies or attractions to anything that will block or in any way hinder our spiritual progress–which must be constant and unbroken. The second is to look ahead. The maxim is right: If you fail to plan, you plan to fail. As Jesus said: "Which of you, intending to build a tower, sitteth not down first, and counteth the cost, whether he have sufficient to finish it? Lest haply, after he hath laid the foundation, and is not able to finish it, all that behold it begin to mock him, saying, This man began to build, and was not able to finish. Or what king, going to make war against another king, sitteth not down first, and consulteth whether he be able with ten thousand to meet him that cometh against him with twenty thousand?" (Luke 14:28-32).

Forwarned is truly forearmed. You take it from there.

> **What indeed is a mantra? While one is bound by the idea of 'I' and 'you', and identifies oneself with the ego, the mantra represents the Supreme Being Himself in the guise of sound.** ***If you persevere you find that the mantra is your own Self.***

The *Sanskrit Glossary of Yogic Terms* by Swami Yogakanti defines mantra: "Subtle sound vibration which liberates energy from the confines of mundane awareness and explands the consciousness when repeated." A mantra is both vibration and consciousness. The vibratory aspect purifies and frees our awareness and both opens our consciousness and evokes higher, divine consciousness from within our inmost Self. In a sense it invokes and produces this consciousness, but it also evokes and reveals the consciousness that is the Self.

Ma tells us that in the beginning we think of and experience the mantra as an invocation or link with the Supreme Being manifesting as the divine sound that is the mantra. If we persevere and inwardly repeat the mantra continually letting our mind become absorbed in or pervaded by the subtle sound, we will find it transforming us on all levels and ultimately revealing itself as the Supreme Being Itself about which the enlightened yogis have also told us: You Are THAT.

Do you not see how beautifully certain syllables have been joined together in the Mahavakyas?

The Mahavakyas the "Great Sayings" of the Upanishads, are four in number:

1) Tat Tvam Asi–Thou Art That (Chandogya Upanishad 6.8.7).

2) Aham Brahmasmi–I am Brahman (Brihadaranyaka Upanishad 1.4.10).

3) Prajnanam Brahma–Brahman is Consciousness (Aitareya Upanishad 3.3).

4) Ayam Atma Brahma–This Atman (Self) is Brahman (Mandukya Upanishad 1.2).

These are not just great statements of sublime truth, they are mantras, formulas of spiritual power, that can awaken the sadhaka's consciousness, though they are usually employed only by sannyasis.

You think you are wholly bound, but this is only what your mind believes.

"It is all in your head" can be a sublime truth. Bondage and freedom are states of mind. Slaves can be free in their mind, and free people can be slaves in their mind. Material consciousness binds and limits us, but when our spiritual consciousness is awakened we find that the bondage and limitation is a mirage and we are free in our very being.

So it is the mind that needs to be freed, and the surest and most immediate means to that freedom is the continuous repetition (japa) of a mantra supported by daily meditation.

That is why true Knowledge can supervene at the very utterance of a word of power [mantra], which is composed merely of a few ordinary letters joined together. How mysterious and intimate is the relation between those words and the immutable Brahman!

Therefore it is said by the yogis: God and His Name are ONE. Through diligent sadhana in the form of japa and meditation this is experienced by every sadhaka for himself. At first he has the wisdom to believe it when he is told it. But after devoted japa and meditation he comes to know by his own direct experience its power, its effect and its potential within himself. The various sadhana mantras are also called taraka mantras. Taraka means both delivering-freeing and carrying over something, putting it into an entirely different place. The sacred mantras free our consciousness from bondage and bring it into the glorious realm of Self-realization, the revelation-experience of our own divine Atman within the Supreme Self, the Paramatman. It is truly awesome; and ours to experience through practice.

> **Take for example, the Shabda [Sound] Brahman: merely by the Shabda [Sound] one becomes established in the Self.**

How is this? Because the entire range of relative existence–all the worlds from the lowest to the highest–are composed of vibrating energy, of sound power which the sages called "Shabda Brahman." A mantra is a form of Shabda Brahman.

> **Look, the ocean is contained in the drop, and the drop in the ocean.**

The entire range of existence, from highest to lowest, is a field, an "ocean," of vibrating Energy/Consciousness that is the Absolute Brahman Itself. Consciousness is as much our inner essence as it is the very Being of Brahman. We are points of consciousness within the Absolute Consciousness. Essentially we are one, and it is Shabda in the form of a mantra which through its repetition joins our consciousness with the Absolute Consciousness and makes them One–yet with the distinction of ourselves within Brahman.

The part can never be the whole, but the whole is always the part. It is the same with us. We cannot from our side be one with God, but God can be one with us–indeed has always held us within His Being as part of Him, one with Him and yet distinct from Him. This is an absolute and eternal condition which is impossible for us to fully grasp within our limited intellects. We can experience it, but we can never describe it, for our experience of Divine Reality is a matter of Pure Being which is utterly absolute and beyond relativity–and therefore beyond words that are only limited mental concepts. Brahman–and our own Self–cannot be either conceptualized or put into words. It is like salt. What does salt taste like? Like salt. And there the matter is concluded. Salt does not taste like anything else, and nothing else tastes like salt.

It is the same with the question: What/Who is God? And also: What/Who am I? In the Bible God is described/named I AM. "And Moses said unto God, Behold, when I come unto the children of Israel, and shall say unto them, The God of your fathers hath sent me unto you; and they shall say to me, What is his name? what shall I say unto them? And God said unto Moses, I AM THAT I AM: and he said, Thus shalt thou say unto the children of Israel, I AM hath sent me unto you" (Exodus 3:13-14).

We may not fully grasp all the implications intellectually, but we *are* one with Brahman Who is our inmost nature and being. Therefore Ma asks:

> **What else is the spark, if not a particle of fire, of Him who is Supreme Knowledge Itself?**

This is the truth of all that exist. But the important aspect is what Ma is specifically talking about: the nature of the Name of God as actually *being* God. Therefore, when we repeat the Name of God, God the Absolute is revealed as present in our consciousness. I say revealed, because God is eternally present *as* consciousness *in* our consciousness, the essence of our finite being, but always infinite. This cannot be fully comprehended intellectually, but in an incomprehensible way it can be experienced, and can become our permanent state of consciousness.

> **It is the notion of 'you' and 'I' by which your mind has been held captive all along.**

Duality produces conflict, confusion and the illusion of separation–in other words: samsara. Only in unity is there peace and the cessation of birth and death that are fundamentally illusion, false limitation and bondage. Sri Ramakrishna gave the example of a laundryman who at night would simply pass a rope around the legs of his donkey without really tying it. But the donkey would think he was bound and stand there all night without moving.

In the same way bondage is only an illusion and freedom the ever-present reality. Therefore bondage and freedom exist only in the mind as an idea. Awakening from the sleep of delusion into the reality of the Self is the only thing we really need. It is like a man believing he has been locked in a room, but when he turns the doorknob the door opens and he steps out into freedom. It is the positioning of awareness that is both bondage and freedom. What will free the bound consciousness? Ma tells us in the following words.

> **You should understand that the combination of sounds which has the power to free you from this bondage is the one to be used.**

Continual repetition of a liberating mantra awakens us to the freedom that is a basic attribute of our Self. From illusion we rise in our consciousness into Reality. Both sleeping and waking are illusions, states of consciousness. When by means of the japa of a siddha mantra, which is a vehicle of liberating consciousness–that actually *is* the Self–freedom from all shades of bondage is attained.

> **Verily, it is through sound that one penetrates into Silence; for He is manifest in all forms without exception.**

God is indeed manifest in all forms, but only through shabda, the inner sound of a liberating mantra, is the silence that is the consciousness of the Self entered into and made permanent, the yogi's very state of being by which he transcends the realm of name and form.

The divine shabda is manifesting as all forms, which is why shabda itself is the only key to the Silence that is the Self. For shabda arises from the Self and is resolved back into it through mantra sadhana. The illusion of bondage is dissolved by the divine sound of the mantra. Many virtues and right actions are needed to support and facilitate our sadhana, but only mantra-shabda leads to liberation, to moksha.

> **Indeed, everything is possible in the state that is beyond knowledge and ignorance.**

Unity dispels duality, including the duality of knowledge and ignorance. To the truly liberated consciousness neither knowledge nor ignorance even exist. Only The One that is beyond knowledge and ignorance is present to the mukta, the liberated one.

> **So long as you are not finally established in that Supreme Knowledge, you all dwell in the realm of waves and sound.**

We must rise into that Supreme Knowledge that is also the Supreme Silence that is beyond "the realm of waves and sound."

> **There are sounds that cause the mind to turn outwards, and others that draw it within. But the sounds that tend outwards are also connected with those that lead inwards. Therefore, because of their interrelation, there may at some auspicious moment occur that perfect union, which is followed by the great Illumination, the revelation of What IS. Why should not this be possible, since He is ever Self-revealed?**

"Therefore be a yogi" (Bhagavad Gita 6:46).

FOURTEEN

In the train to Benares, December 5th, 1948.

> **One thing is the full and final Realization of Unveiled Light; but quite another is a realization due to some cause, in which the possibility of its being obscured again still exists.**

If profound insight and even exalted yogic phenomena and states have a cause other than genuine sadhana, then they must in time disintegrate, and ignorance and powerlessness will once again prevail. The Eastern Christians have a saying: Lower then a demon is a fallen monk. But first he must be a real monk. The same is true of a fallen or failed yogi. A drowning person who desperately strives to save his life and reaches and stands on the solid land may again dive into the water and go through the whole desperation and struggle again–perhaps at that time to fail and drown.

Only those who have gone beyond the possibility of regression are really safe and secure. That is why, as I have already recounted, the renowned Gita Press in Gorakhpur, whose magazine "Kalyana Kalpataru" is read throughout India, has the strict rule that they will never print the photograph of, or an article about, any living spiritual figure in that magazine because they know of many respected figures in spiritual circles that fell away and become a disgrace and scandal or quietly disappeared forever.

Sadhana of the highest order puts us in the State that is beyond all states, and which is described as *bhavatitam-trigunarahitam*: beyond states of mind (bhava) and the three gunas of prakriti–and therefore completely out of the ocean of prakriti and relative existence. Anything less leads back to the former conditions.

What is "the full and final Realization of Unveiled Light"? The transcendance of all relativity and the capacity for re-entering that relativity. It is not just reaching "the other shore," it is the permanent emergence from the ocean and total establishment on the solid land of the Self which is itself the Ultimate Consciousness. There is no bargain-counter or reduction-for-this-limited-time-only realization. It is the All or it is Nothing. Since the goal is consciousness, only consciousness can lead to–and into–it. Sadhana may be prepared for by shakti and kriya (action), but real sadhana leads beyond shakti and kriya, making reversion impossible.

Freedom negates bondage; knowledge negates ignorance. Just as the body grows steadily from childhood into adulthood and makes no regression, so genuine, liberating sadhana produces steady evolution into the state that cannot be turned back from. No one falls from Self-realization. Those yogis that seem so high in consciousness but fall back into samsara only had the appearance of liberation. For true liberation is the state beyond the possibility of regression. However, observers often assume a yogi has attained a state which he really has not. The fake yogis of India master mere appearance and deception. Reality has usually never even touched them. But in time the truth of things is revealed.

> **At the time when the play of sadhana was being manifested through this body, it could clearly perceive these various possibilities.**

And so must whoever aspires to the Goal which is reached by sadhana, and yet is beyond sadhana, have the same perception of the possibilities. Only when there is a complete picture can there be complete understanding and realization.

> **You should understand that if a veil of ignorance has been burnt or dissolved, as it were, the seeker will, for a certain period of time, have unobstructed vision. Afterwards it becomes blurred again.**

Here we have to carefully examine the words of Ma. She says, "*a* veil of ignorance," not "*the* veil of ignorance." She is speaking of only a part of the ignorance in our mind, not the entire entity that is ignorance itself–the very state of ignorance. Most liftings of the veil of ignorance end in the falling again of the veil over the mind. Only the permanent lifting and burning-destruction of the veil guarantees the right result. Often in various situations when people expressed the opinion that everything was settled and permanent She would simply say: "Let us wait and see…." This always implied that the situation or change was only temporary and the old condition would again arise and usually remain.

Ma was the embodiment of the Truth that is Reality. Several times in my pilgrimages one or more people would begin instructing me in Ma's presence as to what I should be doing or what our ashram's activities, disciplines or observances should be. I would look at Ma as they were going on and on. She would usually be looking somewhat upward and separating Herself from the whole matter. So I would always later on ask Ma for her instructions or opinions and She would explain to me the error of their words and tell me the truth of the matter as to what I should do.

Here is an example. Ganges water is an important element in ritualistic worship and Ma had said our ashram should daily have such worship. So one time in Varanasi I asked Ma what to do if our Ganges water was used up. Immediately some people, including a very renowned pandit of Varanasi, began telling me that I only needed to keep adding ordinary water to the Ganges water and by the touch of the Ganges water that water would become Ganges water. I looked at Ma, and she was looking a little upward with an expression on Her face that told me the advice I was getting was utterly wrong. So later I privately asked Her about this, and she replied that to put ordinary water in Ganges water was like putting dog's urine into the Ganges water! When I asked what to do when it ran out, She told me the simplest solution: Come back and get some more. Quite some time later I discovered the mantric ritual for invoking the spiritual vibrations of the holy rivers of India into water. Ma said that it was acceptable and I need not bring Ganges water back–that water would be sufficient.

> **All the same–what will be the result of such a glimpse? Ignorance will have become less dense, and true Knowledge gained**

greater prominence; in other words, by the momentary lifting of the veil, the individual's bonds will have been loosened.

Not totally removed, just loosened in hope of eventual removal if the sadhaka perseveres.

In this condition, there is a semblance of the attainment of real Knowledge; in fact, it is also a state of achievement, although quite different from the state of final Self-realization.

Therefore it is a step toward the final realization and itself of supreme value as long as the progress toward the final state is continued.

The veil has here been suddenly dissolved or consumed–just as in the story of the ten men, when the Mahatma said "You are yourself the tenth!"

Ma refers here to the following well known Vedantic parable:

"Ten men had to ford a river by swimming. To make certain that they had all safely reached the opposite bank, one of them counted the lot and, to his consternation, counted only nine. To make sure that he had not been mistaken, another one of them counted the men, with a similar result. Each one of them counted in turn, confirming that there were only nine left, although they could not make out which of them was missing. A Mahatma passed by and they told him what had happened. He made them stand in a line, hit each one with his staff and asked them to count as he hit. To their joy and amazement, they at once realized that none of them had been drowned. 'Each one of you forgot to include himself,' explained the Mahatma."

There is a Realization, after which the possibility of its being obscured again by a reappearance of the veil of ignorance simply cannot occur: this is true and final Self-realization.

There is a vast difference between partial realization and total realization. Here Ma points out that one point of difference is that partial realization can be lessened or even lost–actually by its nature it is almost guaranteed to be lessened or lost. Many people receive a temporary opening of awareness that fades in time or is dissolved by their own subsequent actions that darken their consciousness which had momentarily been expanded or clarified. I have through the years seen people momentarily gain spiritual insight and then have it become dimmed or even totally eliminated because they did not act upon it immediately or willfully ignored or suppressed it because there were aspects of that intellectual opening that they did not like, especially in the realm of the obligations incurred by expanded or clarified understanding. There is a sombre maxim that increase of knowledge is increase of sorrow. Sometimes the increase of sorrow is the consequence of not acting according to that knowledge–or even a specious denying of the truth of that knowledge or denial of the need or viability of taking action in response to that knowledge.

But when the realization is deep-seated or even total, it will be permanent and demonstrated in the individual's subsequent outlook, thought and action. In other words, it will be a permanently life-changing insight.

So according to Ma genuine realization cannot be reversed, so there is no ignoring it or falling away from it. The sadhaka's subsequent thought and life will be the evidence of its reality (or its non-occurrence).

Lightning comes in a flash, but the light of day continues steadily.

There are people who undergo (or claim to undergo) an instant illumination or insight. Here Ma tells us that continuation of the expansion of the sadhaka's insight will follow a genuine enlightenment experience. It will not be the proverbial flash in a pan. There can be no reversal of true enlightenment. Furthermore, the change and expansion of the sadhaka's insight will continue in a smooth and unhindered manner until perfect enlightenment is attained.

There is such a thing as a "lightning strike" experience in spiritual life, but that is when positive samskaras developed in previous lives suddenly arise in the sadhaka's consciousness as a recovering or remembering which continues to last.

> **Out of your union with this infinity spring your actions, feelings and thoughts, at the present time or in the future, in whatever form He may be pleased to assume.**

It is the permanent advent of our own divinity. Notice that Ma is implying that this will be the experience of Her hearers. False teachers go on and on about their great enlightenment and divine mission to teach others. But Ma urges us to move on to our own enlightenment–yes, to eventually no longer even need Her for guidance. Many people used Ma as a kind of good luck charm or substitute for their own interior life. Therefore when Ma left this world they just wandered around empty and aimless, just as they had through the previous years with Ma. In Varanasi a man told me that he had once said to Ma that those who continually travelled with Her must be of a high spiritual level. She simply replied, pointing to Her forearm: "Baba, even flies sit on this body!"

> **Just consider: The Infinite is contained in the finite, and the finite in the Infinite; the Whole in the part and the part in the Whole. This is so, when one has entered the Great Stream. He who attains and that which is attained are one and the same. It is not merely a matter of imagination through ever fresh channels. He is perceived in ever new forms.**

This is so wondrous and profound that I will not mar it or distract from it by any comment.

> **Having entered that unbroken Stream, it is only natural that yoga, the hidden union of the individual with the All, should become Mahayoga.**

There are two profound principles enunciated here by Ma. First, is the fact that there is a constant stream of Atmic Consciousness that flows upward to the goal of perfect Self-realization. It is a permanent fact of the universe. It is always there. Second, that entry into that stream is natural to the yogi and his own present, though unexperienced, union with the Absolute will be manifested in the state of Supreme Unity–Mahayoga.

> **Infinite is the diversity of creation, infinite are its modes of being, its changing movements and static states, revealed at every single instant. It is impossible to put into writing all that a seeker after Truth experiences.**

So when we read accounts of someone's "enlightenment experience" and subsequent revelations, we can safely forget all about it. For if something can be described, then it is merely part of samsara. Our own Self, like the Absolute–Which is the Self of our Self– is beyond defining or describing. As the upanishad says: "He who knows tells it not. He who tells knows it not." It then goes on to say that if someone says, "I know" he does not know; but if he says, "I do not know," there is a possibility that he does know. It is good to keep all this in mind.

> **Furthermore, it is quite certain that Reality is beyond speech and thought. Only that which can be expressed in words is being said. But what cannot be put into language, is indeed That which IS.**

So Ma is telling us that nothing She says to us can encompass the Absolute Reality that is the only Truth. How different Ma was from the fake gurus that assured their dupes that they were telling them the highest truth.

Also, Ma did not mind being wrong. One morning in Hardwar when I went to Bhagat House to see Ma, She was animatedly telling something to the devotees and laughing. Swami Vijayananda had come from Almora to be with Ma, and the night before She had begun thinking that his sensitive digestion must be upset from eating the ashram food. So She woke up some of the ashramites and told them to seek in the neighborhood and find Vijayananda and bring him to her so any stomach troubles could be corrected. Several people went around the neighborhood knocking on doors, waking people up and asking them if they knew Vijayananda. Finally they knocked on one door and woke up Vijayananda who had been sleeping very well without any stomach problems. So Ma was laughing at how She had made all this fuss and just ended up disturbing everyone's sleep–not just Vijayanandaji's. Now, the groupies were sitting there all sour-faced, not at all liking Ma making fun of Herself. Why? Because they were not devotees, they were parasites hanging around Ma with the idea that the greater people considered Ma to be, the greater they would think that they, the groupies, were. But Ma was ruining Her and their reputations. Yes: they were just flies sitting on Ma's body for their own ego-inflation.

In accord with the progress of the sadhaka, spiritual experiences will occur of themselves.

Multitudes of "spiritual" people are avid to have spiritual experiences that will reveal their spiritual advancement–to themselves and others. I recall a young Italian man who dressed in some self-created "sadhu" rig and hung around Ma like a blissful devotee. One time during a particularly inspiring evening of devotional music Binudi, the sister of the King of Nepal, began playing a flute along with the singing. When it was over, this man looked very solemn and asked us, "During the kirtan, did anyone hear a flute?" "Of course," I said. "Binudi was playing her flute along with our singing." Glum deflation was the instant effect.

Now Ma is saying here that sadhakas will have spiritual experiences which indicate their spiritual level, and sometimes which will have some message or lesson for them. Therefore a sadhaka should pay attention to his experiences and scrupulously analyze them to see what they indicate about himself and his sadhana. There is a saying, "You cannot put hot coals in your bosom and not be burned." So true sadhana will certainly make changes in the sadhaka, and he should be alert to detect and rightly interpret them.

In the nursery rhyme Little Jack Horner "stuck in his thumb and pulled out a plum, and said: 'What a good boy am I!'" This is not the purpose or the effect of sadhana.

> **However, where Enlightenment is complete, there is no more question of important or unimportant experiences.**

This is because experiences are perceptions–objects of perception. But enlightenment is the state of Atmic Consciousness itself. It is a condition of Self-perception, of Self-realization. The sadhaka like everyone else has objective experiences, but the sadhaka goes deep within through sadhana to experience the Consciousness which is his own essential being–his Self. It is not an external object, but his own inmost reality.

> **On reaching the end of one's journey, full Enlightenment is bound to take place.**

Enlightenment is the very purpose of the jiva, the individual person, entering into relative existence-experience. From the onset, it is the journey of consciousness into Consciousness–there is no other goal. There are just two states: unenlightened and enlightened. The wise yogi never forgets this throughout his sadhana, so he is never distracted or deluded by mere experiences.

> **Where the Infinite is in question, the diversity of approaches is equally infinite, and likewise are the revelations along these paths, of endless variety. Is it not said: "There are as many doctrines as there are sages"?**

Basically, since we are so limited, especially by the ego, we like to create in our minds the conviction that someone or something is the only right or true philosopher or philosophy. But Ma tells us that there are virtually an infinite number of paths to an infinite number of revelation-experiences along those paths.

Now Ma does not say that they are all perfect and therefore equal. This we must understand also. There was a comedian in the early twentieth century that said: "When the pay-phone was invented, my grandfather invented slugs." (Slugs are small heavy metal discs the size of coins that dishonest people would put in pay-phones to get free phone calls.) So wherever there is something genuine we often find a large number of fakes. This is simply the way of maya to be wary, but not paranoid, about.

So the sadhaka must intently and carefully scrutinize all spiritual teachers and their spiritual teachings. For duality being the basic state of relativity, there must of necessity be genuine, beneficial teachers and teachings, and false, deceptive teachers and teachings. The ability to distinguish them from one another is part of developing our spiritual intelligence.

> **Unless one has a point of view of one's own, one will not be classed among the sages.**

Therefore there is nothing wrong in working out our own personal philosophy and rules of conduct. This principle also implies that we must develop our own views and the ways to express or embody them. What we must not do is claim that ours alone are right and acceptable. We must literally learn to mind our own business.

> **Surely all this eager searching has for its aim only the revelation of That, which is already Self-revealed. Could there be such ardent yearning and pining for something that is not, that never can or will be?**

The great sages of all eras have sought for that which they intuited was already present and viable. They did not create or formulate, they discovered. Ma is saying that since our essential being is knowing, our search is activated from within by that knowing. Also She implies that the successful search must be eager and ardent with yearning and pining. We must be divinely discontent, satisfied only with realization of the Real–which includes our Self and the Supreme Self. The search is an indication of intuitive knowledge of the object that the search will find. Here the ending is in the beginning.

However we must at all times keep in mind that Ma is speaking of the Absolute as the focus of both the seeker and the search.

> **By concentrating on the problems that arise in the mind, it may be possible to undo the knots that constitute the ego.**

Swadhyaya, self-study or self-analysis, is an essential part of sadhana, of niyama. The sadhaka must always face himself in all aspects and be absolutely frank and open with himself. For many go through life lying to and deceiving themselves. I remember an Eastern Orthodox abbot saying to me regarding a fallen monk: "He was never bothered by demons. He was his own demon." That must not be our story. And we must certainly not be "accepting ourselves" if our thoughts and deeds should be rejected and reformed.

FIFTEEN

Benares, August 17th, 1948.

> **For a Self-realized Being, neither the world with its pairs of opposites exists, nor does the body. If there is no world, there can obviously be no body either.**
>
> **Who says, the body exists? There is no question at all of name and form.**
>
> **To wonder whether a realized Being sees anything outside of Himself is also beside the point. Who is there to whom he can say 'Give, give !' [A play upon words: *deo*–give, and *deho*–body.]**
>
> **Yet this state of wanting is precisely the reason for one's belief in the reality of the body. Therefore, since there is no world and no body, there can be no action either; this stands to reason.**
>
> **To make it quite clear: after Self-realization there is no body, no world, and no action–not even the faintest possibility of these–nor is there such an idea as "there is not."**
>
> **To use words is exactly the same as not to speak; to keep silent or not, is identical–all is THAT alone. There simply can be no question of talking or not talking. Please try to understand this! What actually is it that appears to you to be worldly life after Self-realization?**

This is extremely easy to misunderstand, especially since some people seem to gravitate to various forms of practical nihilism and seem to even desire a negative, hopeless condition. This is a form of intellectual/spiritual self-and-world loathing. When I was in college existentialism was quite the fad among the supposed intellectual sophisticates with empty souls. In Flannery O'Connor's brilliantly insightful short story "Good Country People," the main character solemnly announces: "I see through to nothing."

What, then, does Ma mean by these words? She means that the fully awakened person sees the essence of all things–Pure Consciousness, Brahman Itself–as real, and the world and the body and all "things" as relative, temporary appearances, whose reality is only momentary and even illusory in the ultimate analysis. Yet their inmost being, their essence, is a manifestation of Divine Consciousness. Whatever we see is God, even though we are seeing it as relative and conditioned. The essential being of what we see is the Absolute Itself. And the sages have told us about ourselves: Tat Twam Asi–Thou Art THAT.

The sum of all this is my favorite passage from the Gita: "Therefore be a yogi" (Bhagavad Gita 6:46). For only the yogi can experience and comprehend the truth of all things, including himself.

> **This body [Ma] responds strictly to the line of thought and to the spirit in which a question is asked. Consequently, what is the opinion of this body and what is not?**

In every way Ma's communication with people was unique. A conversation with Ma was not like speaking with anyone else because She spoke directly from Reality. This was why Her statement that She did not have a mind was very important to keep in our minds. She was speaking directly from/as the Absolute. Reality Itself was responding to us at all times, and from Her kheyala, the extension or movement of perfect Consciousness and Being. Therefore every aspect of our experience in speaking with Ma was significant–never merely incidental. I never felt any anxiety that I was not fully communicating with Her or the feeling that I was not "getting across" to Ma what I wanted to say. Every communication with Ma was a fully satisfying, a truly divine experience. I was face to face with the Absolute, Which was not abstract or far above or far distant from me. I was speaking with my own essential being, since She was the Self of my Self. This is not some poetic rhapsody on my part. In Ma's presence I was more real than at any other time. Just entering the room where Ma was produced an immediate and profound opening of my consciousness. Simply sitting and looking at Ma for hours affected my state of consciousness greatly. I experienced exactly what Saint John meant when he said about Jesus: "In him was life; and the life was the light of men" (John 1:4).

Speaking with Ma was like two mirrors facing one another and reflecting one another, since there was not just a unanimity but a unity, even a fundamental identity. Ma became one, even identical, with whomever She fixed Her kheyala on in speaking with them. In Her unitary consciousness there was no separation, so She asks: "Consequently, what is the opinion of this body and what is not?" She was everything. She was both presence and absence. She was Herself the Unity that is the dualities which are only appearances.

> **If there is a line of approach, there must be a goal to which it leads; and beyond it is the unattainable. But where the distinction between the attainable and the unattainable does not arise, is THAT Itself.**

Partly this is because the Unattainable is manifesting as the attainable. So there is nothing but essential unity, the One appearing as two or even many. This was experienced vividly even at the very sight of Ma. But there were many who did not experience this. In fact I have known of people who had known Ma for years and even travelled with Her saying to me and some other devotees: "We wish we could see in Ma what you see in Her!" How was this? As I told someone who asked me why I believed in Ma: "Because She wills me to." There is nothing even at this moment that is not Ma. That includes you and I. At every moment we should embody the aspiration expressed in the song:

> Open my eyes, that I may see
>   Glimpses of truth Thou hast for me;
> Place in my hands the wonderful key,
>   That shall unclasp and set me free.
> Open my ears, that I may hear
>   Voices of truth Thou sendest clear;
> And while the wave-notes fall on my ear,
>   Ev'rything false will disappear.

> **What you hear depends on how you play the instrument. According to your ear is whether the sounds** [a play upon words: *Baje* means the sounding of a musical instrument, as well as meaning "useless" or "senseless"] **you hear her utter make sense or not, is for you to judge.**

It was only natural that we would speak of taking refuge in Ma, even of giving ourselves over completely into Her hands (kheyala). But here Ma indicates that we had to decide the value of Her words, that we were to ourselves judge both Her words and our association with Her. She did not want blind faith or blind obedience, but conscious and intelligent understanding of both Her and Her words. So we should go in two directions at the same time: scrutiny and judgement-evaluation of Her words and total acceptance and conformity to Her words. "With men this is impossible; but with God all things are possible" (Matthew 19:26). In other words, if Ma wanted us to do it we would be able to do it. For Ma's kheyala itself was divine power. And if we followed or conformed to Her kheyala we would be empowered by that following and conformity. With Ma the cart *could* go before the horse.

At the same time we must exercise our own judgment. All this talk of "surrender" in spiritual life is false and detrimental. To obey is to make an act of will, it is not surrender–otherwise it is hypocritical and harmful, not just useless. Therefore Ma wanted us to truly decide what we truly thought about Her and Her words to us. We could not deceive Ma, but we could deceive ourselves as to our attitude and our relationship with Ma.

Plenty of people deceived themselves regarding their relationship with Ma. I well remember two utterly haywire Italian chiropractors that told Krishnapriya, a Swiss devotee of Ma: "We come here and Ma just fills us up, and when we go home we find she is working right along with us, and when we feel the force fading away we come back and Ma fills us up again." Ma would not even look at these women, and when they came to say goodbye to Ma and were standing just ten feet away, Ma forcefully told their intercessor: "There is no time." And kept standing there doing nothing. Why? Because for Ma they did not exist, the truth being that She did not really exist for them. She was just a means for them to brag "back home" about how devoted they were to Her and how kind and gracious She was to them. It was true: all were Ma's children–and one time I saw Ma raise her hand as though to strike a woman while shouting "Chor–Get Out." And She meant it.

One piece of propaganda put out by the Anandamayi Sangha said: "Ma is happy and contented at all times." Really? I have been present when She called two ashram officials and gave them a vigorous dressing down about the way people were crowding into her room day and night, getting kicked out and coming right back. (I was one of them.) "I did not want to come to this place," She said, "but you promised me total privacy so I agreed. And what have I found? My room is like a railway station. I have not had a moment's peace since I got here. No consideration is being shown to me at all!" Gulp. (Brahmacharini Atmananda was faithfully translating all this to me.) I guess "happy and contented at all times" was not the fact, at least in Ma's outer behavior. Even I, who had just met Her that day, knew that She was happiness and contentment itself for those whose hearts were open. But She was putting on a very convincing act. One time in Brindaban Ma told a group of us Westerners to get away and go into the temple. Her manner was very abrupt and intense, even angry in appearance. So we all, like the proverbial whipped dogs, went slinking away, but I was so overcome with gratitude that I was there hearing Her divine voice and being spoken to by Her that I turned around and pranamed, inwardly thinking: "Thank you so much for letting me be here and seeing You." Ma smiled graciously and lovingly and pranamed to me. And I turned and went on with the rest with a glad heart. I remembered the father of a friend of mine saying once, "A slap from a mother is better than a kiss from a stranger."

> **Here [with Sri Ma], the question of striking a chord or not does not arise. You will have to decide whether your Sri Ma is good for nothing or useful, because she is your daughter as well as your mother. Whether she is worthless or of any service, father will be able to tell.**

With Ma there was no thought about being appealing to or being liked by anyone. That was all up to them. The second sentence implies that each one had to decide for themselves "whether your Sri Ma is good for nothing or useful." It all depended on us, on our reaction to Ma and whether or not we ordered and conformed our inner and outer life to Her. That was the only wise and correct response, and that response indicated our true character in relation to Ma–what we were to Ma and what Ma was to us.

> **For this body the problem of difference of opinion in no wise exists.**

First, because Ma truly saw all as The One. Also Ma saw beyond the duality of true/false, is/is not. In divine unity there cannot be two. So Ma was at all times–and had always been–one with us. We were existing only in the very Being of Ma. We were Ma!

SIXTEEN

Benares, August 14th, 1948.

Where Brahman is, the One-Without-A-Second, nothing else can possibly exist.

Therefore nothing else but Brahman does exist now. Furthermore, when Brahman is realized, nothing else is perceived–not only in the absolute form, but everything perceived as multiplicity is directly perceived and experienced as Brahman. Seeing and knowing will not be different.

You separate duality from non-duality because you are identified with the body, which means you are in a condition of constant wanting.

The body has constant demands and actual needs. This gives rise to two conditions: a feeling of lack and the desire to fill and thereby eliminate the lack. However, duality and non-duality are merely relative perceptions. They are both perceptions of the One. So however we may superficially perceive by our conditioned minds, we are only seeing the One.

If you say: "There is only One," when you do not behold Him everywhere: what have you accomplished?

Talk is not just cheap, it is often pointless. Simply saying the right words has no value if there is no solid knowledge and experience behind them–especially if they are spoken just to put up a false front. Sri Ramakrishna said that a parrot may say "Radha-Krishna" over and over, but if you pull its tail feathers it just starts squawking. In the same way I have heard foolish people spouting profound truths, but they could not put one foot after the other spiritually speaking. I well remember during the hip-era yoga boom seeing a strung-out druggie say to someone who had made some philosophical remark: "You mean, like we're all God?" And he was barely human himself.

So Ma is telling us that philosophy and religion mean nothing if they are not based on our own spiritual development and perceptions, that we must not think the ability to cite words of wisdom means we are wise ourselves.

There is only one meaningful criterion in spiritual life: What is the level, the state, of our consciousness itself? True spiritual life is nothing else than the cultivation and expansion of our consciousness until we fully realize and actualize our divine Self. As Sri Ramakrishna said: "One needs sadhana. Mere study of the scriptures will not do. …The almanac may forecast twenty measures of rain; but you do not get a drop by squeezing its pages."

This challenge of Ma has the implication that the aspirant must truly attain higher consciousness–not just talk about spiritual matters but actually experience his own spirit-self. Direct experience of the Self should be our constant goal.

> **All names are His names, all forms His forms, all qualities His qualities.**
>
> **The Nameless and Formless is also He alone.**

But if we do not realize this and actualize it in our constant state of realization and consciousness we are nothing–not even real in the truest sense.

> **A state of being exists where it is immaterial whether He assumes a form or not–what is, is THAT.**

There is a great deal of hullabaloo in India over whether or not God has a true Form, and whether or not we are even individual consciousnesses. Ma indicates that we must attain the state where talk about form or formlessness in relation to God or our Self is pointless. For in the highest Reality form and formlessness are transcended along with all other dualities.

In this case, what is there to express in words? Furthermore, at a certain level the Self may reveal Itself to Itself.

The revelation of the Self to Itself is the only meaningful experience.

At the same time, He does not reveal Himself at all: to whom is He to reveal Himself?

So speaking in such terms is evidence that someone has not experienced his own–and sole–reality.

Where there are neither form nor attributes, what is to be put into language? Where nothing is excluded, how can Oneness be obstructed? In this state of complete poise nothing at all is any longer apart from Him; what is, IS. So, what can be said or left unsaid, since It is entirely beyond words!

What more is to be said? But a lot to be realized!

Suppose you have modeled a doll in butter; whichever aspect of it you may survey–its shape, peculiarity, or appearance–butter it remains, and nothing but butter. As butter, it is one indivisible substance. By division, its integrity would be lost; thus, division is impossible.

Experience of any "state" or the transcendence of any "state" is impossible in the Self. Any such experience is illusion. If we experience duality it is delusion, complete unreality.

There is more in the words of Sri Ramakrishna: "How long does one hear noise and uproar in a house where a big feast is being given? So long as the guests are not seated for the meal. As soon as food is served and people begin to eat, three quarters of the noise disappears. When the dessert is served there is still less noise. But when the guests eat the last course, buttermilk, then one hears nothing but the sound 'soop, sup.' When the meal is over, the guests retire to sleep and all is quiet. The nearer you approach to God, the less you reason and argue. When you attain Him, then all sounds–all reasoning and disputing–come to an end. Then you go into samadhi–sleep–into communion with God in silence."

> **What is called "Nitya Lila" means God's Play, He Himself acting all the parts. Where God is–His Play can never be transient. The actual Eternal Lila exists on the plane of Pure Consciousness. Within the Infinite lies the finite, and in the finite Infinity. He Himself, the One who is the Self, stages a play with Himself: this is called "Nitya Lila."**

What is called "Nitya Lila" means God's Play, He Himself acting all the parts. "Nitya" means perpetual, unending, without beginning or end. It also means play, sport, game, or diversion. God is entertaining Himself through relative creation as it moves through various stages including continual projection and withdrawal. The enlightened Vedic rishis perceived this in their inner consciousness and revealed it in detail in the shastras (scriptures). The books *Sanatana Dharma The Eternal Religion* and *Hinduism The Universal Religion* both have sections on this.

Actually, "creation" is not fully satisfactory a term, because it implies a separation and difference between God and creation, when creation is actually a manifestation of God Who both manifests in and transcends creation. Also it implies a something-from-nothing status which is not accurate. Never has there been "nothing" in the absolute sense. There have been creation cycles in which no thing was manifest, but the essential substance was present and all forms were inherent in it. Further, time and space are illusions, so in one sense nothing ever happens and in another sense everything happens simultaneously. Until our consciousness enters the nitya as its essence there will be no possibility of knowing this in a direct manner–for objective knowing is a function of the limited, temporal mayic mind. We cannot really understand it, but we will know it through direct perception and identity beyond the mind or any "level" of existence. We will not know it–we will be it. And that is the real, eternal state of our being.

Where God is–His Play can never be transient. Where God is fully and permanently present in the consciousness of the individual jiva-person there is eternity and therefore beginingless and endless permanence-establishment in the essential consciousness that is the very nature, the very essence, of the Self.

The actual Eternal Lila exists on the plane of Pure Consciousness. Prakriti, the primal vibratory substance which is the very fabric of relativity, is subject to time, to change, to alternating cycles of rising into manifestation and subsiding into non-manifestation or pure potentiality. The witnessing Self is observing the lila but only appears to enter it and undergo the experience of time, space and change. Really, it is always separate, but can fall into the illusion of identity with relative existence and experience being a part of that illusory existence and therefore come to believe this of itself.

Within the Infinite lies the finite, and in the finite Infinity. This is because they are not just inseparable, they are One. The finite is only appearance, whereas the Infinite is Reality.

He Himself, the One who is the Self, stages a play with Himself: this is called "Nitya Lila." This is a summary restatement of what has gone before.

> **On that plane different appearances befitting different occasions and places are present; for is it not the sphere of Pure Consciousness!**

In the Nitya there is infinite potential, because that is its nature, its very essence. This is necessary, for the Nitya is the field of evolutionary experience which to be relevant must be capable of being shaped into whatever environment is needed for the evolution of each sentient being with in it. And this includes the experiencing of the reaction-results of personal karma. As Pure Consciousness which is therefore Pure Intelligence, it is truly the Mother of all sentient beings–bringing them forth into relativity and making possible their evolution beyond relativity into the Absolute which as their Origin is their own essential nature which is the nature of the Nitya. Otherwise the individuals could not function and evolve within and ultimately beyond the Nitya into the Absolute Non-dual Unconditioned Being.

> **Here even division partakes of the nature of Pure Consciousness, since it is transcendental (aprakrit).**

In essence both ignorance and knowledge, bondage and freedom, are the same Thing. The dualities are like images projected on the screen. They do not really exist and in time disappear and the screen alone remains.

> **When you speak of non-duality, is not the idea of duality implied?**

So we never speak of one thing: duality is always implied. Which means it is as real as the unity, though it comes and goes while the unity remains. It is the unity itself that temporarily appears as duality.

> **But in the realm of Pure Consciousness, if you say "Maya exists," so it does; and if you say "there is no such thing as Maya," it is equally correct; for nothing can be excluded.**

For no statement is really ultimate truth because human beings are incapable of perceiving or expressing the ultimate. The Ultimate Truth Simply IS. And only those who as consciousnesses come to know themselves as consciousness are transmuted into Being Itself–at least in their functioning–which they must also go beyond. It should be evident that, as Ma often said, words cannot express either reality and truth–only approximate and give a hint of them.

> **Non-duality, which cannot be conceived of, is as true as that which one is capable of conceiving. For all is THAT, and where THAT is, there is no contradiction. The false as such must vanish. How can one speak of advaita and include individuals and the world? Since there is non-duality, can there still be individ-**

uals, can there still be the world? In that state, where do these find a place?

So why try to conceive of these things rather than naturally being/becoming them?

Where exclusively Oneness is, how can there be room left for "two"? Nevertheless, whatever anyone may say from any standpoint, everything is right, nothing can be outside of THAT. Whether you say there is or there is not the appearance of Maya–actually speech cannot express it.

Considering our mayic minds, both "one" and "two" are empty words. Silence alone leads beyond them. When we experience for ourselves that "everything is right" we can shut up and BE.

Using words or not, seeing or failing to see, is merely a matter of angles of vision. On the other hand, where THAT is, there can be no angles of vision.

If this is not comprehensible by now we are pretty hopeless.

Problems are born through want of knowledge, due to the veil of ignorance. Until one is established in one's own Essential Being (Swarupa), it is natural that queries should arise. In the realm of phenomena there is much differentiation, such as "above" and "below." But There–what is and what is not?

So we cannot really talk about It, can we? But we can know It since we are already It. Only the yogi can find his way through this maze, even if it is true.

Where ascent and descent can still be spoken of, what will you call such a state? Must you not admit that various directions have remained? If you speak of descent and ascent, it is implied

that there must be a place to descend to; but whither can He descend? To Himself alone of course.

Therefore know the Self. Or more plainly and more to the point: "Therefore be a yogi" (Bhagavad Gita 6:46).

Ascending and descending are one and the same thing, and He who ascends, is He who descends, and the acts of ascending and descending are also He.

After all that has gone before, this needs no elucidation. But it does need to be experienced as true.

Although you speak of Divine Descent (Avatara), He surely does not become divided.

Ma Herself sometimes said: "This body neither comes nor goes." So She never descended or ascended. What had She to do with time or space?

No simile is ever complete [perfect].

Certainly.

But do you not see, every path must come to an end? You should concentrate upon that which will sweep away all other perceptions, and having gone beyond all, there is the revelation of THAT, which you really are.

What a glorious vista! Let's do it.

The beauty of it is that man's very nature is to long for Reality, Supreme Wisdom, Divine Joy, as it is his nature to return home when the Play is over.

Therefore those in whom there is no longing for Reality are unnatural and not fully human. Of course in reality they are not human at all! They are That.

> **The stage of the Play is His, the Play His as well, and so are those who take part in it, friends and fellow-beings–everything is He alone.**

So realize it and enjoy it.

> **The world is concerned with the knowledge that is ignorance.**

Hopefully we have figured that out by now.

> **When you buy clothes you choose durable material, which will not wear out quickly; even this is an indication of your innate tendency to seek the Everlasting. It is your nature to crave for the revelation of That which IS, for the Eternal, for Truth, for limitless Knowledge. This is why you do not feel satisfied with the evanescent, the untrue, with ignorance and limitation. Your true nature is to yearn for the revelation of what you ARE.**

Therefore it is our nature to desire and gain the realization of the Self.

Once again: "Therefore be a yogi" (Bhagavad Gita 6:46). For if you do not become a yogi you do not really desire to gain the realization of the Self.

Seventeen

HE alone IS–so there is no question of acceptance or denial.

This is the viewpoint, the conviction, of the awakened consciousness. It is also the psychological condition of the awakened mind.

Did He ever come into being that there could be a possibility of accepting or denying Him? He was never born.

Simple truth. We either know it or we do not.

According to one angle of vision, it is true that this world does not exist, that Truth is found by eliminating name and form; on the other hand, name and form are made up of the akshara, of that which is indestructible. But in essence, THAT is Truth.

This is why I have often written that those with awakened consciousness are capable of thinking in two directions at the same time, of fully believing two opposite things simultaneously. The Divine Unity is manifesting as duality for the sake of the evolution of sentient beings through countless rebirths until the experience of their eternal union-identity with the Absolute is revealed in their own consciousness. We do not learn it, we experience it through direct realization. And this realization is possible only in the consciousness of the sadhaka. We ourselves are the answer to all questions because we are one with the Totality that is Parabrahman. Self-realization is the necessary requisite for God-realization.

The appearance of the phenomenal world and its disappearance are ultimately one and the same thing: both are He.

And we need to experience this through the purification and expansion of our consciousness through diligent sadhana. There is no other way.

> **Then again there is no question of clearing up error, for there is only He, the One Ground of all.**

Just as darkness disappears at the coming of day, so when That is realized as one's own Self error is impossible.

> **With Him as one's goal, the error that there is such a thing as error has to be uprooted. Talk of this kind is all just by way of helping one to understand.**

And understanding is not enough. Its value is in leading us to the direct, experiential knowledge of The Way Things Are. And this necessitates the direct experience of our own Self, the coming-to-ourself that the Prodigal Son experienced and motivated his return home.

Always when considering this subject I think of the Alto Solo in Mahler's Second Symphony:

> Man lies in greatest need!
> Man lies in greatest pain!
> How I would rather be in heaven.
>
> There came I upon a broad path
>   when came a little angel and wanted to turn me away.
> Ah no! I would not let myself be turned away!
>   I am from God and shall return to God!
> The loving God will grant me a little light,
>   Which will light me into that eternal blissful life!

That little light is our own Self. And we need to heed the words of the chorus that follows: "Stop trembling and get ready to live!"

The study of Scriptures and similar texts–provided it does not become an obsession–can be an aid towards the grasping of Truth.

Our intellect which can lead us astray through specious reasoning can also clear away our misunderstanding when it is purified and reoriented from illusion to reality. The study of holy scriptures and the teachings of enlightened masters can be a great help, but we must not think that the mere intellectual concepts found therein are Truth itself. The Atman-Self and the Paramatman-Supreme Self are the sole Reality. They must be directly experienced within our inmost, highest consciousness–not merely intellectually. This is possible only for the adept yogi, the dedicated and experienced sadhaka. Words are never completely the truth–they only give hints of the truth. The Self and the Supreme Self alone are the Truth. And sadhana is the only way to realize that Truth. It is sadhana that takes us beyond the relative mind into the absolute Conscious-Reality that is our true Self.

So long as what has been read has not become one's own experience, that is to say, has not been assimilated into one's own being, it has not fulfilled its purpose.

Consequently, study of scriptures and philosophical texts are valuable as stimulants to our sadhana, but if we do not also as a consequence take up sadhana to attain Self-realization they are useless–worse than useless if we think that merely learning them constitutes true knowledge.

A seed that is merely held in the hand cannot germinate: it must develop into a plant and bear fruit in order to reveal its full possibilities.

We have to plant the seed of sadhana in the earth of our own subtle bodies. Sadhana then becomes both the sowing and the reaping, for that is the divine nature of authentic sadhana: It imparts experience and enlightenment from the very first moment of our taking it up. But only perseverance to the end, to the complete fruition of the sadhana, will bring us to enlightenment.

> **Nevertheless, in the state where one can neither speak of revelation nor of concealment, there, what appears and becomes, is also ever present.**

When there is a state of continuous, profound awareness, the sadhaka identifies with that within himself that is the continual observer who always remains unchanged, whatever changes may be observed by him. Knowing himself as the observing consciousness, the sadhaka in time realizes that what is observed is also consciousness, and what appears or becomes is already ever-present because in the Self there is no coming or going, no getting or losing–no dualities as absolutes whatsoever, that in every thing the opposite exists as the pole/polarity which is necessary for that thing to exist.

The ever-changing could not exist if the never-changing was not there as its opposite pole or polarity. Unity is the absolute condition at all times but, for the individual person, within the unity the *appearance* of duality is already present as a potential experience–not an actual or absolute reality. In other words, in reality everything is real and nothing is real; duality and unity exist and do not exist at all. For ultimately there is only the One which is beyond duality and unity.

This cannot be reasoned out, but the yogi can know it by experiencing his Self which is both within and without duality and unity. This is why we use the term Advaita which does not mean One, but Not Two. Monism is not Advaita at all. As concepts they negate each other, but as realities only Advaita is real and both monism and duality are illusions. However, the illusive mind is very capable of projecting false experiences of unity. It goes on all the time. So we must divest ourselves of a blanket acceptance of either advaita/unity or dvaita/duality. This is possible only for the adept yogi.

At a certain level one sees glimpses, sparks, as it were, of Reality–this also is one of the states [on the way to complete experience of Reality that is Unity]. One cannot understand what one perceives and therefore is bewildered. There are indeed states and stages without number. The power of fire to burn is one and undivided; but how can there possibly be wholeness and completeness in the so-called glimpses or sparks that one gets?

Only where that wholeness is, there, the question of division does not arise.

This is very clear, and possible of realization.

What is needed is genuine awakening, an awakening after which nothing remains to be attained.

An awakening after which nothing remains to be attained is genuine awakening.

The world of sense objects may or may not be perceived–it makes no difference. A state does exist in which this is so.

The perceiving of an object and the not perceiving of an object are just two ends of the stick of illusion. The state in which these two options are impossible is Reality. That is the state beyond "state." For a state is both a conditioned and a conditioning status, and the liberated sages have told us that liberation is the state beyond condition-unconditioned. For any state or quality of necessity has an opposite state or quality. So only the Nirguna Consciousness that is not a mere state without qualities but the Reality in which qualities or cannot even exist–or be absent from–is Real. And the Self is That.

Whatever anyone does, belongs to the realm of death, of ceaseless change. Nothing can be excluded.

Every action, every "thing," is itself essentially death that involves ceaseless change.

> **In the shape of death art Thou, and in the form of desire. Thou art becoming and Thou art being, differentiation as well as identity–for Thou art infinite, without end. Thou it is who roamest in the disguise of nature.**

This is a good outline of the nature of Mahamaya. But we must not forget that for the diligent sadhaka Mahamaya leads beyond Maya. The non-sadhaka is hopeless until he becomes a sadhaka. Then everything potentially reverses.

> **From whatever standpoint an assertion may be made, I never object to it. For that is to say, if it has not been assimilated into one's own being, it has not fulfilled its purpose.**

Since it is unreal, Ma does not react to it. But She reveals to us that assimilating something into our very being–actually realizing it as an extension of the Self–is the fulfillment of its purpose.

> **For He is all in all, He alone is–the One with form and without form.**

Believing this has no value unless it motivates us to take up and continue viable sadhana so we may realize this by realizing-experiencing our Self as The One that is "with form and without form."

> **In your present condition your divine essence cannot be revealed.**

In our present state we can come to intuit the presence of our divine, essential Self, but the mayic part of our makeup must be purified and transmuted through sadhana. This will reveal to us our own divine

Self that is our divine essence. We to not *have* immortality, we *are* immortality.

You will have to become conscious of your Self in its entirety.

Only through sadhana can we become even partially conscious of the Self. But through prolonged sadhana we can become fully conscious of the Consciousness that is the Self. And since It is one, without any parts, we will naturally perceive Its entirety. There is no such thing as partial Self-realization. There is only total Self-realization since the Self is the Totality of Being.

Nay, to become fully conscious is not enough; you will have to rise beyond consciousness and unconsciousness. The revelation of THAT is what is wanted.

As long as we are in the state where consciousness and unconsciousness are possibilities or options, we are nowhere. We must not just go beyond that state, we must ascend (rise) into the conscious "revelation of THAT" which Itself transcends both consciousness and unconsciousness, bondage and freedom, and therefore is totally beyond them–and consequently can have no relation, positive or negative, with them whatsoever. For no dualities are even possible or conceivable there.

You will have to go on discriminating and make a sustained effort to convince your mind of the fact that japa, meditation and all other spiritual exercises have for their purpose your Awakening.

The mayic ego and the mayic mind intuit that the Self is the light in which they are dispelled like the darkness and illusion they really are. For them, Self-realization is death. And that is so. But for the mind, which is presently blinded by and identifies with them, awakening into Consciousness is considered death. So we must work with the higher mind–the buddhi that is intelligence and insight–so the mind, reflecting the buddhi, will intuit the fact that japa, meditation and all other spiritual exercises have for their purpose the production of its awakening into the realization of the Self. And how do we do that? Simple. *Through japa, meditation and all other spiritual exercises!* For there is no other means of awakening from the sleep of illusion/delusion than those necessary, essential practices. In their realm, practice truly does Make Perfect.

The sadhaka has to take his mind (buddhi) in hand to train it to develop an affinity for japa, meditation and spiritual exercises (practices). Sadhana must be seen as the way to the revelation-realization of the Life that is our Self. And it is sadhana alone that reveals its divine power. Sadhana is the direct process of awakening that can be trusted to produce the spiritual intelligence and will to maintain its practice until the Self is revealed. Then samsara is ended and the Self alone remains as The All.

> **On this pilgrimage one must never slacken: effort is what counts! Thus one should try ever to remain engrossed in this endeavor–it must be woven into one's very being, one has to be fused with one's Self.**

On this pilgrimage one must never slacken. In every aspect of human behavior momentum is a factor–often a decisive factor. Partially because this reveals the strength of the impulse to action, but it also reveals the character of the impulse–whether it is viable and whether its goal is positive or negative. I say this because there are many people who take up the spiritual life with the intention to fail from the very onset so they can justify their entrenchment in folly and evil. "Well, I tried," usually means, "I botched it up so I would have an excuse for continuing on in laxity and wrongdoing." The "I am not strong like you" excuse to remain in the moral and mental swamp is a common ploy–and one which equally negative people welcome as a implied justification for their laxity and moral worthlessness.

Effort is what counts! When I was a child we had a game where we were divided into two groups. At one point a group would go away and decide what they were going to do as a challenge to the other. When they came back and faced the opposing group there was set exchange of words. At one point the challenged group would say, "So get to work and show us what you can do!" Certainly actions do speak louder than words, and reveal a lot more about someone, too. So there are three aspects to this statement regarding effort: 1) what is the purpose or motivation of the effort? 2) What is nature or character, the quality, of the effort? 3) What is the strength of the effort? Because it is true: Nothing ventured, nothing gained. No effort; no result. Little effort; little result. Intelligent effort; intelligent result.

Thus one should try ever to remain engrossed in this endeavor. We must be totally absorbed and one-pointed in our endeavor. Every moment, every aspect of our life, must be oriented as intently as possible on the goal of Self-realization. And sadhana is the endeavor, not philosophizing or giving ourselves, noble, spiritual pep talks. Success in sadhana must be the aim of our entire effort and attention, and our full energy must be constantly put forth for our success. Sadhana must be the sum of our life–actually *be* our life–pervading every aspect of our life. Our every thought and action must be done in the perspective of the ultimate goal of liberation through Self-realization attained through yoga sadhana. To get this fact across Ma then says:

It must be woven into one's very being. Sadhana must not just influence or effect our being: It must pervade the totality of our being! This is what it means to be a sadhaka–one whose entire life is a continual stream of sadhana. For when we are always aware of the divine Goal, that awareness transmutes our every thought and action into sadhana. Mumukshutwa, the thirst, the craving, for liberation must pervade our entire thought and life.

One has to be fused with one's Self. Actually, one has to BE one's Self in totality. And the process of fusion is uninterrupted and unlessening japa, meditation and conformity of our mind and life to the principles of yama and niyama. I think you can see from this that to succeed in sadhana it must totally become our life. Otherwise we will become self-deceived hypocrites.

It is Thou that is crying out helplessly in distress, and it is Thou Thyself that art the Way and the Goal. In order that this

may be revealed, man must employ his intelligence vigorously and unceasingly.

It is Thou that is crying out helplessly in distress, and it is Thou Thyself that art the Way and the Goal. The Psalmist wrote: "Deep calleth unto deep" (Psalms 42:7), the word *thowm* literally means "abyss," a great deep, and was sometimes used to designate the ocean. Saint Paul wrote of "Christ in you, the hope of glory" (Colossians 1:27). Our own Atman, our own Self, is both the Christ and the Glory of Christ–the power than enables the realization of the Christ-Self. Our Self, our Inner Christ, is truly "the way the truth and the life" (John 14:6). We are all avatars in the final and highest sense.

In order that this may be revealed, man must employ his intelligence vigorously and unceasingly. I remember a seasoned ignoramus in California telling a woman that she should not read Ma's teachings because "She is a jnani, and you are a bhakti." But I doubted that he had read a word of Ma's teaching any more than he knew the correct Sanskrit terms. It is not a matter of philosophy or ideas, but of the very principle of intelligence itself: of *applied* intelligence which is both intellectual and intuitive. And it must be applied (employed) *vigorously and unceasingly.* Not just sincerely and tentatively. At every moment we must be intently employing our intelligence to engage in sadhana and point it in the direction in which we should be going. Is this a small or easy thing? NO. It requires the mustering of the entire power of the sadhaka's intelligence and will. For without will power intelligence cannot be directed as it should. The sadhaka must be illumined and empowered by his own Self through insight and endeavor. He must possess and employ both intellectual understanding and spiritual insight-intuition. And always: at all times and in all situations. It must arise from the sadhaka's Self, the finite deep that calls to the Infinite Deep.

A tree is watered at its roots. Man's root is the brain, where his reasoning power, his intellect is constantly at work. Through japa, meditation, the perusal of Scriptures, and similar practic-

es, one progresses towards the Goal. Hence man should bind himself and, fixing his gaze on the One, advance along the path.

Mataji's words reminded me of the Lorica (Breastplate) of Saint Patrick. Actually, a Lorica was a magical incantation-invocation. Saint Patrick's version is that of spiritual wisdom for daily living.

I bind to myself to-day,
The Power of God to guide me,
The Might of God to uphold me,
The Wisdom of God to teach me,
The Eye of God to watch over me,
The Ear of God to hear me,
The Word of God to give me speech,
The Hand of God to protect me,
The Way of God to prevent [go before] me,
The Shield of God to shelter me,
The Host of God to defend me.

And this resolve and endeavor takes place in the intelligent will supported and empowered "through japa, meditation, the perusal of Scriptures, and similar practices."

Whatever ties, bonds or restraints he imposes upon himself, should have for aim the Supreme Goal of life.

Whatever discipline we adopt and practice it must have for its sole purpose the attainment of Self-realization, "the Supreme Goal of life."

With untrammeled energy one must forge ahead towards the discovery of one's own Self.

Ma is speaking in Bengali, so there is no way to know what word the translator renders as "untrammeled," but its English meaning implies this definition: "Not limited or restricted; unrestrained. Not hampered or impeded; free." Right away we see that our energy we put forth must be: total; unlimited; unrestricted; unbound. For only such energy can accomplish our perfect freedom, the freedom of the Self. We arouse and gather this power from within and aim it toward the knowledge of the Self: Atmajnana. That is the only goal to have in mind. It is not a matter of top priority, but the Only Priority. This demands entire conformity of mind and will focussed on the sole aim: Self-realization. When this is employed continuously Self-realization is assured.

> **Whether one takes the path of devotion, where the 'I' is lost in the 'Thou,' or the path of Self-inquiry, in search of the true 'I'–it is 'He' alone who is found in the 'Thou' as well as in the 'I'. Why should one's gaze be fixed, while treading the path? The gaze is He and the 'why' is He also.**

Therefore unity, the true nature of things, is revealed and experienced. The fixing of the gaze on the goal is itself the going toward the goal. For the Self is ever-present. Therefore the mere thought of the Self makes the Self present to the mind and heart of the sadhaka. And sadhana fixes and makes that awareness permanent.

> **Whatever is revealed or hidden anywhere, in any way, is 'Thou,' is 'I'. Negation, just as affirmation, are equally 'Thou'–the One.**
>
> **You will be able to grasp this fully only when you find everything within yourself; in other words, in the state where there is nothing but the Self.**
>
> **This is why you should direct your gaze towards the Eternal while on the way. Where you see limitation, even this is a manifestation of the Limitness, the Infinite. In essence it is none other than your own Self.**
>
> **So long as this fact has not been revealed, how can one speak of full Realization–complete, perfect, all-comprehensive–call it what you will!**

Then again, how can the question of perfection or imperfection, of completeness or incompleteness, still arise in such a state of Fulfillment?

I hope you do not think I am being lazy in not commenting on this, but it is so perfect and complete it needs no comment.

But a great deal of perseverance in sadhana is required to understand and realize/experience it.

EIGHTEEN

Raipur, Dehradun, September 6th, 1948

Inquirer: You say all moments are combined in the One Supreme Moment. I cannot understand this.

> **Sri Ma: The moment of one's birth conditions the experience of life...**

This fact is the basis of astrology and the reason an astrological chart is drawn up at the birth of most children in India.

Each one of us is an integral part of the universe, and our birth occurs at the exact time in the solar system when the positions of the planets in their respective zodiacal signs reflect the karmic forces which bring our birth about. Until this karmic mirror occurs we cannot be born.

I am an example. When my mother was in the hospital and went into labor our small-town doctor was fifteen miles away at home undergoing a mild heart attack. So when the hospital called him for advice he told them to forcibly delay my birth until he could recover enough to drive there. Until then my mother was in terrible agony. Eventually he came to the hospital and they permitted me to be born.

Now all this was a manifestation of karma–which is what the astrological positions mirror. They delayed my birth until the first degree of Gemini was coming up on the horizon. The rising sign reflects the person's mental makeup and characteristics as well as the appearance of the physical body. I am a typical Gemini psychologically and physically. That is not the effect of being born when Gemini was rising, but a reflection of my mental and physical karma. So I do not have the all-over-the-place mind because I was born when Gemini was rising, rather I was born when Gemini was rising because that was the kind of mind I was bringing into this incarnation.

If that seems tangled, just consider the gas gauge in an automobile. When the gauge says Full that does not make the gas tank full. Rather, the full gas tank makes the gauge say Full. We must not confuse the cause for the effect or vice-versa.

The magnetic vibrations of the reflected heavens truly do condition the person, but the cause is karma. Therefore an astrological birth chart is a chart, a portrayal, of the newborn's karma–his karmic "face." It is a matter of interdependence. So the moment of one's birth both reflects and conditions the future of his incarnation. This is why an adept astrologer can outline the general life story of anyone. This is especially true in India where astrology has been a major science for thousands of years.

> **...but the Supreme Moment that is revealed in the course of sadhana leads to the completion of action, and therefore of one's karma.**

The sadhaka alone is living his life fully and meaningfully, bringing his very purpose of birth to fruition. For the moment of Self-realization is the culmination, the very purpose, of his incarnation. But we must view the cause-effect situation correctly. It is not his karma that brings about his enlightenment-realization, but it is his enlightenment-realization that ends his karma.

Why, then, does not the sadhaka drop the body the moment he attains perfect Self-realization? Some do. But for others it is in their karmic pattern to live out their life as illumined yogis. However there are records of some yogis living only a very short time after their enlightenment. But their death was by their enlightened will. Death is conquered by Self-realization, so a yogi leaves the body solely by the force of his will. He is not ejected by his karma, but departs through his liberated will. Even his death is a manifestation of life.

> **You should understand that one who is engaged in action is subject to nature–prakriti.**

Engagement in action is possible only by the force of our karma, and karma is an energy-manifestation of our Self. So there are two kinds of actors in this world: those who are impelled by their karma to act, and those who act solely through their enlightenment-empowered will. Prakriti determines the conditions and path of the ordinary person, but consciousness–atma-chaitanya–determines the conditions and path of the enlightened yogi. Most people are subject to prakriti–energy force–all their life, their death being involuntary. The adept yogi, however modifies his karma if he wishes and dies only by the force of his empowered will. The lives and deaths of yogis through the centuries demonstrate this.

The constitutive elements of nature are called guna [a play upon words: the word 'guna' means 'to multiply' as well as 'quality'], because they multiply themselves; for this world is not of the eternal.

Since this world is "not of the eternal" it is the realm of multiplicity and therefore of difference, change and conflict. The world is the realm of the many, whereas eternity is the realm of the One and those who have realized and united themselves with the One. The perfected yogi both ends the many and enters the One and yet at the same time himself turns the many into the One. It is all a matter of viewpoint, but only those who perceive directly without any intermediary such as mind or intellect can manifest unity, the state of the eternal–whether they leave this world or remain.

The perception of the world that consists of the three gunas is in time and transitory. Looked at from this point of view the world will be recognized as perishable.

But the enlightened see through the veil of the world into the Eternal and Imperishable. As Ma was wont to say, no simile is perfect, but it is very like what I witnessed nearly eighty years ago in the local movie theater. Since regular theaters had curtains, so did the movie theaters, but with a difference. When the intense light of the motion picture projector shone on those curtains they became translucent, so you saw the screen through a kind of veil (sometimes with a slight pattern) and could see the opening credits–but your view was clouded or dimmed to a degree. Then the curtains would withdraw to the sides and the screen would be viewed clearly and directly as the motion picture continued. (Sometimes the curtains would open and close a few times.)

Sadhana clears the perceptions of the yogi so he, too, "sees through" illusion into the underlying reality that is both the Atman and the Paramatman, the Self and the Supreme Self.

Vairagya can consume and bhava, bhakti, melt what is impermanent in human nature.

There are two processes in enlightenment: consuming and dispelling. Limitations and karmas are consumed or incinerated, and the mere appearances and illusions of maya are dispelled or melted away so nothing remains but the witness-Self.

Vairagya is non-attachment; detachment; dispassion; absence of desire; disinterest; or indifference–indifference towards and disgust for all worldly things and enjoyments. It is wisdom-insight that consumes or incinerates ignorance, including delusive/deluded attachment.

Bhava and bhakti involve both insight into and realization of the nature and aspects of something. It is seeing true. Therefore they both reveal and eliminate (melt) what is impermanent in human nature by revealing what is permanent–namely the Self and its inherent quality of intelligence which produces clear-sightedness of the intellect. So dispassion either arises or is strengthened by bhava and bhakti. We have a tendency to mistakenly think of bhakti is emotion or "love" when it is really a stabilizing insight and dedication. True love (prema or bhakti) is not at all blind; it is divine, clear sight into the truth of something or someone.

The basic point is that these three elements free the mind and intellect from delusive attachment and produce practical jnana which by its very nature is objective and clear-sighted.

But the moment in which burning and melting are impossible–that Moment is eternal.

This is because that Moment is itself the entry into objectivity which is untouched by any reaction, but is itself clear sight: penetration into the reality behind all appearance. And that Reality is Eternal and Eternity Itself, both aspect and entity. And the Moment of realization is eternal, so insight and comprehension are everlasting in the Self-realized yogi.

To try and seize that Moment is all you have to do.

The difficulty is this: that Moment is not objective at all, but is itself the realization/revelation of the Self which is the eternal Subject. Therefore only the consciousness that transcends both the observation/awareness of the subject matters. For all objects are ultimately unreal, even non-existent outside our mind. It is the primal Subject, our Self, that is the constant, ever-present reality. Ultimately there is only the observer that is real, the observed being essentially unreal.

In reality this is THAT–everything perceived is THAT–how can THAT be apart from anything?

I told you so!

So there is no practical utility or reality in wanting anything to be negated or dissolved. For all is THAT. And: Tat Twam Asi–You Are That.

"Therefore, become a yogi" (Bhagavad Gita 6:46).

This is so when one has entered the Stream; for such a one, how can there still be the division of present, past, and future?

The Stream is the dynamic life that is not an object but That which is essentially the subject, the yogi himself. It is both cosmic and individual. Every sentient being is a wave in the Infinite Life–which is The Stream in Its dynamic aspect. It is the evolutionary stream of external and internal consciousness. It includes every experiencer and every experience. It is infinite, but contains finitude. It has no "essence" because It IS The Essence Of All Things–and therefore IS all things. The sadhaka simply lives in It knowing that It is his own essential life. Evolution of consciousness takes place in it until the individual realizes that It is his own Self. What is beyond words and concepts is directly perceived and experienced as The Self. So nothing can be said or need be said.

> **A yogi can get something that is on the other side of a wall merely by stretching out his hand. When this is possible, the wall is not there although it exists, and even if no wall exists, yet it may function as an existing wall.**

The simple character of these words render them inconceivable. But the fully-realized sadhaka experiences this and knows it cannot be spoken because it not longer needs to be conceived. It simply is Reality.

> **Behind the veil lies the thing, but before you is the veil. The veil was not there previously, nor will it be in future; hence it does not really exist now. From a certain standpoint it is like this.**

"That which is non-existent can never come into being, and that which is can never cease to be. Those who have known the inmost Reality know also the nature of is and is not" (Bhagavad Gita 2:16). It is the second sentence we have to work on.

> **You should understand that the yogic process, due to which the veil has no power to hamper the free activity of a yogi, is analogous to the method by which he perceives an ordinarily invisible object.**

It is all in the mind. The very mind that deludes and confuses us from like to life is the means to dispel delusion and confusion. It is a matter of how we direct and use it. A surgeon's scalpel can save life or end life, depending merely on how it is directed and used. That which binds can also set free. Sri Ramakrishna said, "The mind is everything." It harms us and it heals us according to our use of it. Sadhana is the right, the best, use of the mind. The will saves and destroys according to its direction and application.

In Wagner's mystical opera *Parsifal*, King Amfortas was wounded in his side by the spear that pierced Christ's side also. The wound could not be healed and he suffered continually for years. Then Parsifal, holding that spear, declares: "That which wounded can also heal," as he touches the side of Amfortas, which is instantly healed. In the symbology of *Parsifal* the spear represents the will which either wounds or heals according to our use of it.

The yogic process is an act of will–an act, not just an idea or aspiration or emotion. Sadhana is the healing, restoring action. The will which accomplishes merely mundane and often pointless or useless things can bring about the yogi's total transformation by employing it in liberating sadhana. It is that simple. Not easy. But simple. Right will and right action are the whole picture. Willing to be liberated and engaging in liberating yoga sadhana–japa and meditation–is the whole picture. Doubt will not hinder us at all. Doing is the one thing needful. Then our experience of the resulting change will encourage us to continue. Doing, doing, done. It may not be that quick, but it will be inevitable. Faith and belief have nothing to do with it. Let me given an example.

My very dear friend, Hari Dutt Vasudev, told me that one of his friends was a devotee of Anandamayi Ma and considered Ma his guru. Hari Dutt used to pester and mock him on many occasions, saying: "Could you not find a man for your guru? Are you really so hard up that you had to make a woman your guru?" Over and over he did this. His friend would only say: "Meet Her for yourself and then you will understand." After a very, very long time he took Hari Dutt to where Ma was visiting in Mumbai (Bombay). When they got there, they were told that Ma was on the roof of the house where She was staying. His friend said, "Go on up and see for yourself." So he went up the stairs, and the moment he saw Ma he shouted,

"O my Mother!" and fell down at Her feet. And his heart remained there. His wife, Amrit, also become a devotee of Ma and a great sadhaka. She attained a very exalted spiritual state. I remember her holy countenance very well.

The same mind that deludes us is the instrument of divine knowing for us. It is all in what we do with the mind. In the Bible we find instances where the invitation to higher life and consciousness was simply: Come And See. Just Look.

"Come and see the works of God" (Psalms 66:5).

"He [Jesus] saith unto them, Come and see" (John 1:39).

"Philip saith unto him [about Jesus], Come and see" (John 1:46).

"I heard, as it were the noise of thunder, … saying, Come and see" (Revelation 6:1).

"I heard the second beast [a supernatural creature] say, Come and see" (Revelation 6:3).

"I heard the third beast say, Come and see" (Revelation 6:5).

"I heard the voice of the fourth beast say, Come and see" (Revelation 6:7).

Not once was the aspirant told: "Believe and you will see." Through continual sadhana we turn the mind in the right direction, focus it and See For Ourselves.

Furthermore, motion and rest, although each remaining what it is, lose their distinction for him who can see.

When the consciousness is absorbed in constant japa and meditation it is not the mental actions that are perceived but the resulting perception of Reality Itself. So the two processes merge into one unbroken awareness of the Real.

In that state there are unlimited possibilities.

The Self is limitless because it is essentially part of the Infinite. Therefore when we are established in awareness, the consciousness, of the Self, there are no boundaries. Potentially, Infinity opens up to us in the realization: I Am That (Soham). The process of opening to that realization is outlined in *Soham Yoga: The Yoga of the Self.*

> **But this body does not always have the kheyala to tell everything. All this belongs to the realm of the marvellous (chamatkara [inner vision]).**

And ultimately the aspirant need not be told of anything because through perfection (siddhi) in sadhana he sees everything for himself.

> **To return to the 'moment': the moment that you experience is distorted, whereas the Supreme Moment contains being, becoming–everything. Yet nothing is there, although everything is there.**

The "moment" that is a point in relative, samsaric time must inevitably be perceived in a distorted manner because it is perceived through the distorted lens of imperfect perception–the mind.

Though we may not be aware of it, sadhana by its very nature right away begins transferring the focus of our mind into a higher realm.

> **Then again, there can be no question of either the Supreme moment or the moment that is a particle of flowing time.**

Because time is an illusion. There is only the eternal Now. But we project our inner illusion outward and see it on the screen of samsara.

Later the topic of the 'moment' was again raised.

> **Moment means time, but not what you call time. Time (samaya) means Swa-mayi, the state where everything is seen as the Self alone, where nothing whatsoever can exist beside the Self.**

Ma often spoke of The Great Moment, meaning the point in time where the Timeless Eternal is revealed as both the Supreme Self and the individual Self.

Inquirer: You say there is rest (sthiti) in movement (gati), and movement in rest. What does this mean?

> **When the seed becomes united with the earth, when the two have mingled, at that moment there is rest; but the process of germination sets in immediately, and this surely implies movement. To move means not to remain in one place. Nevertheless, it was in one and the same place–it still is! Each stage in the growth of a tree represents a point of rest, yet is also a passing one. Again, the leaves grow and then fall off, which marks a change of condition; it does and it does not, for after all it belongs to one tree. The tree potentially contains the fruit: this is why it will yield it–'will' means 'does'.**
>
> **No simile is ever perfect in all respects.**

Then again Sri Ma said:

> **In reality, there is nothing but the One Moment all along. Just as one single tree contains numberless trees, innumerable leaves, infinite movement and untold static states, so does one moment contain an infinite number of moments, and within all these countless moments lies the One Single Moment. Look, there is motion as well as rest in that Supreme Moment.**

And all of our lives, all of our inner and outer doings, are oriented toward that One Supreme Moment when the Real fills our entire range of consciousness–that that is our own Reality, also. We awaken to and into That irrevocably. Then the Goal has been reached.

> **Why then should the revelation of the Moment be spoken of?**

> **Because, misled by your perception of differences, you think of yourself and of each and every creature or object in the world as being apart from one another. This is why, for you, separateness exists. The sense of separateness in which you are caught, that is to say, the moment of your birth, has determined your nature, your desires and their fulfillment, your development, your spiritual search–everything. Consequently, the moment of your birth is unique, the moment of your mother's birth is also unique, and so is that of your father's and the nature and temperament of each of the three is unique.**

This is the background in which our perceptions are arising.

> **In accordance with your own particular line of approach, each one of you must seize the time, the moment that will reveal to you the eternal relationship by which you are united to the Infinite–this is the revelation of Mahayoga, Supreme Union.**

Somewhere I read years ago: "There are many ways to the One Way." We each have a unique mode of approach to the realization that is the One Goal of all existence.

Please be aware from these words of Ma that the individual sadhaka is the essence, the point, of everything She is saying. Philosophically, theoretically, it is universal in scope, but individual in practice. And every path to its realization will be characterized by the empowering and developing of the unique, individual character of the sadhaka. This is extremely important to hold in mind.

In Sanatana Dharma, and therefore in Yoga, the individual is the focus, the aim of everything both philosophical-theoretical and practical. Each Self has an innate, unique individuality which will continually emerge as sadhana is maintained unbrokenly. We are all destined to become consciously united with The One, but our eternal individuality will only be confirmed and developed as the Goal is increasingly being attained. Every true yogi I have met has had a strong self-identity resulting in a pronounced individuality-personality. Ma Herself was strikingly unique. Both Ma and Swami Sivananda were absolutely One Of A Kind. And powerfully so. And the more we progress in sadhana the more individual we shall become. So when someone refers to you as "a real character" and "something different" they are endorsing your progress as a yogi whether they know or intend it or not. "Weirdo" and "Freak" are acceptable, too. For we are not members of The Herd. We are genuinely striking out on our own, for as I have mentioned a few times before, the path to divine realization has been called "the flight of the alone to the Alone." After all, God is one and unique. How could the godly then be otherwise?

> **Supreme Union signifies that the whole universe is within you, and you are in it; and further, there will be no occasion to speak of a universe.**

Language is limited at all times, but especially when speaking of that which cannot be conceived intellectually and therefore cannot be expressed at all. So Ma's words can be a real puzzle, but I think She means in this instance that if we were not already in the state of union-identity with the universe we could not enter into or experience union with it. The last clause means that in the consciousness of complete union there cannot arise the mistaken idea of the universe as outside us in the most profound sense.

> **Whether you say it exists or does not exist, or that it can neither be said to exist or not to exist, or even beyond that–as you please.**

Whatever or however we wish to conceive and speak of the universe or any external object is perfectly all right–as long as it is honest and truthful (not necessarily correct in all ways). Because words are just that–not realities. This perspective is good to maintain. Furthermore, because of the vastness and variety in the external world, whatever we say about it will be true in some manner or perspective. We also have to realize the since duality is fundamental, anything we affirm can be denied from some viewpoint.

This is why words are only secondary in value, while direct insight is of great importance–though the insight may not be communicable to others through words.

> **What matters is that He should stand revealed, be it in whatever form.**

Juggling words, topping one another in metaphysical conundrums and Old Zen Master type absurdities are worthless mind games that reveal childishness of mind and shallowness of intellect. Only one thing matters, as Ma says: the revelation of the Self of all Selfs: Parabrahman. "Be it in whatever form" indicates that The One has many forms which are valid and through which It stands revealed–while yet transcendent in Being. This revelation is the only thing that matters to the sadhaka. And that revelation is totally personal–never public. That is why: "He who knows tells it not. He who tells knows it not." It is simple fact.

Therefore the wise aspirant focuses on the revelation of his own Self and, as the old song advised, will "let the rest of the world go by."

Ma implies that the forms in which The One is revealed will be many.

Only one thing ultimately matters: that we have The Eyes With Which To See. And that they be opened and activated. Sadhana is the means for this.

> **At that 'Moment', at that point of time–when it is found–you will know your Self. To know your Self implies the revelation (at that very same instant) of what your father and mother in reality are, and not only your father and mother, but the entire universe. It is that Moment which links up the whole of creation. For to know yourself does not mean to know your body only; it signifies the full revelation of That which eternally IS–the Supreme Father, Mother, Beloved, Lord and Master–the Self. At the moment of your birth, you did not know that you came into being. But when you have caught the Supreme Moment, you suddenly come to know Who you really are. At**

> **that instant, when you have found your Self, the whole universe will have become yours. Just as by receiving one seed, you have potentially received an infinite number of trees, so must you capture the One Supreme Moment, the realization of which will leave nothing unrealized.**

Awesome.

> **The sense of want, of emptiness (abhava), and one's true being (swabhava), are in exactly the same place–in fact, they are THAT, and THAT alone. What is this 'sense of want', and what 'true being'? He, nothing but He. For the simple reason that there is one single seed, which is the tree as well as the seed and all its various processes of transformation–truly the One alone.**

Absorption into the One Point is to expand to the infinity in which Here and There do not exist, which is One and Many simultaneously. Only the yogi can enter into this consciousness and become established in it.

> **You attempt to appease want by want; hence want does not disappear, and neither does the sense of want. When man awakens to the acute consciousness of this sense of want, then only does spiritual inquiry become genuine. You must bear in mind that when the sense of want becomes the sense of the want of Self-knowledge, then only the real Quest begins. Whether you call it the One, the Two, or the Infinite, whatever anyone may say, everything is all right.**

When we awaken to–comprehend–the sense of want, its cause and its objective, and its resolution-fulfillment, then alone can we find the way to ultimate fulfillment in Self-awakening and Self-knowledge. It takes a great deal of awakening just to realize there is a lack; and a great deal more to realize the way to ultimate fulfillment in Self-awakening and Self-knowledge; and a great, great deal more awakening to finally become truly Awake.

Sadhana is the essential means in all these stages until sadhana itself reveals the Goal that is our Self. The real search for ultimate realization is the process of reawakening to and regaining that which was never lost–only forgotten. Seeing is just a matter of opening our closed eyes. The faculty was always there, but inoperative. Sadhana is awakening to and the empowerment to Seek The Seeker. The Self then takes over completely the seeing, the seeking, and the finding. It is itself the beginning and the end. It is truly the One Thing Needful: Thou Art That.

NINETEEN

Benares, October 26, 1948

Inquirer: I have heard it said that a yogi can, by the power of his yoga, lengthen a man's life to the extent of one or two months at most. The average yogi's power cannot achieve more in this respect.

> **Yes, at a particular stage this is so. But the fact that human life has been lengthened, even by a month or two, only shows that a further increase might but be a question of greater yogic power.**

Samsarins love limitations because they seem to excuse and justify their lack of inner development, but yogis know that limitations are illusions to be dispelled by awakening their inmost consciousness.

> **One method of increasing the duration of one man's life is to take a period from another's.**

This would be a great evil: a form of murder.

> **Then, there is also a method by which the prolongation of a man's span of life can be effected without deducting the period from someone else's.**

There are several ways, called kalpana, by which this can be done. But eventually death comes to all relative modes of life. But the Self knows no death–so why not become established in that? Then external physical death will be no more than kicking off an old shoe.

> **Yogis who are able to use their powers in this way do exist. But where Creative Power is unobstructed–this is quite a different matter.**

It is a matter of release, of actualizing potential. True sadhana does this quite steadily and naturally. Authentic sadhana is extremely easy–therefore the mayic mind pretends to find it both incredible and impossible, and so excuses itself from real sadhana to preserve its false life. Why should it not be so? The yogi should be clear-sighted at all times and in all circumstances. Furthermore, the yogi must be thoroughly self-motivated and self-empowered at every step of the way. The truth is this: Like Jesus said (John 14:6), the Self is The Way, The Truth and The Life.

Inquirer: Does it then follow that the physical body can be immortalized?

Another inquirer: Without a doubt. If He is conceived as being omniscient and omnipotent, how can anything be impossible for Him? Nevertheless, not a single example of the immortalization of a physical body is to be found in the Shastras. Hanuman and some others are said to be immortal, but we are told they also have to change their bodies from time to time with the help of their yogic powers.

> **In the Supreme State everything is possible, as well as impossible. To say "this or that has never happened," is merely to speak from the worldly point of view of the individual.**
>
> **If the body has to be retained in one and the same condition, this too can be and is being done.**
>
> **Consider the matter now from another standpoint: bodies give rise to bodies, trees to trees, and so forth.**
>
> **In a certain state there is being and non-being. Where all that has just been discussed exists is manifested, and will continue to be manifested, there–what is, and what is not?**
>
> **Besides, when you say that no example can be found in the shastras, the reason for this is, that where Truth stands re-**

vealed–to the extent at least to which it is revealed–those things are known by direct perception.

Read all the foregoing carefully, but do not put much brain power in attempting comprehension since understanding it does not count for much pragmatically/practically speaking. However, if it entertains you, who am I to block your fun? Go ahead. No good will come of it, but no real harm, either.

The very last words are what is meaningful: "Those things are known by direct perception." They are not thought out or comprehended by reasoning or logic. Only to the direct perception of the yogi who has opened his inmost consciousness–which is his own real Self–can these things be known without any intermediary or faculty. For the adept yogi Being Is Seeing/Seeing Is Being. Nothing else really can be said. Anyway, it is realization alone that matters, that accomplishes anything.

Therefore Be A Yogi.

Some people have too much time on their hands, as the following question reveals.

Inquirer: I have heard you say that one individual may have many bodies. If this be so, a man may simultaneously practice yoga with one body and experience the pleasures and pains of life with another. For a yogi this may be practicable; but how can this happen in the case of an ordinary person, who is still in ignorance?

See what I mean? But Ma can make sense of nonsense.

Yes, quite so. This can be done by means of yogic powers; for the ordinary person it seems impossible.

And to the spiritually intelligent person it seems pointless. It is.

Look! When you see the bud of a flower, you perceive the bud only; whereas actually the full-blown flower, the fruit, the seed, and the whole plant, are contained in that little bud.

It is only a matter of potential needing to be actualized. And that is our state right at this moment. Within us is limitless power and consciousness, and sadhana opens and reveals that power and consciousness. The sadhaka may choose not to open and reveal them, but he will have awareness of and potential access to them, for as Ma often said about Self-realization: "There nothing is left out."

> **Manifestation is universal and unlimited, but your vision of it is partial, from one angle, dependent upon what, at a certain time, appears before your eyes. Look with an all-round, comprehensive vision and try to find out who a particular yogi, a particular individual, in reality is!**

If this were not possible, Ma would not recommend it. But only the yogi can possibly do it, and he would have to be a very adept yogi with long experience, whether in this life or in previous lives. Furthermore, this ability can be a nuisance to the yogi whose aim is Self-realization and not psychic abilities.

There was a time in my sadhana when I knew someone's name as soon as I saw him–even people on television. When I walked down the street I could see through the walls into the rooms and see the people inside there. When I looked at a person with any degree of attention, pictures of his daily life would start appearing in his aura. Sitting in a room by myself I might see translucent figures come in and leave, and in five minutes or so they would physically come in and do what I has seen them do and go out.

I did not like any of this and intuited that it could be detrimental if I let it go on and began to develop it. But what could/should I do? I remembered hearing that if someone tells about psychic experiences they often stop, so I began telling people I knew about these phenomena and they did stop. Later I learned how to turn off such perceptions at their onset. Finally the whole phase ended.

The yogi must direct his experience inward to his inner, higher consciousness and cultivate that through japa and meditation. This is the only worthwhile endeavor. The realm of the psychic is always unstable and subject to misperception and so are those who habitually dwell in it. In contrast the yogi calmly and steadily immerses his attention in his Self through japa and meditation. The way is outlined in *Soham Yoga: The Yoga Of The Self.*

> **Your body was first a child's body, then became a young man's, and later will grow aged. Childhood, youth, and old age are contained within you. If it were otherwise, from where could they arise?**

Everything about us is the fruition of our karma, the unfolding of our inner karmic destiny. We alone created it and we alone can either fulfill or dissolve it through Atmabala–the power/force of the Self. Only the adept yogi fully understands this.

> **You hear people say that as a child your face was such and such. This proves that your face as a child is present at this moment as well; otherwise, how could it be thus described? In a similar manner, your body in every one of its phases is always present: as it was in the past, is now, and will be in future. This is so where past, present and future are experienced as being ever-present.**

Time is an illusion, just one of the illusory attributes of samsara. But the yogi can awaken within samsara and remain awake and even master it to some degree if that is needed. Eventually he will become free within samsara and live accordingly, leaving it when he so wills. He will no longer be compelled to return, but can return if he wills. All possibilities are at all times available to the adept yogi. Therefore wisdom, awareness and vigilance are essential elements in his life. Otherwise disaster is a very real possibility. Few things are more tragic than a fallen and deluded yogi. The fictional Dracula was quite right when he said, "There are far worse things awaiting man than death." And a yogi multiplies these possibilities by developing his consciousness and its control. Everything is dual, with a positive and a negative side–sometimes indistinguishable to a person. So the motto Yogi Beware is not paranoia but safety. Caution is wisdom.

> **Time devours ceaselessly. No sooner is childhood over than youth takes its place; the one swallows up the other. This cannot be grasped by ordinary perception. Change is observed only to a very slight degree.**

This is profoundly true. The yogi must move himself out of this inexorable stream, and that is possible only through development and expansion of consciousness and control through diligent and continuous sadhana. Then he sees both clearly and completely and can put forth his will to literally become master of his destiny. "What is man's will and how shall he use it? Let him put forth its power to uncover the Atman, not hide the Atman: man's will is the only friend of the Atman: his will is also the Atman's enemy. For when a man is self-controlled, his will is the Atman's friend. But the will of an uncontrolled man is hostile to the Atman, like an enemy. That serene one absorbed in the Atman masters his will, he knows no disquiet in heat or in cold, in pain or pleasure, in honor, dishonor" (Bhagavad Gita 6:5-7). That is how it is done.

> **Actually appearance, continuance, and disappearance occur simultaneously in one Place.**

Again we return to the fact that time and space are illusions–but very real as illusions. The pictures on the screen in a theater are real, but insubstantial. They both exist and do not exist in the sense that the objects they picture are not there, just a visual image. And in the film in the projector everything happens–is present–simultaneously. Think of a author whose mind can create an entire novel in a single second–beginning, middle and end in the same moment. So it is in the Cosmic Mind. Every creation cycle is the thought of an instant. How do we know this? Because the teachings of the ancient and modern sages of India reveal it. If you have not done so, I recommend that you read both *Sanatana Dharma The Eternal Religion* and

Hinduism The Universal Religion. The facts contained in them, especially about the cosmos, are profound and were known only by the Indian rishis for untold ages. And they did not just have brilliant intellects, they were Self-realized yogis whose sadhana had opened and empowered their minds so they could determine these eternal facts of existence itself.

> **Everything is infinite–infinity and finiteness are indeed the same.**

Because they are just traits or elements within the Consciousness of The Sole Reality: Parabrahman. You and I are dreaming the Cosmos along with God.

> **In a garland the thread is one, but there are gaps between the flowers. It is the gaps that cause want and sorrow. To fill them is to be free from want.**

Unbroken realization of the Self is the one thing needed to end all suffering, lack and fear. Yoga is the sole means to this, the sole possibility of unceasing Knowing.

TWENTY

Benares, March 21, 1949.

Someone declared that Vedanta and bhakti were two entirely different doctrines or lines of approach.

> **Where doctrines are, there "all-inclusiveness" cannot be.** [A play upon words: "Vada" means doctrine in Sanskrit. The Bengali word "bada," means exclusion. The letters "V" and "b" sound alike in Bengali).]
>
> **What is emphasized from one point of view will be rejected from another. But where is the state in which bheda-abheda, difference and non-difference, have ceased to exist? Some maintain that the conception of Radha-Krishna is completely Vedantic, for Krishna cannot be without Radha; nor Radha without Krishna–they are two in one and one in two.**

No need for comment.

Inquirer: It is said that God's Eternal Lila is based on duality.

> **The assumption of duality is also within Oneness; some advocate this opinion.**

No need for comment.

Inquirer: What is the actual significance of the terms dharma, lila, parikara?

[Lila: Play; sport; divine play; the cosmic play. The concept that creation is a play of the divine, existing for no other reason than for the mere joy of it. The life of an avatar is often spoken of as lila.

[Dharma: The righteous way of living, as enjoined by the sacred scriptures and the spiritually illumined; law; lawfulness; virtue; righteousness; norm.

[Parikara: Who or what helps or assists; multiplicity.]

> **They say that even in the midst of this Lila, Oneness remains unimpaired.**

Duality is an experience, but it is not a reality–it is a dreamlike illusion. It is a part of the lila, the divine play, of the transmigrating, evolving individual Self. Obviously the Oneness of the Absolute remains, but so also does the inmost oneness of the individual jiva undergoing the dualistic experiences of relative existence. Oneness is always the truth of all Being.

> **What is enjoyed in Lila is rasa** [emotional experience]**, which is unique; and in Vedanta too, duality is out of the question. Although duality appears to manifest itself before the eyes of the bhakta, nevertheless, here also there is nothing but oneness. If one does not view things through the spectacles of the bhakta, this cannot be grasped. Seen from his angle of vision, it appears thus.**

Mostly because the true devotee-bhakta considers that all is God Who can manifest any appearance or condition according to the Divine Will. As Jesus said: "With God all things are possible" (Matthew 19:26; Mark 10:27). The Divine Lila is a kind of psychic training film to prepare the individual for unlimited consciousness.

> **Suppose when giving initiation the guru instructs the disciple to practice the formal worship of Radha-Krishna, and to regard himself as the servant, and Radha-Krishna as his Master.**
>
> **By regularly engaging in worship and service of this kind, the following development may take place:**

First of all one feels that the room in which the worship is being performed has to be consecrated to the Deity, and He has to be worshipped with lights, incense, etc. (arati).

As one continues day after day to carry out these acts of worship, one begins to question: "Is my Lord as small as this little image? Does He dwell only in my shrine-room and nowhere else?"

By performing His service one gradually comes to feel that all is His. This feeling grips one and spreads like an infectious disease.

Someone once said: "Do not venture near Anandamayi Ma, there are small-pox germs around her."

Ma is outlining how the lila of dualistic worship has within itself the seed of non-dual consciousness which is developed through genuine devotion (bhakti). Fake non-dualists have contempt for ritualistic/dualistic worship, but that is because they are caught in their own externalized, dualistic minds. When the mind is fixed on and absorbed in sacred imagery and worship, their roots in the Divine Unity are revealed and the formerly dualistic experience of the sadhaka is transmuted into the experience-consciousness of enlightened unity. That is why, as I have cited before, Swami Sivananda used to say: "Bhakti begins with two and ends with one." But only the yogi will come to this insight, for only sadhana purifies and frees the mind for such direct non-dual inner realization.

Regarding the last sentence about avoiding Ma, I well remember a long-time devotee of Ma remarking to me: "Beware of the cobra!" By that he meant that just as the inner poison of the cobra takes life, just so the inner Reality That was Ma, if touched, would impart life and change my earthly, supposedly "normal" consciousness and life. Ma had "bitten" him many years before, so he knew by experience.

Single-minded devotion engenders deep thought, which expresses itself in action.

Profound insight and eventual realization result from true devotion and pervade the sadhaka's entire inner and outer existence. A genuine bhakta in time becomes a jnani as well. And a genuine jnani becomes a bhakta as well. Then they are complete. And their interior states manifest in and through external actions. Genuine interior attainment is always externalized. Always.

> **The Lord's Light descends on the devotee, His Power awakens in him and, as a result, profound inner inquiry blossoms forth.**

When the Light of the Self manifests in the consciousness of the devotee, the divine power of the Self is awakened in his buddhi, his higher mind, and his outer mind turns inward and unites with the inner consciousness that is the Self. This is the "profound inner inquiry," the Atmavichara, that blossoms forth in the form of Self-realization which is not attained but revealed as the sadhaka's eternal state and consciousness of Being. Though the awakening seems to come from without, it is really the manifestation of the sadhaka's internal divinity which comes to fruition as simultaneous inner realization and outer manifestation.

> **Then follows a stage, where it happens that one may have a vision of the Beloved–for instance, while scrubbing the vessels used for puja, or one may lie asleep and see Him standing near one's bed.**

This is the realization of the perpetual Divine Presence that has accompanied the sadhaka from the moment he entered relative existence, samsara, as a single atom of hydrogen. The journey has been long to reach this point which will unfold and manifest continually until infinity is revealed as the sadhaka's inmost and outermost state of being. For Reality is ONE.

> **Look, at first one believed the Lord to be present in one's prayer-room, but by and by one is able to perceive Him here**

and there. At a further stage, not anymore in particular places, but wherever one turns one's eyes: He is seen sitting in trees, standing in water; He is perceived within animals and birds. However, even here one's vision of Him is not uninterrupted.

This is our eternal destiny.

Then comes a time when the Beloved does not leave one anymore; wherever one may go, He is ever by one's side and His Presence constantly felt.

This is the purpose of the jiva's entry into relative existence. This is Self-realization described in terms of a bhakta, but it is the identical experience of a jnani as well.

What now is the next stage like? The form, variety, appearance of the tree–all is the Lord. At an earlier stage one perceived Him within all objects; but now He is not seen within the objects anymore, for there is nothing but He alone. Trees, flowers, the water and the land–everything is the Beloved, and only He. Every form, every mode of being, every expression–whatever exists is He, there is none beside Him. It may occur that a sadhaka continues in this state for the rest of his life.

Perfection was a living trait seen in Ma at all times. And these words as well as this entire document embody Her perfection in verbal communication.

Now Ma investigates the expression of the active sadhaka's moving into advaitic perspective and eventual actualization-realization of that.

If everything is the Lord and nothing but He, then one's body must also be He–the One Existence. In this state, when one is deeply absorbed in dhyana, no physical activity–be it the

> **performance of ritual or acts of service–is possible. For He alone IS. One no longer exists apart from Him.**
>
> **What would the Vedantists say? "There is only one Brahman without a second."**
>
> **Nevertheless, for some who have attained to this condition, the relationship between the Lord and His servant remains and is felt thus: "He is the Whole and I am part of Him, and yet there is only the One Self (Ek Atma)." If the Brahman is described as the splendor of Krishna's body–why should one object? Verily, everything is identical, undivided. To realize this means to be immersed completely into the Ocean of Oneness.**

Realization arises internally and naturally and easily becomes revealed or manifested outwardly in various forms according to the personal character of the realized sadhaka and his personal environment.

> **After this has been accomplished, one can again do puja and service, for the relationship between Master and servant persists.**

Enlightenment is a single thing, but it embraces and pervades both duality and unity in the yogi's consciousness and personal realization. It is interesting that Ma implies that although non-duality is sought for and attained, the objectification of that enlightenment manifests as what is considered dualistic actions. But for the truly enlightened duality has ceased and all is recognized as The One in all action.

> **Mahavir [Hanuman] said: "He and I are one; yet He is the Whole and I am part of Him; He is the Master, I am His servant." One experiences Wholeness as well as the status of the Lord's servant. If, after the One Self has been realized, the relationship of a servant to his Master still continues, why should anyone object? At first this was the path to one's Goal. After Realization it is He, the One, who serves. This is real service–call it Mukti, call it Parashakti, call it what you will.**

If the consciousness is complete it must include/embrace all possible modes of consciousness. All must be functional in the sadhaka. For the character of both non-duality and duality is inherent in the Self. The One sports as the Two. God sports with his own Self the way a creative child assumes more than one role in his solitary play.

> **The spiritual Teacher gives instruction. For Him doing or not doing japa is exactly the same. It does not involve a contradiction. Calling Him 'World teacher,' how can one still find fault with Him?**

Both action and inaction are essentially one in the consciousness of the ever-present ever-pervading Self. And frankly, since the student's doing or not doing sadhana has no effect whatsoever on the teacher, to him they are the same. What is to be realized is the Consciousness that is present in both action and inaction. For action and inaction cease when the body falls away and the Self remains. .

Inquirer: After having realized the Oneness of all, due to what need or imperfection does it become necessary again to worship a particular deity?

> **In that state there is no need or imperfection.**

Nor need for comment.

Inquirer: But then it cannot be service or worship, as we understand them!

> **You may call it anything.**
>
> **The point is this: Sukadeva was a liberated Being; why then did he relate the Srimad Bhagavatam? What reply have you to this? The need or imperfection that prompted one to serve and worship at the initial stage has no place here.**

> **The Vedantists discard one thing after another, saying 'neti, neti' ('not this, not this'). Indeed, you see a beautiful flower, and a few days later it has been reduced to dust; therefore what they say is perfectly true. What is subject to change will most certainly change.**
>
> **On the other hand, expressed in the terms of those who believe in the reality of name and form, one may say: "All names are Thy Name, all forms Thy Form." Here name and form are also real.**
>
> **Again, it may be argued: "What is bound by change is the world. By persevering in the practice of discrimination, one finally becomes established in the One Reality." When there is only the One Ocean–nothing but water–one cannot see oneself as separate from the All. This is full immersion.**

Why comment on what Ma has made so clear–even self-evident? Ma did not teach the truth; She revealed the Truth.

> **Nevertheless, if outwardly or inwardly, even so much as a hair has remained dry, it signifies that complete immersion has not yet occurred. When a seed has been fried it can never sprout again. Just so, after realizing Oneness, you may do anything–it no longer contains the seed of karma.**

The Self has no karma because its ever-transcendent nature simply does not do what generates karma. It is mistaken to say it cannot–only that it does not. For the Self is not in the realm of can and cannot. That is the province of the false ego.

> **Where this [capacity to create or generate karma] is not present, there, all form and variety are but THAT.**

This is the state of authentic Realization where Doing is simply meaningless as either concept or action.

Look, by intense devotion as well as by Vedantic discrimination one has arrived at the One Essence.

Genuine bhakti and genuine jnana lead to the One. Considering them opposed to or even differing from one another is erroneous. But the ego loves to frolic in spurious versions of both.

Does then 'to merge into IT' mean to become stone-like? Not so, indeed! For form, variety, manifestation, are nothing but THAT.

This is extremely important, because increasingly in India people are being declared "munis" and "in a state of non-dual consciousness" when they are mentally impaired. I know of an man in almost total dementia who was not only being bowed to by a trickle of "bhaktas" but openly worshipped on occasion.

Some charlatans–or tools of charlatans–become total "munis" simply so no one will discover they are either ignorant or outright stupid. This I have seen myself.

I am sorry to say that Bhagavan Sri Ramana Maharshi is often presented as one of these when he was just the opposite. He spoke little, but he was totally aware and his intellect was supernormal. I have observed that when people are determined to not engage in sadhana or even learn the basic tenets of authentic Advaita–and certainly to never be bound by moral principles–they particularly pretend to be followers of Sri Ramana.

Of course there are those who have become adept at producing a stream of non-dual jargon that stymies any attempt to either make sense of them or determine their actual spiritual state.

So we have two kinds: those that do not speak and those that do not speak rational good sense so they will be thought profound and beyond the understanding of ordinary people.

The characteristic features of each person's particular path will of course be preserved; yet, what is attained is the One, in which no doubt, no uncertainty can survive.

Since the purpose of sadhana is the realization of The All, each sadhaka's path will be distinctly his, for sadhana reflects the individual sadhaka's characteristics which in turn increasingly reflect the characteristics of That which is the goal.

Sadhakas will–and should–be of a variety of personalities and modes of external life. Oneness is not uniformity, but oneness of consciousness pervading a virtually infinite range of even very marked differences. The sadhaka that is on the right path will be seen to become more distinct and developed in his characteristics, for the Infinite that is his goal possesses numberless characteristics or qualities that may come to be seen in him in varying degrees as his sadhana progresses. There is a difference between nothing and the No Thing. Those on a false path either become extraordinarily distinct in an exaggerated manner or fade out into virtual blankness and emptiness.

The sadhaka may seem inexplicable to non-sadhakas, but the problem is from the non-sadhakas' side alone, reflecting their deficiency. Everything advances in the genuine sadhaka, whereas the deluded non-sadhaka often erases himself through wrong practices that are not true sadhana. I think we can see from all this that truly: "Sharp as the edge of a razor and hard to cross, difficult to tread is that path [so] sages declare" (Brihadaranyaka Upanishad 1.3.14). But it can be traversed by day-after-day steady and profound sadhana. Without sadhana nothing is possible for the aspiring yogi. That alone frees him from doubt and uncertainty, as Ma says.

> **In fact, what is there to be attained? We are THAT–eternal Truth. Because we imagine that it has to be experienced, realized, it remains apart from us.**

It is an absolute requisite that the sadhaka understand that his primary endeavor is to know and enter into the full awareness and function of his divine Self. He does not "find" the Self, he manifests the Self which has been his true identity from the beginningless Beginning. And he cannot approach the Self as separate from himself, for it IS his Self, his existence. As long as he seeks his Self as an object and not as the witnessing subject-Self he will remain deluded for lifetimes.

As long as we think we must become something in some manner, we are blocking our realization. We must enter into the consciousness of the Self which we are and have been from beyond time. It is the inmost experience, the only lasting truth: the Truth of the Self. We do not experience the Self as an object, but realize It as That which is manifesting as both subject and object simultaneously.

On some levels this point of view is valid, but on others it is not.

According to the evolutionary development of the sadhaka's inmost consciousness which illumines the ever-present Self, this viewpoint is valid or invalid. Truth can be misunderstood and truth can be misapplied until the inmost consciousness is fully revealed. For ultimately the only truth is our own individual Self within the Universal Self–which is the truth of truth itself.

We must become The Truth to even know relative truth effectively. The Bauls in Bengal sometimes ask a person: "What station are you dwelling in?" meaning the level of consciousness in which that person is established. For it is not our beliefs and opinions that matter, but our absolute Knowing in the Self. Since Brahman alone is absolutely Real, we are not truly real until we know that Brahman as our Self.

The Eternal ever IS.

Once Swami Kriyananda had spent a long time with Ma. When he returned to the ashram where he lived he found a telegram asking him to immediately return to Ma. The ashram was in view of the railway station so he just picked up his suitcase, went to the station and got the next train to where Ma was staying. When he got back to Ma he saluted her and then asked: "Why have you called me back, Ma?" "Oh," said Ma, "I just wanted to see you." He was truly flabbergasted and objected,

"But Ma, you always see me!" "Yes," replied Ma, "but you don't really *know* that!"

So it was only what a person truly knew about Ma that mattered. Please note that I speak of knowing *about* Ma, not fully knowing Ma Herself. No one knew Ma but Ma, for She was Purna Brahma Narayana Itself. (Once Ma was asked what was the true[est] Name of God, and She replied: "Purna Brahma Narayana" which means full, complete, relative Divinity and Absolute Divinity: God pervading creation/relativity and God transcending creation/relativity–and beyond even That.)

The important thing is this: the Self is on a finite level everything that God is on the Infinite Level, including ISness.

What is styled "the veil of ignorance" signifies continual motion. Motion means change, incessant transformation.

It is interesting that this concept is in Judaism, where the world or creation is referred to by *gilgul,* a word that mean "rolling." Continual motion means not just change but arising and subsiding of forms. Appearance and disappearance perpetually alternate. Every phase of coming into and going out of manifestation is part of, inherent in, "the veil of ignorance." It is like a motion picture screen on which a vast number of things appear and disappear yet leave the screen untouched or unaffected in any way. What seemingly exists ceases to exist. The only stable or abiding thing is the screen itself.

Consciousness is the basis of everything, the screen which itself generates an endless series of perceptions and stages of perceptions–coming and going. Therefore illusion is arising from reality, though it is the advent or touch of reality that dispels the illusion which rises from it. There is not just constant flux and change, there is constant ignorance of the What, How and Why of the flux and change and the illusions that arise. But the realization of that is insight that is itself real and implies and eventually produces the resolution of all appearance into actuality. What appears becomes real, yet eventually dissolves and reveals its fundamental unreality. It really is a kind of existential Ring Around The Rosey.

Yet again, no change takes place where there is non-action in action. For such a one duality does not exist; who then eats, and what can he eat? In this state, how can there be theories or disputes?

Non-identity with action is non-action even if there is apparent action. As Ma said: "I neither come nor go." We can understand this intellectually to come extent, but we cannot explain it because it is a state beyond the scope of the mind–but not beyond enlightened intuition, for that is direct knowing beyond the mind. So theories and disputes do not even exist there. We cannot conceive that which is beyond conception, but the adept sadhaka can know it in an immediate manner when the mind is not involved.

If someone argues that, since a certain person speaks, he cannot have attained to this state–what does he speak and to whom?

Here we confront a tremendous problem: understanding the words of a liberated jnani. If someone speaks to us there does seem to be an obligation to listen and understand. But what if he speaks to us from a level of consciousness, of genuine realization, that is vastly beyond us and which no one can comprehend but someone of equal realization? The wise acknowledge their limitation and try their best to glean some glimmers of truth from the jnani's words. The egotistical pipsqueaks create a special vocabulary and formulations couched in their own jargon that hopefully sounds as abstract and obscure as the jnani's words. They pick out a truly great person such as Sri Ramana Maharshi–the most abused at this particular point in time by the blowhards of "silence"–formulate an intellectual ring-around-the rosey verbiage that means nothing and therefore can be considered legitimate exposition of the No Thing, and make a reputation for themselves as either disciples or even successors of the jnani. They may write a few very short books or articles, but they mostly like to wander around giving lectures and playing verbal games with "sincere inquirers."

Unless, of course, they find a place to settle and gather a tiny community around themselves that supports and adores them. As Sri Ramakrishna's great disciple Swami Brahmananda used to say: Just See The Fun!

Who is the one to whom he speaks?

Exactly. As Yogananda sometimes would sing over and over: "He who knows–he knows. None else knows."

This is so when full Realization has come about.

Case closed.

When trying to explain this to others, one comes to see that they have not understood it.

If they had, it would not be worth experiencing, and anyway they would not need any explanation.

Does realizing that someone has not understood imply that one has oneself reverted to ignorance?

This is most intriguing, a version of It Takes One To Know One. Anyone can say: "N. has attained perfect Self Realization," but how is that person qualified to make that statement? Sometimes in scriptural accounts of very high philosophy we find the declaration that if someone speaks or hears the supremely high principles or truths "his head will fall off."

Silence is the language of Knowing.

One has realized both: being able to understand and being unable to understand.

Although the Self is the immortal consciousness which is the core, the true identity, of every sentient being, it is joined to–in a way merged with–the human complex of body, mind and soul, and develops the individuality of each separate spirit-soul, which includes the mind of the senses, the manas, and the mind of the intelligence/intellect, the buddhi. Therefore the sadhaka is a kind of link between spirit and matter, and although he is ultimately spirit alone, he presently works through the body, mind and intellect complex. First there is perception, then attention and then comprehension.

Each one of us "sculpts" ourself as we fix our attention on every aspect of our being and condition or direct the various faculties we possess, especially the witnessing consciousness that is our true, fundamental Self. We experience both knowing and unknowing, both comprehending and not comprehending. For our own development we eventually wisely choose knowing and comprehending, and use these as tools with which we condition and shape our personality.

The truth is, when a certain level of evolution is reached it becomes our task to create or recreate ourselves. This not always done with profound introspection, so it is not always satisfactory. But there is no evading the necessity to become thoroughly aware of our inner mechanism and its powers and apply them. In other words, we become a yogi, a sadhaka.

Until that moment comes we are just like a leaf being blown about by the winds and tides of relative existence. Until that point is reached we have not become truly human. For humanity is the gateway to divinity, though nearly everyone on this earth wastes lifetimes bumbling around and suffering inevitably. Until we take ourselves in hand very literally we have no future. That is why the prime message of the Bhagavad Gita is this: "By struggling hard, and cleansing himself of all impurities, that yogi will move gradually toward perfection through many births, and reach the highest goal at last. Great is that yogi who seeks to be [one] with Brahman, greater than those who mortify the body, greater than the learned, greater than the doers of good works: therefore, Arjuna, become a yogi" (Bhagavad Gita 6:45-46).

He who is limited by the point of view of the world is in bondage.

The world is not purely material, but it is such a good illusion that a great many people consider it to be so. Now where does "the point of view of the world" come from? Our own mind! And how reliable is that? Not much–observation reveals that. So not only is the world limited, the mind which encounters the world is both limited and ignorant of its true nature and the meaning of the phenomena that is taking place within and outside it. Like the book title we truly are "strangers in a strange land." But what if we move out of that limitation and "see" the world in an entirely different way? Then the world itself will be entirely different!

In a certain esoteric association its members are told: "Every revealing is a further veiling," meaning that when one veil comes off we are faced with another veil that underlies it. In Hindu cosmology the observer keeps on peeling off layer after layer to get at the Reality which exists at its basic level. So the yogi progresses through a series of "veils" inner and outer to get at the perception of the underlying Reality.

The worst bondage is intellectual bondage, and materiality by its nature either hides or distorts what our mind perceives–or thinks it perceives. The world is itself a prison, with a dual function: it blinds and binds. But the world is not the ultimate reality–it is only the first step or level. Our physical eyes cannot see beyond its surface, but the inner mind is itself an "eye" that it is an instrument of our higher, subtler perception.

Further, there are higher and higher reaches of our mind, each with its own set of senses. Therefore the yogi works to "see through" the layers of the world-substance and see the Divine Life that is its source. For we are ourselves not just in that Field of Life, we are an integral part of that Life-field.

He who sees with the outer eyes is blind, but he who sees with the inmost eyes truly sees. Yoga sadhana first develops our ability to perceive, then the inner instruments of perception are developed and activated, then we come into touch with them and become able to function through them and See True. Until that happens we are hopelessly and helplessly bound.

But freedom lies just beyond our limitations, and sadhana releases us from them and activates our inner mechanism, the antahkarana, and the more we exercise the inner eyes the more we see, both wider and deeper, until we see That which has always been there as a divine basis and potential.

The yogi enlightens himself through his sadhana. The secret is within and therefore can only be found within.

> **But where the vision of THAT is, there, the knowledge of ignorance and the knowledge of Knowledge stand revealed in their fullness.**

These are two interesting terms I have not encountered before: "the knowledge of ignorance and the knowledge of Knowledge." Basically this is the prospect of intelligent discrimination–viveka: knowing what is ignorant/ignorance and knowing truly what is knowledge–both the quality of knowledge and the factual side of knowledge, understanding. The nature of the Self is Light, so when the Self begins to manifest in our consciousness we both perceive and comprehend knowledge, for knowledge is an experience, a perception, and the content/comprehension of the experience.

Both of these elements will be immediately present in the intellect of the sadhaka who has truly entered into the state of Knowledge/Knowing which is Atmadarshan, the vision/perception of the Self.

> **There, the question of viewing knowledge and ignorance separately can simply not arise.**

This is because knowledge and ignorance are a single entity or experience seen as two because in essence they are two aspects of the same thing–not two separate things. Unity always prevails however dualistically our experience of that unity may be. In the highest sense, duality cannot exist as a reality, for only Unity is Real. So duality is a product of the mayic mind that is itself formed from illusions such as duality.

> **Actions such as eating, and so forth, have now become action in inaction.**

Prakriti never stops changing, but Purusha never changes. So if our consciousness is fundamentally focused or centered in Prakriti, there is nothing but change–in our experience. If, though, our center of awareness is our true Self, our Purusha, then although the appearance of action and change continue, there is unchanging awareness of our Self, our Reality. Therefore our experience is determined solely by us once we have come to the level where sadhana is known and we have chosen the Yoga Marga, the Path of the Yogi. The positing of our consciousness is in one sense the only thing that ever happens to us: everything that follows is a result like a domino effect. Naturally this is incomprehensible to anyone that is not a yogi. But sadhana reveals everything in time.

Whether one still performs ceremonies or not, what difference does it make?

Busybodies that are also bullies always make demands of others: "You must do this!" "You must not do that!" So there are those who insist that ritualistic worship or observances are absolutely necessary, and those who insist that they are completely irrelevant and should not be bothered with. They think their inflexibility is the proof of their rightness! But Ma asks what difference is made by the rituals–implying that none produce significant results. Also, since it is our mind and will that shows our basic character, rituals at best can only reflect or hint about our inner character. At the same time Ma seems to be saying that both are equally valuable/viable, according to one's inner disposition: bhava. At the same time, since they are external, what internal effect will they have? And what value is there in performing anything that is without definite positive effect?

The Gita says: "The ancient seekers for liberation could safely engage in action. What is action? What is inaction? Even the wise are puzzled by this question. You must learn what kind of work to do, what kind of work to avoid, and how to reach a state of calm detachment from your work. The real nature of action is hard to understand. He who sees the inaction that is in action, and the action that is in inaction, is wise indeed. Even when he is engaged in action he remains poised in the tranquility of the Atman" (Bhagavad Gita 4:15-18).

Further, since it is the state or level of consciousness that really matters, it should be determined whether an action is effectual or ineffectual for the yogi. Also the sadhaka must be looking at the actual effects his actions have and judge them accordingly.

> **Knowing and not-knowing in their entirety are now contained within oneself. But to understand this state is difficult indeed.**

It is essential to keep in mind the Law of Opposites as a fundamental fact of both external and internal life. They are within us as our very nature. They alternate in manifestation. Therefore it is crucial that we fully comprehend all the aspects and implications of these states and set about to establish them in this right order–for one cannot exist without the other, like inhaling and exhaling, opening and closing our eyes. So the question is both what should we do or not do, and when should we do or not do them. This helps to understand why Karma Yoga, the Yoga of Action, is the basis of intelligent, responsible and effective life.

> **It is easy to comprehend a particular line of approach or level. But here, there is no question of attainment or non-attainment, and therefore, even non-attainment is no shortcoming either.**

The thing to ponder is the effect or non-effect of action. For action is neutral–only its motivation and actualization (result) determine its character in relation to us. We must also correctly understand the character and therefore the effect of the force, internal or external, that produces action: is it wise or unwise, dharmic or adharmic? For the character of the moving force will be revealed in the character of the result of the action. There is a kind of circular movement-effect involved in all action. In the beginning is the end, and the end somehow seems to have called forth the beginning. This is because our entire life is a manifestation of Consciousness–of Intelligent Shakti.

However, if the very slightest attachment has survived, it signifies that this Sublime State has not yet been reached.

And how will we know the truth about this? For we easily delude ourselves or ignore that which produces or reveals the character of our action.

What is sublime about non-attachment in action? Because it permits our Atmabala, our soul-force, to manifest and change our outer experience without really controlling or determining the effect of the result. Ma said that She did not have a will or determination regarding anything, that rather there was a spontaneous movement that manifested as action but did not involve desire or will. We must mirror this to some extent and make our inner and outer action a manifestation of spontaneous, direct consciousness. This cannot be reasoned out since its very character is spontaneity and no thought or will process is involved. It is best to leave this matter here, as further explanation or description would no doubt cloud everything by our words and desires directing those actions.

By selling imitation goods people may become rich. Why are imitation goods purchased at all? Because they resemble the genuine ones; this is the wonder of it! But by using them the deception will come to light, and then one will again search for the genuine article.

Since this world is the product of maya, of illusion, there seems to be within us a natural affinity for the false–the mere appearance of something rather than its core reality. My parents' generation was the first to become absolutely enthralled with the "wonder" of artificiality. They loved artificial flavors and various forms of synthetic foods. Many times I have heard people say about a flower: "O, it is so perfect it looks artificial!" Not a very high standard.

Ma says that selling imitations is a path to wealth, as in the motion picture "Lady From Lisbon" that I mentioned some time back. But however well they may sell or make money, Ma points out that they could never have any value or attraction if there was not an original, genuine article whose value is unquestioned. Further, She indicates that by becoming familiar with these synthetics by using them, their inferior, spurious character becomes revealed. Therefore experience of this world must end in disillusionment and disappointment which arouses the search for "the genuine article."

This is because however intense the power of maya can be, it is the very purpose of maya to awaken and lead us to The Real. In time our own experience of disillusionment will impel us to turn from the false and intensely desire and seek the Real which we shall absolutely find if we persevere. So in a sense we awaken and guide ourselves to higher reality through our natural aversion for the false and evanescent. As Ma Herself remarked in a conversation: "Have you not seen what life in this world is?" So we mistakenly think that disappointment and disillusion are only unhappy experiences or states, when for the wise they are the call to Reality.

> **Having realized the One Self, and that there is nothing outside of It, one knows that the image one has worshipped is THAT in a particular form.**

This can only be true of the devoted yogi. Sadhana alone opens and clarifies his consciousness and reveals to him the truth of the One Self that is The All. Therefore all the objects we mistakenly considered of lasting value were themselves teacher-revealers of their actual nature. So although the momentary delusion arose from within us, those very objects of our ignorance produced the insight by which we perceived the truth of their illusory nature. So Maya attracts and deludes and then grants insight into Its own nature, and so frees us from the spell it cast upon us initially. Truly, we are at every moment being led From The Unreal To The Real, however circuitous the route may be. For illusion is a momentary manifestation of the Real in our path to Seeing True. At one point we may indeed be saying Neti Neti–Not This, Not That, but after a while we will discover and declare: All This, All That, is The Real.

> **Having found Reality, one perceives it in this particular guise: The deity I worshipped is none other than the One Self,**

the Brahman–there is no second. Thus, the One is the Lord I worshipped.

There is nothing more to add.

When one has dived into the depth of the sea, water is known to be He in one form.

Again, we progress from Not This to All This. What a glorious fulfilment.

The aspirant who advances along the path of bhakti will, when he has attained to the vision of his Master, become a true servant.

For theory becomes realization as we "see for ourselves" the truth of things. Therefore the bhakta becomes a jnani if his path is a true path. If this does not occur, he is not a true bhakta or jnani, just a philosophizing samsarin.

The methods of 'not this, not this' and 'this is Thou, this is Thou' lead to the One Goal. By proceeding in one direction It is reached, and by taking the other direction, one also arrives at the very same Goal.

The paths of bhakti and jnana, of devotion and insightful wisdom, lead to the One Goal, for they are the two simultaneous aspects of the one inner call to the Supreme Self.

Those who follow the path of surrender to Shakti, the Divine Energy, and those who worship the image of Shiva, both must finally attain to the one Shakti, the one Shiva.

For it is The One that manifests as Energy (Shakti) and Consciousness (Shiva). If one is truly known, then knowledge of the other is automatically manifested. This is how we can discern genuine bhakti and jnana: they are really one. Where there is one the other is necessarily present, otherwise it is only mayic illusion.

> **Those who advance along the line of Vedanta will find that ice is water, that there is no form, but only the formless; whereas the bhakta comes to realize that his Beloved is but the one Brahman–everyone has his own method of approach.**

If these truths are not realized by the aspirant either his path or his seeking are false.

> **Equality, Oneness must come and become the permanent state.**

There we have it: the beginning and the ending. This is not Advaitic belief or outlook, it is non-dual realization-consciousness. That alone is Real, that alone is genuine Realization.

> **Having achieved it, if someone says: "I am renouncing liberation," or: "I am giving up the worship of my Ishta"–even though he may give it up, nothing will be lost; for in this condition there is neither renouncing nor retaining.**

These statements will only be in relation to the sadhaka's external life in maya. But in his true, internal life of the Self, the very idea of giving up or retaining something is impossible, for such a perspective cannot arise in the illumined consciousness which is essentially non-dual.

> **It may be asked, why there cannot be one and the same path for all?**
>
> **Because He reveals Himself in infinite ways and forms–verily, the One is all of them.**

Therefore there is really only one path for all, manifesting in countless ways and modes. Difference is only in appearance, or our misunderstanding. When Ma said: "There are many ways to the One Way," She meant this unity beneath the appearance of the many.

In that State there is no "why."

There is no reason behind the principle of Being. There is just IS without any possibility of Is Not.

> **Quarrels and disputes exist merely on the way. With whom is one to quarrel? Only while still on the way is it possible to have disputes and differences of opinion.**

That is perfectly clear.

But there is one thing we must remember regarding all the foregoing: Direct Realization is the only true knowledge/knowing. There is no discussing of Reality–just comprehending It. There is either direct knowing or there is no true knowing at all. Therefore the jnani never argues and the ajnani does nothing else but argue–even with/within himself.

TWENTY ONE

Inquirer: Are there as many names of God as there are creeds, or is there in reality only one creed and one Name?

> **Discussion and controversy belong to the path, but actually everyone is in his own home.**

This is one of the most wonderful and valuable of Ma's words in response to questions: She goes right to the implications of the questions that are most relevant to the subject.

Throughout the world–and in India whose philosophy is the most detailed and complex of all–there has been from time immemorial the seesaw of: Is there only one true Name of God? Are there many Names of God? Are all Names attributed to God True Names? Are there many views or creeds that are equally valid or is there only one view or creed that is valid? Naturally there are those that say all Names of God and all creeds are valid, and there are those that say some Names of God and some creeds are valid; and there are those that say only one Name of God and one single creed is valid. Such questions can only be resolved by every individual, for one of the unique aspects of Sanatana Dharma is the insistence on the validity of each individual's outlook–that all views are valid and those that would try to cancel out other views are mistaken. Yet they are free to do so.

Ma indicates that this is the situation when an individual is on the path to realization, but actually even now and in the future each person is exactly where he ought to be–is in his own home: his immortal, eternal Self. Silencing of discussion and controversy cannot and may not come from external pressure or coercion. Rather, personal realization and centering in the Self ends all conflicts. Samadarshana, Equal Vision, includes the acknowledgement of all viewpoints as well as the understanding that Reality transcends all viewpoints as well. The fundamental value of sadhana is its ability to reveal the True and the Real to each individual. Although there is fundamental unity of all sentient beings, at the same time realization is experienced and expressed in an intensely individual manner by each sadhaka. Unity and Diversity are present in all aspects equally and permanently. And "everyone is in his own home" right from the beginning and clear through to the end. Oneness is the fundamental state of being at all times. Therefore Ma even said that whatever anyone says is true for him, so no one is wrong at any time. Yet there will be continual change as the individual's mind expands and reveals countless facets of perception and understanding. At the same time everything and everyone are always exactly as they should be, for all is/are ONE.

> **The same path is not for everyone. Brothers of the same family will each have their different inclinations and likings. Vedanta may appeal to some, Vaishnavism to others, and the cult of Shakti to yet others.**

All human beings are of the One Family, but as they evolve they change and become increasingly individual and unique while remaining at all times fundamentally and unchangingly ONE. This is a matter of vision, not intellectual formulation. It is solely a matter of evolution of consciousness and therefore cannot be taught or dogmatically imposed. It either arises or it does not. Each individual should fix his inner eye on the One Goal and single-mindedly pursue it, keeping his attention on his unfoldment and caring for that alone. The intelligent sadhaka is keenly aware of the validity of every individual's viewpoint and response to that viewpoint. Keeping oneself intent on the Goal and moving constantly toward the realization/manifestation of that Goal is the sole necessity for each person. This is the only way to "live life."

> **Therefore it cannot be said that there is only one path.**

In India they often rightly say: "There are many ways to the One Way." There is one path, but it manifests as unique to each person. This is diversity that is really unity. It is a matter of individual awareness of the One Reality. So it is both utterly individual and utterly universal. For just as God is One and Many simultaneously, so are those who follow a way to the One Way. The sadhaka sees both unity and diversity as innate in/to both himself and the One.

> **In fact, seekers after Truth are moulded each in a unique way, different from others as well as from one another; but they all will have to pass through the gate of Truth.**

Now this is very important: in the West the herd mentality not only prevails but is imposed. That is fine for those who like it, but the genuine sadhaka must realize that the more he comes closer to The One, the more unique he himself becomes. Every yogi becomes increasingly individual and distinctive. His personality does not become attenuated, but rather it develops and becomes increasingly stronger and unique–but within himself, not with a big outer display. However, he will not be effacing or invisible, but beyond ordinary perception. The yogi is increasingly and literally a Person of Power. Otherwise he can never become one with The Sole Reality. His individuality must match the uniqueness of the Infinite which is everything and yet one at the same time.

Inquirer: Then, are the creeds really different from one another?

> **You can see for yourself that one guru has any number of disciples. Are you trying to convert every one of them to the same creed? In spite of this, how many sects have not been founded, just as people have abandoned their own.**

There is always a attempt at uniformity in associations that are founded on personal ideas and purposes. (These are the people that often refer to their institutions or activities as "The Work.") But Ma is pointing out that diversity and difference are the natural way, and that attempting to control the ideas of another person is against the fundamental nature of evolution: diversity and individuality. Again I want to say that an essential characteristic of a sadhaka, a yogi, is increasing individuality, increasingly distinctive characteristics (traits) of personality and mode of thinking and acting. When these are natural and positive they are very easeful, natural and quietly strong. But they have deep roots and do not fade or waver. Calm assurance is a cardinal trait of a genuine yogi.

Before my first pilgrimage to India I came across a magazine printed by the Jesuit Order. The lead article was about India. The Jesuit missionary author complained intensely about the marked individuality of Indians and commented that even when there is a huge crowd of Indians you are aware that each one is a distinct individual at all times. This did not please him at all, but it was a wonderful thing to my mind and I intended to become part of that crowd.

Diversity in unity is a sign of integrity and realistic outlook. Ma indicates that continual, expanding diversity is the right way when it is spontaneous and based in the Self–actually expresses/reveals the Self.

> **What you said, Pitaji is very true indeed–but where? In that, which emerges when everything is given up. What then emerges? He Himself–THAT.**

Ma is referring to the previous two questions: "Are there as many names of God as there are creeds, or is there in reality only one creed and one Name?" "Then, are the creeds really different from one another?"

She is saying in reply that the Divine Consciousness arises from the depths of the sadhaka's very being, his Self, when all that is not the Self is eclipsed by the vision of That Which Alone Is. Then the sadhaka is face-to-face with Divinity Itself which is his own ultimate Self. The solution to all problems, the answer to all questions, is the Divine Vision. How is that gained? "Be a yogi" (Bhagavad Gita 6:46). Everything comes back to this over and over. It is inescapable. This primal truth must be faced by, and reflected in, the consciousness of the sadhaka. The very statement Thou Art That, implies that the Self is nothing but THAT. The only purpose of sadhana and all the disciplines that support it is the revelation-realization of the Absolute Self.

Inquirer: My opinion is a borrowed one, derived from what I have heard various people say.

> **Why have you adopted this particular point of view? This body presents the matter from the standpoint of the IS and munis, from the line of approach that they have indicated.**

Why have you adopted this particular point of view? Affinity for an object can reveal the character of the urge toward something or even a person experiencing that affinity. In other words, Ma is telling the devotee to examine his own viewpoint and motivations and discover what his choice may reveal about himself. Ma knows whence the viewpoint arose, but the devotee does not, and so She urges him to self-discovery by self-analysis.

This body presents the matter from the standpoint of the IS... Ma was never "in the game." She was always out of the game and not just an observer but the knower of every aspect of the game. Indeed, the game itself was Her manifestation. In Ma's presence a discerning person knew he was in the living presence of the Infinite, that Ma was beyond all conception. This was not just a perception on his part, but the revelation to him of Ma through Her kheyala.

...and munis, from the line of approach that they have indicated. The sages naturally act according to the level of perception in which they are established. The very deeds of the enlightened are conducive to the enlightenment of those who observe or experience the results of their actions. The muni embodies his illumined consciousness and therefore extends it around himself to those in whom he comes in contact. Many years ago I read of a man who was immersed in materialism and ignorance. He went to a very holy person and asked for his blessing. When the saint blessed him, the man jumped up and shouted: "No more sin! No more world!" And from then on he exemplified the path of enlightened awareness. Ma often spoke of The Moment in which forces from previous lives and this present life meet, combine and produce profound and lasting change seemingly in a moment. But they really had long roots into the past awaiting the right moment when they would coalesce and manifest for lasting upliftment and change.

I am reminded of Swami Sivananda's words: "I always travel throughout the world in subtle form, and those who are quick catch me." During my first interview with him I said, "You know, I saw you in America." His response was to smile like a mischevious little boy being caught out. Later in that interview the friend I was with told him of a very serious problem he was having. Sivanandaji looked at us both like a little boy about to whip out a snake from his pocket. Then he said with great force: "Just say God's Name! Japa will do everything!" How simple and how divine.

Truly Sivananda was a presence of God in this world, as were other great ones (mahatmas) whom I was blessed and privileged to meet in India and in America when they were visiting here. As my beloved friend, Sri Hari Datt Vasudeva, said to me: "They are the real glory of India." And he was one, as was his gloriously holy wife, Amrit. Once a man in India said: "I am not a saint; but I have seen saints." Yes. Indeed.

Countless opinions and schools of thought exist in the world, but these will not serve the purpose of a seeker. The method that the guru prescribes for him is the one to be adopted: by following that current he will be carried towards the Ocean.

Countless opinions and schools of thought exist in the world, but these will not serve the purpose of a seeker. Why? Because they are "in the world." Intellectual concepts begin and end in samsara. Only that which transcends the world can enable to aspirant to move beyond this realm of illusion and enter into his own true being whose nature is unconditioned consciousness. Authentic sadhana is immaterial and unconditioned right from the start. Since the sadhaka is at all times essentially the Self, his sadhana can from the moment of its onset begin revealing the Self to his awareness. We end up with what we begin with. Every step to the Real must from the beginning be a revealing of that Reality. Naturally the sadhaka's scope of insight and experience is limited in the beginning, but it is the nature of true sadhana to continually increase the sadhaka's level and scope and depth of awareness.

So straight is the gate and so narrow
The way to eternal day,
And few are the pilgrims who find it,
Too great is the price they must pay.

Salvation is free, yet to gain it
The soul must leave all things behind;
Deny self and follow the Savior,
The way straight and narrow to find.

How rugged the path, yet God's glory
Attendeth each soul on that way;
And brighter and brighter it shineth,
Revealing a glad, perfect day.

But it's worth all it costs to be holy,
It is worth all it costs to be true;
God's blessing and honor shall crown thee
With power thy life to endue.

I can never forget the first time I heard that sung. I hear it even now when my memory turns back to that moment. Each word was so true that I took it to heart.

The method that the guru prescribes for him is the one to be adopted… This applies to both the method prescribed by the external guru or the method to which the sadhaka's inner guru, his Self, naturally attracts or draws him. But it must really come from his Self, not his ego-clouded mind. The eventual result of the sadhana reveals its actual character and value. It is true that the sadhaka must be guided by the inner guru, but he must ever be wary and deeply cautious lest he deceive himself through his own negative karma and perspective. He must continually study and analyze himself, for in the final analysis he has only himself to monitor his sadhana and progress.

...by following that current he will be carried towards the Ocean. This is a sure thing, but the wise sadhaka continually examines and, yes, even questions his progress. I well remember two men to whom Ma said with great force: "Sitting here in the presence of God [they were seated before a temple shrine], this Body tells you that the mantras you were given at your initiation are the true mantras for you." But it still required their own continuous practice to reveal that truth to their inmost being. Also, it is not enough to "be carried towards the Ocean" only part way. It must move onward unerringly to its end in Kaivalya Moksha: total Self-realization.

Inquirer: Ultimately, when the process of time comes to an end, will all have to merge in that Ocean? But how can it be that those whose aims are so entirely different, as for instance the Vaishnavas with their salokya, samipya, etc. and the Vedantists with their 'Self-poised state', should end up by merging in the one Ocean?

Another Inquirer from the audience: Puffed rice and "murmura" are names for one and the same thing!

> **If puffed rice and murmura are the same, why should they be called by two different names? There must be some element of variation in the two–although essentially both are just rice.**
>
> **The sense of "mine" and "thine: has remained. What do you say, Pitaji?** (Laughter).

Of course no reply is given to Ma because She has perfectly revealed the true situation. Unrealized, merely theoretical Advaitins like to go on and on about how all is one, but if that is so, to whom are they speaking, and about what? And why?

> **When discussing creeds and paths, remember: it is only while on the path that one speaks of paths.**

Therefore he that has come home to his own divine Self and is fully living in the consciousness that is the very nature of his Self, does not speak of "paths" concerning himself because he has left all paths behind by entering into his Self and abiding there. So those who wrangle and discuss about paths have attained nothing but self-born confusion. Withdrawal in silence is the most potent statement the sadhaka can make in such a situation.

Inquirer: When one has reached beyond the level where every creed represents a different line of approach, there is no more talk and controversy.

> **In "there is–not," "there is" is also implied–for without it, how could the "is not" have arisen at all?**

I well remember being amused at seeing a restaurant in New Delhi called "The A and J Cheap and Clean Restaurant." One would hope that such a name would not be needed by those that entered there. There are those like this cited "Inquirer" who think that by repeating slogans that sound profound they can silence intelligent discussion. When I was in school, especially "junior high school," there were people who would stop all discussion by popping up out of their seat and saying: "I rise to a point of order," which apparently had some profound relevance in "Robert's Rules of Order" which none of us had agreed to adopt. Why this ruse worked I never figured out, but its mindlessness succeeded every time. What a perfect way to stifle simple good sense and realistic outlook!

Ma is pointing out that by the absolute rule of duality in every aspect of our samsaric existence, the opposite of any position or concept can instantly be invoked just by a statement of opinion or fact. The proof, then, of genuine wisdom is in the keeping of silence. There Is No Dharma Higher Than Truth is indeed true. But the highest expression of truth is often in saying nothing–just going ahead on the chosen path, leaving discussions to those who really do not plan to get anywhere–just discuss and appear intellectual. Authentic non-duality is silence, contented silence that needs not prove itself because duality has to arise for discussion or argumentation.

Walking away can be a marvelously easy way to be at peace. When I was living next to the Hollywood Self-Realization Fellowship Church, one of the faithful attendees at the church was a loud, spiteful woman whose name in her native language meant "The Sweet One." Every Sunday after the service "Sweetie" usually had a surrounding coterie listening to her blather. No one dared make a comment or leave and offend her. But one Sunday enough was enough. "I do not have to stand here and listen to this," I told myself, so with great courage I dared to perhaps be noticed and very quietly and slowly separated from the group and walked off the grounds and went home. I was in shock at my forward and bold actions. But it felt good and I resolved to continue not enduring nastiness because I foolishly wanted to avoid conflict. Self-assertion was a trauma, but a healing one. The sadhaka must know when to stop enduring oppressive nonsense and quit being a virtuous coward.

Some years later in India Ma showed me how it was done to lasting effect. A Mahamandaleshwar–head of an association of several ashrams–was often invited to speak at spiritual conferences sponsored by the Anandamayi Sangha. Never in east or west have I endured such an empty, boring and tiresome speaker. I do think that he could have made a stone cry from boredom. But he had lots of money under his control so he was greatly honored and was a usual fixture at important events. And one time in Brindaban he was present for an event, and I was dreading the inevitable droning.

One morning when I went to the ashram, I found an interesting scene. The Mahamandaleshwar was stalking around with a very sour look on his face as ashram officials kept running up and kowtowing to him in an agitated and fawning manner. His face was a chubby thundercloud. Ma was observing this in Her usual tranquility.

As I stood there one of the ashramites came and explained the situation. At the morning satsang which I had mercifully missed, the Mahamandaleshwar had given a long answer to a question from the audience. At its conclusion, Ma had said very forcefully: "Only a person with no knowledge of the subject could have given such an answer!" Explosion! Consternation! Confusion! So everyone was trying to atone for Ma's words. I, of course, was delighted. And Ma seemed quite content, too. As Uncle Bill Swearingen from my little hometown used to say: "Some folks just need tellin'." Ma knew how!

> **People claim to belong to a particular sect. But where there is no question of any doctrine, nor of controversy, there is He at the root–He who is present in all these innumerable forms.**

When mere intellectual busyness is absent, then insight into divine mysteries becomes possible.

> **Whether you speak of the many or of the One, it is a matter of outlook.**

We like to think we are speaking the truth, when it usually is only our opinion, although sincere. Pure objectivity is rare–that is the truth of the matter. So we should always be aware that no matter how sincere or correct we may consider our words to be, they only express a particular, personal viewpoint. We are not fountainheads of Truth, but can only express our opinion. This should be understood and accepted. There is rarely a Last Word on any subject. Language rarely conveys pure truth, only approximation. There is wisdom in knowing this.

> **One seed is sown, and a tree grows with countless flowers and leaves, displaying infinite ways of becoming and numberless stages of rest; yet essentially it is one.**
>
> **To see through the multiplicity to the unity is a rare gift, indeed-one that only sadhana produces since it is rooted in the One by its very nature.**

Ma is implying that the practice of sadhana arises in the consciousness of the aspiring yogi from his own Self: the One. And further that only sadhana produces the perception of the One. What, then, can be more valuable to the yogi than his sadhana?

> **Every creed, every school of thought, has its particular method of approach. So long as you advance along one special path, there is, for that period, only one path for you.**

It is imperative that we understand there is rarely only one right view or course of action, but it usually is necessary that we focus our attention and action in a single-minded way. But the alternate possibilities should not be ignored or unseen by us.

> **Very well, let us leave this point now. You asked, did you not, Pitaji, how those who aim at entirely different goals, can ultimately, when the process of time comes to an end, merge in the one Ocean?**
>
> **When you speak of an "end," this is within the limits of time; yet where time is, there is also something beyond it. But where the question of "end" or "time" can no more arise, There, all will be united.**

This is matter of consciousness, of the condition of the mind that considers our situation. Our mind is like a mirror that only reflects a small part of the reality which surrounds us.

Time produces change, therefore transcendence of time is the only way to perceive the Changeless Reality both within and around us. That is extremely easy to say, but to step out of time into eternity for even a second requires profound purification and reorientation of the mind. Here, too, sadhana is the only means of success.

The fact it this: those without regular sadhana practice have no possibility whatsoever of realizing these profound truths within their own consciousness and ultimate transformation. Ma's words are simply mere noise in the ears of those without regular personal sadhana practice. People often expressed discontent with the state of consciousness that prevailed in the people that usually surrounded Ma. But being in Ma's presence was nothing if a person's consciousness was not affected by Her divine consciousness which was really their own essential being. Most people never really met Ma. They just had a vague, unfocused and minimal experience of "something." Very few people ever met or saw Ma.

Inquirer: So long as one speaks and discusses, does it mean that some sort of imperfection still persists?

> **Yes; he who is still within the domain of speech, that is to say, worldly talk on worldly matters, is in the boundary of ties. But 'There,' the question of speaking does not arise.**

Speaking takes place in duality. Unity is revealed in the silence of Being that is the Self. When Ma, spoke, She was always in the Consciousness of Unity. Therefore Her words had an effect on others that was unique. Just the sound of Ma's voice conveyed deep inner awareness to those who listened to Her in the inner silence of their own Self. Just to see Ma was a profound and exalted spiritual experience. So many times I have seen people come into Ma's presence and stand there with tears of relief streaming down their faces. Just the sight of Ma brought peace and healing to their hearts, as does Her remembrance even now. Ma often said that She was always with us–we were never separated from Her. She was Universal Existence Itself. At the very sight of Ma we became inwardly more alive than we could have imagined possible. Ma was the Absolute Reality revealed.

> **This is why the aforesaid does not apply to a real World-teacher. What a World-teacher says is not like the speech of this world.**

Everything about Ma was pure consciousness. Her every word was the reality of what She was speaking about, not just a linguistic symbol. Therefore Her every word conveyed a direct communication with us. But for this to be so, there had to be an openness, a direct and deep connection with Her. She made this possible by Her grace, but each individual had to desire that communication.

I have met many people who saw nothing in Ma whatsoever because there was nothing substantial or real within them. Two of my friends were visited by a man whom they had known well before they went to

India and met Ma. They showed him a photograph of Ma which was one of their favorites, hoping he would "see something" in it. He stared at it for a while, then said: "Stringy-haired old broad, ain't she?" They were impressed.

As I have mentioned before, although Sri Jyotish Chandra Roy's book was originally called *Mother's Darshan*, it was wisely renamed *Mother As Revealed To Me*. For this was true: only those to whom Ma revealed Herself really ever saw Her. And I have observed people who seemingly could not even see Ma. More than once I have seen people nearly walk into Ma, only turning aside at the last moment. And even then it was obvious that they had not seen Her at all. Ma said that no one could see Her if She did not will it. So many times I have sat looking at Ma and thinking: "She wants me to see Her." Jai Ma!

Inquirer: Please explain the nature of worldly and divine happiness.

> **Divine Happiness–that which you call parama sukhadam [supreme happiness]–is pure, unalloyed bliss, happiness in its own right.**

This arises from within, from the deep inner state of the Self. When we saw Ma, that wondrous experience filled us completely. Ma was Herself the divine eye through which She saw us and we saw Her. This is a great mystery, but it certainly was experienced by us always.

Inquirer: But surely, there is happiness in the world too

> **Then why do you make this remark?**

Because there is the refusal to honestly reply to Ma's question: "Have you not seen what life in this world is?" Certainly they have seen, but do not want it to be so. They want to fixate on this world the way a dog gnaws and gnaws on an old, dry bone. And God and Ma lets them do as they please.

Inquirer: Why do people run after material happiness?

> **You know this happiness from experience, and hence your question. But God is gracious and makes you see that this so-called happiness is not happiness. He kindles discontent and anguish in you, which is due to the absence of communion with the Divine. Worldly happiness is derived from the countless manifestations of God.**

We can only be satisfied in the direct and permanent experience of the Self. Yet human beings do not care for the truth about this. It is like the movie in which a man has a dream about meeting God. At one point he says: "You are God. I can't fool You, can I?" And God replies: "You can try." So it is. We make the choice. Always. That is why, as I have mentioned before, that in India they say: "When someone chooses God you can know that God has chosen him first."

> **People talk and marvel about those who renounce the world, but in actual fact, it is you yourself who have renounced everything.**

Here Ma speaks straightforwardly as usual, though people had a great capacity for ignoring and forgetting Her words. For example, the very first day I met Ma, I was outside Her room waiting for even a glimpse of Her. Her door would open and we would all rush in, then get put out, wait and rush in again when the opportunity arose. A moment's glimpse of Ma was worth a million glimpses of anyone or anything else. At one point two young men asked to speak with Ma, and they told Her they were pondering whether or not to take sannyas.

[Here let me pause for one of my favorite stories of Sri Ramana Maharshi. Once a young man asked Sri Ramana if he should become a monk. Immediately Sri Ramana replied, "No." "Why not?" objected the man, "You did." "Yes," replied Sri Ramana, "And I did not need to ask anyone if I should."]

Ma told them that it was not just a matter of taking up an external identity, rather it was a matter of choosing a one-way ticket out of this world or a return-trip ticket back into it. The life of sannyas was the one-way ticket and life other than sannyas was the return-trip ticket. The matter was simple: They should choose which they preferred. But see the words of Ma here! She says that those who do not renounce the world are renouncing EVERYTHING!!! There are only two options open: Renounce and Receive or Accept and Lose. You cannot have both. Very few people will acknowledge this truth.

What is this "everything"? God!

The sannyasi is able to possess God through the exclusion of the world. The non-sannyasi cannot avoid the world, and therefore loses the possession of God. Ma is saying this, not me. But I certainly do agree. Never will I forget the night when I was speaking with Ma through a translator. Ma was walking up and down as she answered my questions. My last question was about taking sannyas. The moment I began to speak the question, Ma stopped walking and stood looking at me with a radiant smile. When my question was translated, She vigorously replied: "Yes! Do so!" And walking over picked up a silk cloth which She handed to me, saying that I should get it dyed gerrua and have that used in my sannyas ceremony. What a relief! A reprieve from samsara!

Leaving Him aside, everyone is literally practicing supreme renunciation.

And what an ignoble renunciation! Rejection of God to possess the world until death takes that away inevitably! What a fool's bargain! Everything is lost to the worldling. That is why Ma says non-monastic life is supreme renunciation, for it is renunciation of the Supreme! Take it or leave it, but do not lie about Ma's true opinion of the matter.

It is only natural that the sense of want should awaken.

Those who are not sannyasis cannot evade "the sense of want" pervading their life. Earlier I cited Ma's declaration: "He who does sadhana automatically becomes a sadhu." That implies that if a person does not become a sadhu he is not doing sadhana, but only faking it! And as I have said before, one time in Ranchi Dr. Ghosh, a devotee of Ma, brought some Catholic nuns to meet Ma. Ma said to him: "Tell them that this body also is a nun." What could be clearer?

Even in the midst of comforts and pleasures, one feels homesick in a foreign land.

Only the Self is our "native land," our true home. When the waters of the Great Flood were abating, Noah "sent forth a dove from him, to see if the waters were abated from off the face of the ground; but the dove found no rest for the sole of her foot, and she returned unto him into the ark, for the waters were on the face of the whole earth: then he put forth his hand, and took her, and pulled her in unto him into the ark" (Genesis 8:8-9). If we are doves in the spirit we will have no place is this world to settle. We must be like those that Saint Paul wrote of as "strangers and pilgrims on the earth" (Hebrews 11:13), divine misfits. Ma was clearly one of those, too, and it is wise to join Her company.

There is distress even in happiness, one's possessions are not really one's own–this is what He causes man to feel.

The truth is that human beings are not at home on earth. We come from a higher world and are intended to return there having gained the evolution needed to ascend there and nevermore re-enter samsara.

It is said, is it not, that on being hit one recovers one's senses, [awakens]. One learns by receiving blows.

But how long will we will have to be beaten up to get the idea and escape the inevitable blows of life in this samsara?

"What are you running away from?" is the accusatory question of the enmeshed worldling to the aspiring monastic. Once a pagan ruler was riding through the streets of Alexandria when he saw a Christian monk hurrying along. He had the monk brought to him and asked where he was going. "I am leaving this place which you and others like you have set on fire!" replied the monk. The ruler said that the monk should be detained until he could return and "deal" with him. But the ruler was killed in battle and the monk was set free to depart and elude the fires of the world of corruption.

As a character in the Pogo comicstrip once said: "Cut the philosophy and RUN!"

> **When He manifests Himself as worldly happiness, one does not feel contented, for along with it He appears as the sense of want.**

Deep inside we know that we do not belong in this place of continual change and uncertainty. For this world is the realm of death and we intuit our immortal nature. It is like a song I sang long ago in church:

> Have you heard a voice from heaven,
> Calling in a solemn tone,
> "Come, my people, from confusion,
> This is not your native home"?

I did not hear it then, but when I found Sanatana Dharma and Yoga I certainly heard it with my newly-opened inner ears. And I found refuge that has lasted through the years.

> **But divine happiness, even the tiniest particle of a grain of it, never leaves one again; and when one attains to the Essence of Things and finds one's Self–this is Supreme Happiness.**
>
> **When it is found, nothing else remains to be found; the sense of want will not awaken any more, and the heart's torment will be stilled for ever.**

What a glorious prospect! What a wonderful destiny! And sadhana alone brings us to the state described in the second paragraph of this passage.

> **Do not be satisfied with fragmentary happiness, which is invariably interrupted by shocks and blows of fate. But become complete, and having attained to perfection, be YOURSELF.**

By this time no comment is needed by me. Just continual dedication to continual yoga sadhana. Then all is assured. For completion and perfection is our nature. Take the yogic key and unlock the treasure.

TWENTY TWO

Inquirer: Why does one not remember one's former lives?

Through ignorance. There is no knowledge, due to the veil that hides it.

Since we take on a new body, and therefore a new brain, in every life we naturally will have no memory of previous lives. But the so-called subconscious mind is the mind/brain of the astral body and does carry both memories and conditionings from many lives. So if the subconscious can be activated or accessed, past life memories will arise. The yogis know this very well.

It is also to the benefit of the individual that past lives are sometimes not remembered, otherwise past memories and conditionings would continually clutter up and intrude in our present mental functioning.

However, an intuitive and introspective person may spontaneously remember elements from previous lives. As the yogi develops his mind he often, even usually, recollects fragments of previous lives which reveal to him the elements from his past lifetimes that are shaping his present life and mental makeup at the present time. This takes many forms.

Our mind has been totally shaped by previous-life experiences, and for the yogi the arising of memories often clarifies his present situations and can even indicate the course of action he should be taking in response. When I was studying in the university, one day I heard the footsteps of someone coming into the room. I began to smile even before I looked up, and there I saw a beloved sister from centuries before. We were instant friends and knew each other's mind completely.

The yogi has such experiences since his sadhana is lifting the veil of the subconscious to illumine his present situations and experiences in this life. This is a necessary part of self-understanding.

Inquirer: But why should there be a veil? After the body dies, the mind continues, for one's samskaras live on. Since these samskaras persist, and also because one is able to remember what has happened today and yesterday, why should the events of one's past lives be forgotten?

> **Having entered the kingdom of forgetting, everything is forgotten. This world is the abode of non-remembrance.**

But for the yogi this does not have to be so, and hopefully remembrance of previous lives will develop further into awareness of his own present, eternal status as the divine Self. This is the ideal knowledge for which we are all born.

Inquirer: Why should so very much be forgotten? A small portion might at least be remembered!

> **You say, do you not, that the Lord Buddha talked about the events of five hundred of his previous lives. Can you recall everything that you experienced in your present birth, from your childhood until now?**

This is the way it should be, otherwise our mind would be so full of past experiences it would distract and even cloud our perceptions in this life.

> **You die at every instant without being aware of it.**

Every experience is a kind of birth, and the ending of that experience is a kind of death. Furthermore, elements in our body are continually dying and being replaced by others which will in their time "die" and be succeeded by others in a continuous sequence.

This instability should motivate us to center our awareness in that aspect of our being which is neither born nor dying, not arising or subsiding. When Ma said, "I neither come nor go," She was hinting at this as Her continual situation. For Her there was no beginning or ending. We could not comprehend that intellectually, but the moment we entered Ma's presence we entered to some degree into what She termed the Eternal Moment. It was indescribable and incomprehensible, but nonetheless a definite awareness, a hint of Ma's Eternal Being.

> **At present, you are neither an infant, nor a child, nor a youth. No sooner is a baby born than he starts of his own accord to drink his mother's milk, and when he has drunk, he feels happy and satisfied; by this he has already given full testimony of former births.**

I well remember how in science class in junior high school the teacher dogmatically declared that science knew there was no such thing as instinct, that there was just reflex. This was the unsatisfactory explanation of the fact that the newborn infant instantly begins to nurse at the first touch of breast or bottle. I had great respect for our teacher, but I never believed him for a moment. Even adult life is pervaded by instinctual reactions that are really reflexes from previous lives. Without insight into reincarnation, human life and experience are incomprehensible, and life cannot be lived completely intelligently and insightfully.

Writing this I remembered when I was five and my cousin Larry was four. We went to a funeral home where the casket of a newly-departed relative was placed in a kind of viewing room. The moment we entered, Larry said wonderingly: "Why that is where they put *me* when I died!" At the time I did not believe him, but I do now. There are many aspects to Growing Up spiritually, and recognition of reincarnation as a fundamental fact is part of it.

> **Now also, whenever your hunger has been appeased, you experience a similar sense of well-being and contentment as you did in your early childhood, although you do not recollect what you felt at that time.**

So it is.

Inquirer: How is it that samskaras persist?

Through the force of sustained practice (abhyasa yoga).

This is very interesting. Samskaras persist and become life-shaping elements through the opening of consciousness brought about by sadhana. Only for the sadhaka are the presence of samskaras comprehensible and meaningful. Only the yogi is fully awake and functional in his life. For yoga is the science of consciousness itself.

> **Direct your efforts towards God-realization, and His remembrance will come to you automatically at the moment of death.**

Ma is getting right to the heart of things. Remembrance of previous lives is valuable, but the supremely necessary remembrance is the remembrance of God throughout life and at the moment of death. "Therefore, become a yogi" (Bhagavad Gita 6:46).

> **The individual is that which is bound, and the world** [is] **perpetual motion.**

The individual jiva experiences two opposing states: personal bondage-confinement in a static condition through the body and the constant, unceasing change and mutation of the world around him. He is both bound and tossed about, unable to move and unable to stop being thrown about. This results in total confusion and misery. The suffering individual can find ways to artificially close down his awareness of this condition, but in time it always impinges on his experience and shapes it into the prevailing condition of change and instability. For the individual is meant to be established in the Absolute instead of being immersed in and deluded and confused by the perpetual changes of relative existence. This condition is known as *gilgul* in Hebrew, meaning "rolling" in the sense of constant motion and instability. It includes the concept of continual reincarnation with its attendant miseries and confusion.

Whatever appears in this world of creatures is the manifestation of the One.

And this includes us. God is the very essence of our being. We are distinct from God, but we are never separated from God for an instant. It is this divine essence that carries us onward from life to life as we experience and evolve through countless births: beginning as an atom of hydrogen and culminating in total liberation as a wave in the ocean of Divine Being. This cannot be conceived or described, but it is attained by all sentient beings after long ascent upon the ladder of ever-expanding evolution of consciousness. It is inconceivable but attainable.

"Beloved, now are we the sons of God, and it doth not yet appear what we shall be: but we know that, when he shall appear, we shall be like him; for we shall see him as he is. And every man that hath this hope in him purifieth himself, even as he is pure" (I John 3:2-3). Sadhana is the way of self-purification that reveals our eternal, innate divinity.

The fact that you die at every moment, in other words, that Brahma, Vishnu, and Shiva are ever at work, becomes evident when the body expires.

Just as in the creation, so in the life of each one of us the preservation-maintaining-dissolving action of Brahma, Vishnu and Shiva are manifest. For we are ourselves THAT from which they, too, have arisen and will ultimately merge back into at the end of the evolutionary journey which takes place in the winking of an eye, but appears to involve creation cycles.

As yogis we can attain direct experience-knowledge of divine being, of the eternal immortality that our own apparent death will reveal to us. "Behold, I show you a mystery; We shall not all sleep, but we shall all be changed. For this corruptible must put on incorruption, and this mortal must put on immortality. So when this corruptible shall have put on incorruption, and this mortal shall have put on immortality, then shall be brought to pass the saying that is written, Death is swallowed up in victory"

(I Corinthians 15:51, 53-54). Life Itself is the essence of our being, for we are eternally part of the Divine Life outside of which nothing really exists.

Writing this I can vividly see the joyful countenance of Mr. Bajoria, a disciple of the great Himalayan master, Sri Tapovan Maharaj. Mr Bajoria had lived his life for the welfare of others. When I met him he was very old, and often his memory would slip a bit as he spoke with me. At such times he would laugh and say: "The body is going, the senses are going, and even the mind is going. But I shall never die!" Immortality vibrated in those words of such a master yogi.

> **So long as you wander about in the world of forgetting, you must of necessity forget.**

So the choice is ours. Sanatana Dharma and Yoga lay that out before us in living detail. The rest is up to us. The path of the yogi is the sole path to manifestation of our immortality. "In this yoga, even the abortive attempt is not wasted. Nor can it produce a contrary result. Even a little practice of this yoga will save you from the terrible wheel of rebirth and death" (Bhagavad Gita 2:40).

> **Now what is a samskara? Take for instance the samskara of a temple; that is to say, what had already existed [as a concept] becomes revealed [as an objective reality]. Then again, whatever you do, consciously or unconsciously, leaves an impression on your mind, whether you are aware of it or not. This is styled samskara.**

"Samskara" is an impression in the mind, either conscious or subconscious, produced by action or experience in this or previous lives. Therefore right action continually engaged in produces right consciousness.

> **He who has the capacity to see will be able to discern that these imprints or samskaras pertain to previous births.**

Past life memory comes naturally to the persevering yogi, for self-understanding is a requisite on the path to Self-realization. Often the yogi finds that when he is faced with a turning point in his life, especially if it requires a choice of action on his part, a past-life memory will surface in his conscious mind so he will understand the best choice of possible reactions. Light from the past illumines his present situation. It also sometimes reveals to him why/how the present conditions have manifested as they have, and what meaning they have for him. The life of a yogi is a life of continual discovery of those things that the non-yogi cannot even conceive, much less encounter and experience. It is the yogi, not the exploitive materialist, that lives life to the fullest extent.

> **A yogi can perceive the impressions of a great number of past lives. One may see the events of thousands of one's former births, but when the realization has come of what creation with its ascending and descending currents in reality is, what will he see then?**
>
> **He will see, and also not see: and neither will he not see, nor see.**

When the nature and purpose of life itself is seen by the yogi, then he experiences this seemingly contradictory state of mind. I cannot really explain or describe it, only repeat the words of a great yogi who used to sing in ecstasy: He who knows: knows. None else knows!

> **Where everything that exists is revealed in its fullness–this is called Self-revelation, THAT Itself, the Self-luminous One–call it what you will.**

What more is there to say?

> **All that exists anywhere in the world, be it trees and plants, insects, reptiles, or any other living thing–their birth is indeed your birth, and their death your death.**

We are at all times one with the Absolute Reality, even when we do not realize it. We are not just part of, but ONE with the entire range of existence, relative and absolute. Therefore every change in the universe is a change in us, and any change we bring about in ourselves as sadhakas is a change in universal existence and life. Consequently, when we purify and deepen our consciousness, the consciousness in every atom of our manifested being is purified and deepened. That is why the yogi is a supreme benefactor to all the worlds and every sentient being within them.

So never let some ebullient (and inwardly discontent) busybody hassle you about being "selfish" as a yogi. You most certainly are–and self-centered, and self-involved, too. And never attempt to justify yourself to them. Just say you see the matter differently and get away from them. They hate the light and hate you for bearing the light within yourself, for you prove them false. Never try to placate or pacify them. As Saint Paul counseled Saint Timothy: "From such turn away" (II Timothy 3:5).

> **On the level where everything is contained within you and you are present in everything, there is only the One, and He alone.**

Therefore realize that "the One, and He alone" is your friend. Be friendly to all, but realize that God and the friends of God are your only real friends. Love all if you can, but entrust yourself to no one.

> **Suppose you are able to visualize [perceive] a few of your previous lives: your vision is limited by number.**

Therefore it is of little use. It is the knowledge of your Self as the only real life you have ever had or ever will have, that is the treasure you must attain and guard assiduously. And you cannot share it with anyone. Each person must gain it by his own effort. It is a good thing to have friends who aspire to the same goal as you, but understand that the path to Self-realization truly is "the flight of the alone to the Alone." Spiritual association is good, but spiritual dependency is deadly.

When I began the yoga life I had more friends than ever before in my life because I moved to where there was a yoga center. We meditated and sang and read holy books together. But every one of them eventually abandoned the yoga life for the delusions of the world and were destroyed by their own choice. They did not just crash: they crashed and burned. Yogananda said that in the spiritual battle people will fall to the right and left of you, but you must go on.

> **If you recollect the history of your former births, it means that you know only the course of your own individual lives, in their own particular times and places. But you are not aware of your various movements and static states in the whole universe.**

So what we must do is seek and find the answer to the question: "Who am I?" And the answer is the realization: "I Am That: Soham."

> **You see 'the many'; how will you go beyond this multiplicity? By finding your Self in the many.**

How easy to say and how rarely is it done.

> **Who is that Self? HE, and none but He. So long as He, the Self, has not been revealed, you are imprisoned within the boundary; boundary means ignorance, and therefore there is forgetting.**

This does not please the ego, especially the philosophical, "wisdom" ego. So such an ego speaks out to Ma in a challenge:

Inquirer: Are you suggesting that we must reach the state of Divinity (Ishwarakoti)?

> **The question of reaching that state does not arise at all so long as the veil of ignorance persists. Whether what has been said refers to Ishwarakoti or Sadhakakoti** [the state embodying

Ishwara or the state embodying a sadhaka], **you yourself must ascertain!**

So Ma implies that according to the individual's understanding is the meaning of Her words. It all rests on the sadhaka's shoulders. Although it is called "nonsense verse," Edward Lear's poem "The Jumblies" says it very well.

They went to sea in a Sieve, they did,
  In a Sieve they went to sea:
In spite of all their friends could say,
On a winter's morn, on a stormy day,
  In a Sieve they went to sea!
And when the Sieve turned round and round,
And every one cried, 'You'll all be drowned!'
They called aloud, 'Our Sieve ain't big,
But we don't care a button! we don't care a fig!
  In a Sieve we'll go to sea!'
    Far and few, far and few,
      Are the lands where the Jumblies live;
    Their heads are green, and their hands are blue,
      And they went to sea in a Sieve.

They sailed away in a Sieve, they did,
  In a Sieve they sailed so fast,
With only a beautiful pea-green veil
Tied with a riband by way of a sail,
  To a small tobacco-pipe mast;
And every one said, who saw them go,
'O won't they be soon upset, you know!
For the sky is dark, and the voyage is long,
And happen what may, it's extremely wrong
  In a Sieve to sail so fast!'
    Far and few, far and few,

Are the lands where the Jumblies live;
Their heads are green, and their hands are blue,
And they went to sea in a Sieve.

The water it soon came in, it did,
The water it soon came in;
So to keep them dry, they wrapped their feet
In a pinky paper all folded neat,
And they fastened it down with a pin.
And they passed the night in a crockery-jar,
And each of them said, 'How wise we are!
Though the sky be dark, and the voyage be long,
Yet we never can think we were rash or wrong,
While round in our Sieve we spin!'
Far and few, far and few,
Are the lands where the Jumblies live;
Their heads are green, and their hands are blue,
And they went to sea in a Sieve.

And all night long they sailed away;
And when the sun went down,
They whistled and warbled a moony song
To the echoing sound of a coppery gong,
In the shade of the mountains brown.
'O Timballo! How happy we are,
When we live in a sieve and a crockery-jar,
And all night long in the moonlight pale,
We sail away with a pea-green sail,
In the shade of the mountains brown!'
Far and few, far and few,
Are the lands where the Jumblies live;
Their heads are green, and their hands are blue,
And they went to sea in a Sieve.

They sailed to the Western Sea, they did,
  To a land all covered with trees,
And they bought an Owl, and a useful Cart,
And a pound of Rice, and a Cranberry Tart,
  And a hive of silvery Bees.
And they bought a Pig, and some green Jack-daws,
And a lovely Monkey with lollipop paws,
And forty bottles of Ring-Bo-Ree,
  And no end of Stilton Cheese.
   Far and few, far and few,
        Are the lands where the Jumblies live;
      Their heads are green, and their hands are blue,
        And they went to sea in a Sieve.

And in twenty years they all came back,
  In twenty years or more,
And every one said, 'How tall they've grown!'
For they've been to the Lakes, and the Torrible Zone,
  And the hills of the Chankly Bore;
And they drank their health, and gave them a feast
Of dumplings made of beautiful yeast;
And everyone said, 'If we only live,
We too will go to sea in a Sieve,—
  To the hills of the Chankly Bore!'
   Far and few, far and few,
        Are the lands where the Jumblies live;
      Their heads are green, and their hands are blue,
        And they went to sea in a Sieve.

Going to sea in a sieve is hardly a likely prospect, but the Jumblies did it. Yet it is certainly true that the places where Jumblies do this wonder are "far and few." Furthermore, they have green heads and blue hands! So who wants to be a Jumblie? Surely they are considered comic freaks by those who neither can nor want to sail the sea in a sieve. To step out of the common ranks with a green head and blue hands and sail off in a sieve takes a great deal of confidence and resolve. Who is ready to sail?

The book of Daniel in the Bible tells a true story of superhuman courage and resolve. In Sunday School as a child I sang:

> Dare to be a Daniel!
> Dare to stand alone!
> Dare to have a purpose firm!
> Dare to make it known!

One of my aunts, hearing this song as a child, thought the words were:

> Dare to be a spaniel!
> Dare to have it known!
> Dare to have a purple spine!
> Dare to have it shown!

Funny as it is, my aunt did get the basic idea. Those who will succeed in spiritual life have to dare, act, persevere and be considered a freak or a fool. Every yogi must be a Jumblie/Daniel. The yogi has stepped out from the unheeding herd and said with Isaiah the prophet: "Here am I; send me" (Isaiah 6:8) on the quest of the Divine Self.

Inquirer: Surely, one who has become established in the Self will naturally forget the world?

In the kingdom of forgetting one forgets.

The sadhaka does not put the world and its ways out of his mind in hope of forgetting them. Rather, he becomes increasingly aware and perceptive in his view of the world. He sees through the false appearance of the world into its reality as just that: false and untrue. And he unceasingly keep this in mind as through sadhana he cultivates the faculty of "seeing true" at all times. The yogi establishes himself in the world of inner awakening while others sleep the sleep of death in their often intentional unawareness.

> **So long as you are identified with the body (deho), it is your very nature to call out: 'give, give!' ('deo, deo!').**

Aware of our utter emptiness in this false and empty world, we turn toward the Reality of the Self which is Fullness Itself. There alone will we find satisfaction and fulfillment.

> **You say 'give!' because you are in want. Where want exists, there must needs be error and ignorance; and where error and ignorance abide, there will most certainly be forgetting.**

One of the most heard mantras in Bharat is the following:

Purnamadah pūrnamidam,
 purnāt purnamudachyate.
Purnasya purnamadaya,
 purnamevāvashihyate.

That is the Full [Complete] and this is the Full,
 The Full has come out of the Full;
Having taken the Full from the Full,
 Only the Full remains.

It presents the great mystery of relative existence within the Reality that is the Absolute, transcending relativity–which is then seen as unreal.

> **When in the midst of all this you practice sadhana in order to realize your Self, or rather, when by God's Grace sadhana comes about–for to be able to engage in sadhana is itself the Grace of God–then, after having worked through layers and layers of ignorance, you discover: "I am in fact the whole."**

This paragraph merits careful reading more than once until we get the complete message about relative existence itself. How perfectly Ma expresses it. It is truly a marvel. Ma was the fountainhead of truth and wisdom. She was Herself Truth and Wisdom.

> **I am–this is why there are trees and plants, and everything that exists, however manifold. Every single form is in fact "I."**

These are the words of the Great I of the Self–not the little I of the ego. Explanation and description are impossible, so wise silence must suffice.

> **Where I am conscious of separateness, my natural expression is to want. Even in this condition, I am infinite.**

As long as our consciousness is not centered in the pure consciousness of the Self, sense of lack or deficiency, need and want are inevitable.

> **In the very form of the human body lie moods [bhavas: states of consciousness] of endless variety and numberless modes of expression.**

No end can be found in a single lifetime to the endless chain of possibilities that present themselves to the samsarin, the dweller in samsara.

> **Indeed, all existing forms are infinite, and I am likewise infinite.**
>
> **All forms and distinctive marks I see to be myself; eternally, therefore, I exist.**

This only follows as the truth, since Infinity Itself is the fundamental nature of relative existence in all its aspects. This is the play of Maya at all times.

> **So then I have discovered this, and that I am of many forms–infinite forms indeed, with infinite modes of appearance. They**

> **exist within me in ways of infinite diversity, and yet I myself am all of these. Within me exist the separate modes of display–in endless variation none are excluded.**

This is a perfect encapsulization of the interaction of the Nitya and the lila, the Infinite and the finite.

> **When the like is directly perceived and all manifold aspects are recognized as a [single] whole, then the One will certainly be revealed. How can the One be distinct from the infinite multiplicity? The many exist in the One and the One in the many.**

So unity and multiplicity are the same thing reflected in one another in the way two mirrors facing one another reveal an entire series of reflections that are really only variations of the two originals.

> **This is why, when you can visualize five hundred of your former births, you are still limited by number; for there is so very much more than this!**

Since we begin relative manifestation as an atom of hydrogen and proceed onward from there in increasing complexity for countless creation cycles, there is no way our births/deaths can be counted.

> **When you have discovered yourself [your Self] in all the untold forms, you realize that the Lord is present in every one of them.**

This is no small statement. To realize the universal presence of the Divine we must see that Divinity in all forms. And this seemingly objective experience will result in the subjective experience of our own Self as identical with the Supreme Self–though as a part of the Whole.

> **When the essential nature of infinity and finiteness becomes fully revealed, you see that there is finiteness in infinity and infinity in the finite.**

For they are manifestations of the One Reality which appears to us as finite and infinite–and is beyond those designations. There is a dimension beyond dimensionality, for it is not an experience but a state of being. So yoga sadhana is the way to experience that sublime state. Sadhana does not produce the experience, but opens our consciousness to perceive it as an ever-present reality.

> **Now** [having attained the just-mentioned revelation] **you are in a position to resolve the polarity of Sakara (God-with-form), and Nirakara (God-without-form).**

And to directly experience them as One, not as a duality/polarity at all.

> **Look, if there were no veil of ignorance for the individual, how could God's Lila be carried on? When acting a part one must forget oneself; the Lila could not proceed without the covering veil of ignorance.**

The Show Must Go On, because it is essentially the path to perfect realization and the transcendence of any kind of forgetfulness or ignorance. The illumined yogi is not under the spell of Maya, but uses Maya as a helping hand in its transcendence. A frequent simile is that of using a thorn to extract a thorn that has pierced some part of us by accident.

There are times when the sadhaka must just jump right in the Kiddie Pool and splash around to see what develops–or what does not. For both can be informative. Always the yogi is looking at the world and himself in the world through his intelligence, his buddhi clarified by sadhana.

> **Consequently it is but natural that the veil should be there. So the world is the perception by the senses of what is projected: Srishti-drishti.**

Srishti is manifestation, and drishti is its perception, including insight and understanding of what is observed.

> **To be a separate individual means to be bound, and that which binds is the veil of ignorance: here is the clue to the forgetting about which you asked.**

To feel completely separate from everything around us is to be bound–confined–in body consciousness. Lack of insight or understanding is the root of such bondage. Forgetfulness of our wider mode of existence as a part of universal life confines and stifles us as a result.

Unless there is arising/awakening into our unity with all things–of actually being an inseparable part of all things in the sense of the unified field of vibrating, ever-changing energy that is itself the field of experience within matter–we are bound in misperception of both ourselves and all that surrounds us. Separation is the cause of our forgetting the unity in which we live and evolve. To say, "I am one thing and all else is another" is to immerse ourselves in isolation and even fear of all that surrounds us as opposing or attempting to overwhelm and confuse us. We suffer from two fundamental simplistic illusions: that we are absolutely part of everything and that we are absolutely separate from everything.

The pairs of opposites delude us because they blind us to the underlying Unity that is the Universal Self. Thinking, "I am part of all this" and "I am not a part of all this" alternately according to the prevailing impressions of the moment deludes and confuses us. For both statements are true, although we must come into realization of that which is a third facet: that part of us which transcends "I am" and "I am not" in relation to the world in which we find ourselves seemingly without purpose.

Only the inward orientation of the mind which is opened to us through yoga sadhana can enable us to directly perceive the truth of our situation as both part of and separate from what we experience. Ma often remarked that there was an alternative to both the idea of unity and the idea of separation, that our mind needed to comprehend the third state of awareness that includes both and yet reaches beyond them. That is why the term advaita is so important. It means Not Two, but not One in a simplistic manner. Unity in duality and duality in unity is the right vision. As I think I have mentioned before, if we cannot think in two opposite directions at once we will never get even a hint of the way things are.

When you speak of previous births you intuitively feel: "Was there ever a time when I was not?"

It is interesting that this is true. When we attempt to understand that we have lived many lives before now, we find that we cannot conceive of a moment when our existence in the universe began, that we have always been "here" in relativity and rebirth. The question is: how much of our experience is merely created by our limited consciousness and how much is genuine intuition arising from our Self? Only the yogi is able to separate these mental states and reach beyond them to the actuality that transcends our usual pedestrian and dualistic misperceptions of the way things actually are.

True creativity arises from the Self of the creative person. Therefore artists and poets often grasp and express what ordinary people cannot. As an example, here is part of "Ode: Intimations of Immortality from Recollections of Early Childhood" by William Wordsworth.

There was a time when meadow, grove, and stream,
The earth, and every common sight,
To me did seem
Apparelled in celestial light,
The glory and the freshness of a dream.
It is not now as it hath been of yore;—
Turn wheresoe'er I may,
By night or day.
The things which I have seen I now can see no more.

The Rainbow comes and goes,
And lovely is the Rose,
The Moon doth with delight
Look round her when the heavens are bare,
Waters on a starry night
Are beautiful and fair;
The sunshine is a glorious birth;
But yet I know, where'er I go,
That there hath passed away a glory from the earth.

Whither is fled the visionary gleam?
Where is it now, the glory and the dream?

Our birth is but a sleep and a forgetting:
The Soul that rises with us, our life's Star,
Hath had elsewhere its setting,
And cometh from afar:
Not in entire forgetfulness,
And not in utter nakedness,
But trailing clouds of glory do we come
From God, who is our home:
Heaven lies about us in our infancy!

It is you who speak in terms of "before" and "after," since you are confined within the realm of time. But really there is no question of "in time" and "out of time"; nor of day and night, "before" and "after."

So long as one remains enslaved by time, there will be birth and death.

This is a compulsion arising from the universe itself in which we have taken birth. Yet:

Actually, there is no such thing as rebirth.

For life is by its nature a seamless continuity, but samsara and the samsaric mind and its limited perceptions produce in us the convictions of many lives, though life by its very nature in its pure state is a unity.

In a very real sense, birth entails dying to the truth of the individual's inmost life of the Self. The Bhagavad Gita expresses it this way: "You dream you are the doer, you dream that action is done, you dream that action bears fruit. It is your ignorance, it is the world's delusion that gives you these dreams" (Bhagavad Gita 5:14).

Still, at some stage the memory of previous lives will most certainly occur, but what is the significance of "before" and "after" since I exist throughout eternity?

This is not a matter for the intellect or reason. Only direct intuition arising from our own Self will solve this seeming problem. The yogi will certainly perceive hints of his previous lives and in time will actually remember at least fragments of some of them, according to what he needs at a particular moment in his life. The past life experiences of the yogi arise into his awareness only at the time they are of practical value, and will often clarify for him the meaning or the background of what is happening to him at the moment. Nothing is for entertainment or mystification. Everything in the yogi's life is practical and useful.

Inquirer: If someone advances along the path of advaita, will he acquire vibhutis (supernormal powers)?

If you speak of a sadhaka who aspires to the state of unqualified Oneness (advaita sthiti), then, even if supernormal powers come to him, he will not accept them.

This is because the intelligent and understanding sadhaka aims solely for the goal of Self-realization in which supernormal powers are meaningless and even distracting and potentially harmful. But they will naturally arise in reaction to his endeavors and are an indication of his sadhana being effective.

> **Whereas the aspirant who worships God with form and attributes will accept whatever psychic or super-psychic powers are granted to him, regarding them as manifestations of the One.**

This, too, is one response, but one that should be done only after careful observation and analysis. Often such experiences arise because of past life samskaras or karmas. This arising indicates the sadhaka is definitely affecting his subtle bodies and the samskaras inherent in them. His reaction, however, should always be one of caution, since exercise of such powers can be distracting and even detrimental to the sadhaka's spiritual development. For powers (siddhis) such as this are centered in the astral bodies where many samskaras both positive and negative are inherent.

> **Such powers are bound to be developed in the course of sadhana, since they represent the fruit of one's efforts.**

Nevertheless, these powers will manifest and are an indication of correct practice. But correct response to these powers is crucial for the sadhaka. Wisdom is always necessary, but especially so for the sadhaka.

> **The word "vibhuti"** [manifestation of supernormal power(s)] **signifies the various manifestations of the All-Pervading (Vibhu). For this reason it is only natural and certain that vibhutis should come.**

The wise and observant sadhaka must be careful in his response to these supernormal powers, for wherever there is power there is the possibility of using that power wisely or foolishly, beneficially or to one's detriment. Caution is urged upon the sadhaka, and usually ignoring and not using these powers is the wisest and safest response.

> **The aspirant must however take care not to be possessed by these powers, because his progress would then be arrested at that stage.**

This is a mild warning. Most people who have let themselves be distracted from serious sadhana and enticed into egoic use of such powers have eventually become deluded and even mentally impaired if not outright insane.

> **The seeker following the path of advaita will not accept duality.**

The use of vibhutis is based on a dualistic attitude, an acceptance of the vibhutis and their exercise as fundamentally real. There is great danger in this matter. At one point in my sadhana certain powers began to manifest. I had heard that talking about such things could end them, so I told several of my yogi friends about them and asked them to pray that they would cease. And those experiences stopped almost immediately.

This is one of the reasons the Katha Upanishad (1.3.14) says regarding the yogic path: "Sharp as the edge of a razor and hard to cross, difficult to tread is that path [so] sages declare." The sadhaka should not be fearful, but he must be very cautious.

> **On the other hand, one who contemplates God-with-form will not accept non-duality, yet, in the course of his practice will arrive at the understanding that the One Supreme Form is revealed in all forms.**

Genuine sadhana reveals the entire spectrum of spiritual realities, so the sadhaka must be ready to learn and unlearn a great deal.

> **What is termed Nirguna, the Attributeless, must also become fully revealed. Thus the resolution of the apparent discrepancy between Sakara [with form] and Nirakara [without form] must come.**

Then the sadhaka knows they are fundamentally the One appearing as two.

When, on attaining to a certain state, multiplicity disappears, this must not be mistaken for Self-realization.

For it is only a discerning of the underlying unity of the entire range of relative existence. The fully advaitic, non-dual, vision is a further advancement in realization beyond mere numerical or simplistic unity.

To those who advance by the method of advaita, the realization of the One Self must come through viveka and vairagya.

This is crucial. The sadhaka must at all times be aware that partial understanding can be as perilous as complete misunderstanding. Also many states can arise which the inexperienced sadhaka can mistake for much higher and deeper realizations than they really are. Regarding this Sri Ramakrishna said: "Men often think they have understood Brahman fully. Once an ant went to a hill of sugar. One grain filled its stomach. Taking another grain in its mouth it started homeward. On its way it thought, 'Next time I shall carry home the whole hill.' That is the way shallow minds think. They don't know that Brahman is beyond one's words and thought. However great a man may be, how much can he know of Brahman? Sukadeva and sages like him may have been big ants; but even they could carry at the utmost eight or ten grains of sugar!"

How can the aspiring sadhaka be sure his perceptions are true and complete? Ma says that such realization "must come through viveka and vairgya." Viveka is right intuitive discrimination: discrimination between the Real and the unreal, between the Self and the non-Self, between the permanent and the impermanent. Vairagya is non-attachment; detachment; dispassion; absence of desire; disinterest; or indifference–especially indifference towards and disgust for all worldly things and enjoyments.

Both of these states of mind are necessary for the sadhaka to avoid self-delusion. For once we start lying to ourselves, who can help us?

> **When all differences have been burnt up and everything has merged into the One, this marks a state of achievement that some may call advaita sthiti, the state of unqualified Oneness.**

Unqualified Oneness is the essential state of Consciousness Itself. For pure consciousness is absolute Unity in every aspect. Indeed, pure consciousness is the very nature of the individual Self and the Supreme Self, their only difference being that the consciousness of the Supreme Self is infinite, and the consciousness of the individual Self is by its very nature finite. It is the difference between lightning and the reflection of lightning in a mirror.

To convey to us some approximate idea of this exalted state, Ma continues:

> **The ever-changing world, with its varying movements and states of rest, and all diversity, have completely vanished; only the One remains. Here the 'many' are simply non-existent; there is only One Supreme Reality [Brahman], One Self [Atman]. This is styled the state of Advaita [Non-duality].**

It is the perception of duality in the mind of the sadhaka that has vanished, leaving only perception of the One to remain. It is the sadhaka that has changed, not the world around him.

> **Expressed from a different point of view, all is Pure Consciousness (Chinmayi) and nothing but that. Nama, dhama–everything; form, diversity, appearance–are actually Consciousness and in fact non-material (aprakrita).**

This is the way it would have to be, for in the beginning there was just the One Pure Consciousness. Then, as the Brihadaranyaka Upanishad (2.4.10) says, "From This, indeed, are all these breathed forth." So nothing is separate from The One; nothing is outside It. Everything IS The One. So Ma continues:

> **In that state there are no "others," only He alone exists as the One Supreme Form. Diversity, as perceived from the worldly point of view, has no place here.**

Ma certainly knows how to say it and say it straight to the point. That was a quality in Ma that I admired throughout the years. No one could honestly misunderstand Ma's directives and statements. Clarity was always their outstanding character. Further, profound wisdom and practical good sense were embodied in everything She said.

Ma was perfection itself in manifestation through Her every aspect. I had the good fortune through Her blessing to always see Her divine nature. The very presence of Ma was the Presence of the Infinite. Again I have to insist that it was pure inspiration that had the English translation of *Matri Darshan* (*Mother's Darshan*) entitled *Mother As Revealed To Me*. For without inmost, divine revelation no one could "see" Ma to any significant degree.

I recall one very interesting time during a Samyam Sapta, an annual week-long assembly where many scholars and mahatmas would speak throughout the day, which would end in the evening with a Matri Satsang in which Ma would answer questions. At one point if anyone prefaced a question by saying to Her: "Ma…," She would immediately respond: "No! The Self alone is Ma!" With this in mind, I still said to Ma in a private talk: "I want to wear out your ears calling 'Ma!'" She immediately replied: "You cannot wear out these ears calling 'Ma' because that is what they are for!"

As I said earlier, when people asked me, "Why do you believe in Anandamayi Ma?" I would simply tell them: "Because She wants me to." For She gave me the capacity to see and hear Her divine presence.

> **The word "vibhuti" consists of "vibhu" (He alone as the One Form), and "ti," which stands for "Tini" (He), and signifies that the Almighty reveals Himself in the many as the One Supreme Form–just as there is ice in water and water in ice.**

How simple and how equally profound.

If there were no water, out of what could ice have formed?

As water is the essence of ice, Brahman is the Essence of everything–including us.

> **If it did not lie in the nature of water to become solid under certain conditions, how could ice come into being? In other words; all is in Him and He in all. This is expressed by "Sarvang khalvidam Brahman" (All this is Brahman).**

It is the very nature of the Absolute to manifest as the relative. In a sense everything is supernatural and at the same time everything is divinely Natural.

> **When the seeker realizes himself as the eternal servant, this is a state of non-duality. "Eternal servant" denotes that there is nothing transient in this relationship. THAT manifests as forms and modes of being.**

This implies that the extreme non-dualistic cant of many "advaitists" is just that: empty blather meant to impress and mystify. What Ma says here is the only genuine, authentic and sensible view, whether one follows the path of bhakti or jnana. Actually, there is only one path to The One, and that includes and transcends both bhakti and jnana.

> **If someone who aspires to the Formless realizes Him as the One-without-a second, but fails to realize Him in the field of His Divine Play, his realization is not complete, for he has not resolved the problem of duality.**

Absolutely!!!

> **Different methods of approach have been described here. But Realization must be all-comprehensive, all-embracing, and one must recognize one's Self in everything.**

We must recognize our Self in everything and everything in our Self. This is the only real non-dualism possible.

> **The tree yields a shoot, and out of this shoot grows a tree. A spreading tree is potentially contained in the small shoot. But as one gets new shoots from this tree, It has again come back to itself. That the One is in all, and that all abide in the One, have to be revealed simultaneously. It is and it is not, yet neither is it not, nor is it–how can this be?**

It is possible to see and not comprehend or understand, but that experience is not illegitimate. In the same way the Absolute can be intuited or revealed in many modes of expression. In a sense all are correct and in another sense none of them are correct. This being so, the wise sadhaka does not employ either logic or intuition, but realizes the truth of the Self and the non-Self as truly One. Then he knows that the Self is Everything and at the same time No Thing. He come to rest in Simple BEING. Having no questions, he has no answers, and so is truly Free.

> **When looking at a seed one sees only the seed, but not the plant, or anything else; but when the tree has developed, it bears leaves, flowers, fruit, there is then an endless variety of growth.**

Therefore, belief or unbelief, expectation or non-expectation, simply do not matter. The tree grows and manifests its full potential by just being. So does the conscious individual. It may take creation cycles, but it inevitably comes about because that is its innate nature, not some destiny declared by an external force or intelligence. Every truly enlightened consciousness is *swayamprakash*–self-illumined. And has been so always. Otherwise enlightenment could not last since what begins must come to an end. The yogi moves outside time and space and stands revealed as what he always was.

> **In the seed as such nothing else exists; therefore one may say "it is not." Yet again, when it is a tree, everything exists. To**

say "what does not exist now, did not exist in the past" is also correct. Nevertheless, it cannot be said that it does not exist, for what has once appeared, is.

Then also, it is not, because it was not.

Can it be said any other way or any more?

How can all this be possible? THAT manifests in an infinite diversity of ways and also as one integral Whole. Where is the language to express all this?

This is why a realized person is a muni–a silent one.

It is said that there is Being, there is Non-being, and yet neither Being nor Non-being.

That is not "the idea," but that is The Reality which cannot be merely believed but can only be known. This is why it is said: He who tells knows it not; he who knows tells it not. This is why the insightful simply opened themselves to Ma and let what happened happen. As the Christmas carol says:

How silently, how silently
The wondrous gift is given.
So God imparts to human hearts
The blessings of His heaven.

The same inexpressible Truth is experienced in two ways: as Self-luminous Silence, or as the Eternal Play of the One: He Himself playing all the parts.

Nothing more need be said.

In the aforesaid a state has been described where everything is burnt and transformed into the One, so that no trace of it

can be found in spite of all searching. To say that everything has been transformed into the One, means that here an element of obscurity has still remained; for this, surely, is not Self-realization–the Kingdom of Pure Consciousness has not yet come. There is no knowing when one may emerge from this "state of obscurity."

It is good to read this through carefully at least three times. And then let it alone.

When the kingdom of Pure Consciousness has been attained, Form is revealed as the Essence Itself.

That is it. But it does not end there:

What was sorrow from the worldly point of view is now viraha, separation from THAT, in other words, the agony of existing in a particular form.

Viraha is defined as "burning agony due to the separation from the Lord." The sorrow ordinarily experienced by human beings is based on their frustrations experienced in relative existence when their desires or aspirations are not fulfilled and the opposite is experienced instead. But this is not the sorrow experienced by the intent yogi who refuses to be satisfied or pacified by the world, but demands nothing less than union with the Absolute, because this really arises from his own Self as in the Biblical saying: "Deep calls out to deep" (Psalms 42:7).

The divine calls to the divine in two manners. One: The divine depth of being that is the Absolute Self calls, summons or attracts the divine depth of the individual Self that is one with It in essence. Two: the individual Self, because it is essentially one with the Absolute Self, equally calls to the Infinite with the same intensity.

The separation is only in the illusions of the individual Self, but its pain, its agony, is absolutely real and can only be calmed and fulfilled when there is union of the consciousness of both sides, the finite and the Infinite. As Saint Paul wrote: "Now we see through a glass [mirror], darkly [obscurely]; but then face to face: now I know in part; but then shall I know even as also I am known" (I Corinthians 13:12): finite divinity and Infinite Divinity that are essentially one, united in complete, total Knowing and Being. At first we see only reflections of each other, but in time through yoga sadhana we meet and know each other face-to-face in the eternal union of Being that is the true nature of both divinities.

But until this union and identity of essential being is permanently established:

> **This "separation" is without end, and manifests in ever new ways.**

Since the "separation" is only in the illusion-ridden mind of the individual Self, there is simply no end to the illusory separation until the condition of illusion itself is abrogated by the conscious awakening of the individual Self into its True Being that is the Absolute Self, and therefore has always been one with that Absolute Self. That separation is ended by the endeavors of the individual Self. It alone experiences separation while the Absolute is itself Conscious Unity in which separation cannot exist even as a concept.

> **By a mere stroke of God's imagination this vast universe comes into being. What actually is this creation? He Himself, the One.**

The entire universe is a concept within the Infinite Consciousness, arising therefrom and ultimately resolving back into It. And that concept itself is a manifestation of God, the Sole Existence.

> **Why then are there distinctions, why should there be "others"? There are no "others." The ocean is contained in the drop. How can this be?**

This can only make complete sense to those whose consciousness is illumined by the Supreme Self. The entire range of Infinite Consciousness is the single drop or point (bindu) that is the totality of conscious existence. From that single point everything spreads out as the entire field of relative existence, manifests for a time as the Many and then resolves back into its original state as Ekam Evam Adwityam: The One, Only Without A Second.

When the One reveals Himself as a form (vigraha)–say for instance, as Radha-Krishna–this vigraha exists eternally. Where? In Vrindavana.

Here Ma is referring to the level of divine existence and consciousness that is the Eternal Vrindavana of which the earthly Vrindavana is a feeble reflection/extension, however wondrous it is. Time does not exist for the Absolute. In reality everything happens simultaneously as an ideation in the Consciousness of Ishwara. It does not unwind like a motion picture, but happens in an eternal moment. Naturally we cannot conceive of this, but we can intuit it somewhat and therefore perceive it to some degree however slight.

All the divine forms that have ever appeared and ever will appear are present at this moment within the Divine Consciousness, and the adept yogi can perceive them according to the degree of his development. It is all a matter of direct experience, though inconceivable to the ordinary state of mind. "That which is non-existent can never come into being, and that which is can never cease to be. Those who have known the inmost Reality know also the nature of is and is not" (Bhagavad Gita 2:16). Yoga sadhana is the requisite.

For him, whose knots of the heart have been undone, only Vrindavana exists, and nothing else. What you have thus realized as Lila is infinite; and how will this infinity be known? By discarding the world and all that belongs to it?

No. For the world, the entire universe, is divine manifestation.

Sri Ramakrishna Paramahamsa said: "The Great Mother dances."

The entire range of relative existence and experience is the dance of Mahashakti, the Great Mother Whose very life encompasses every sentient being and the sentient realm in which they experience the Mother's dance. For All Is Consciousness.

Who is a Vaishnava [devotee of Vishnu]? One who sees Vishnu everywhere.

The true worshipper of God does not just accept and believe what others teach him about God. Rather, he experiences God everywhere at all times. Obviously, then, the only true believer in God is the awakened yogi who directly knows God through direct experience. For only the yogi's inner eye is opened to perceive the One Reality that is his inmost being as well as the entire range of existence.

The idea that the world has a boundary is delusive; consequently, the conception of many different powers is also an illusion.

The world is infinite because it is inseparable from that Infinity which is the essential being of everything–of existence itself. Furthermore, there is one essence, one existence: Parambrahman. Only the direct experience of Parambrahman, the Paramatman, is real. In her remarkable poem, "Illusion," Edna Wheeler Wilcox describes encounter with God in this way:

God and I in space alone
    And nobody else in view.
"And where are the people, O Lord!" I said.
"The earth below and the sky o'erhead
    And the dead whom once I knew?"

"That was a dream," God smiled and said,
"A dream that seemed to be true,
There were no people, living or dead,
There was no earth and no sky o'erhead
There was only Myself–and you."

"Why do I feel no fear," I asked,
"Meeting you here in this way,
For I have sinned I know full well,
And there is heaven and there is hell,
And is this the judgment day?"

"Nay, those were dreams," the great God said,
"Dreams that have ceased to be.
There are no such things as fear or sin,
There is no you–you have never been–
There is nothing at all but Me."

To use an Americanism: That pretty well sums it all up.

It is you who have created the distinction between the natural and the supernatural; as a matter of fact all and everything is but His Lila. In the All He is to be found. The supernatural is not apart [separate] **from the rest.**

Being one with all that is, God is the only natural thing that exists, so there is no "supernatural" in reality, only That Which IS. God is the only thing that exists–everything else is an adjunct dependent on God for its very existence, Who is its very existence. Understanding or believing this is of no consequence. All that matters is BEING That. Everything else needed will follow in time.

If one remains confined within the boundary, one's heart cannot become Vrindavana.

Only Infinity, our essential, boundless Being, is the inner Vrindavana of each one of us. And when our consciousness, our heart, is centered in that infinity which has no center, we are both Vrindavanis (those who live in Vrindavana) and Vrindavana itself. Then we will be Krishnamaya–literally formed of the Consciousness that is Sri Krishna.

> **When Realization has occurred, there is nothing but Vrindavana, nothing but Va, complete non-duality. Then only can it be said that the entire universe is His Divine Play.**

Otherwise we are only speaking in theory, but helpful theory which arouses us to go beyond words into the actualization of Divine Consciousness as our own being.

> **Prakriti** [the field of vibrating energy in which we experience everything], **which prompts one to distinguish between 'this' and 'that,' is also His.**

And therefore is ours to employ for our conscious evolution, no longer leaving anything to outside influence, but relying on the evidence of our own Self-experience.

> **In the state of Pure Being, the distinction between the natural and supernatural ceases to exist.**

For in Pure Being there is Pure Knowing that *is* the Supernatural. Therefore we say: "I am That." Not "I am Them."

> **When Consciousness is being revealed in its undivided Oneness, some find themselves in a pure Self-conscious Silence (Advaita), while It presents itself to others as His Divine Play.**

This is according to the mental conditioning, the bhava, of the mind. Either experience is right and true.

He is Form (vigraha), and at the same time He is not. The word samagra (whole, complete) denotes that sama (equality) comes first and foremost (agra). If it is not realized that equality comes first of all, it means that one will still observe from the viewpoint of the world, which is not advaita.

This is known as samadarshana: equal vision, seeing all things equally, equal-sightedness, and equanimity. All that. Nothing is left out.

Whereas, when advaita has been attained, this signifies the recovery of one's original state.

It is both Self-discovery and Self-revelation.

In worldly life one had been drowned in sorrow and affliction–drowned means obscured (by the veil)–all this has now been left behind and there is only THAT. His Presence has revealed itself in everything. One realizes that it is He alone who appears as being and also as becoming. Who is the pratibimba (reflection) of Reality? Also He alone.

I do not see any reason to comment on this. Having come this far, surely we easily get the idea.

In this condition–who can cause one pain or trouble? Your whole Being is now in a state of complete integration.

This is extremely important. Being complete, we understand that everything about us, inner or outer, is a manifestation of our own inmost bhava–disposition of mind. It is a revelation of our inner landscape. Being established in that, we neither trouble others nor are troubled by others. For our mind is centered in the unity that is the truth of ourselves and of all things.

The grief that made you miserable today has become the separation from the One.

Without the sense of separation from the Real outside and within us, suffering or misery is not possible. For our true state of being is the embodiment of Satchidananda–IS Satchidananda. Truly: Soham–I Am That.

Worldly sorrow comes through the sense of want, but to pine for God is man's true nature.

The lack of external things causes discontent and even misery, but recognizing the lack of internal realization stimulates us to seek for the Divine that is our true nature: our Self. Thus peace and happiness come to be our unbroken state, for we have at last Come Home.

What are the experiences of a seeker who contemplates God with form and attributes? At first he is engrossed solely in the particular deity (murti) he adores. Then, as he progresses, he begins to question: "Is my Beloved as small as that? No, indeed He dwells in Rama, Krishna, Shiva, Durga, and in all other deities. My Lord has many faces." At a later stage he comes to realize that his Beloved abides in every creature, and every creature in Him.

Here Ma describes the way this inevitable condition arises spontaneously in the sadhaka as he worships a divine form. It will happen if the worship is genuine. So by this we also know the true and the false "seeker." The true seeker finds; the fake seeker keeps on wandering and calling it "seeking."

On this pilgrimage there are many lines of approach, and along each of them there are many states and stages.

So the beginning pilgrim faces a great many choices and the necessity for a great deal of self-understanding through self-discipline. Everything is in his hands. If he does not have a clear concept of his ultimate goal, he is in grave danger of delusion and failure. Once again: "Sharp as the edge of a razor and hard to cross, difficult to tread is that path [so] sages declare" (Brihadaranyaka Upanishad 1.3.14).

As Jesus said: "Strait [extremely narrow] is the gate, and narrow [extremely difficult; extremely laborious] is the way, which leadeth unto life, and few there be that find it" (Matthew 7:14). And fewer follow it, and even fewer persevere and succeed in it. This is my conclusion after many years' observation. "But he that endureth to the end shall be saved" (Matthew 10:22). There are many ways to the one way, and the wise pilgrim walks them all.

> **The development along one particular line is described in the following: To begin with, one is convinced that none can be likened to one's own chosen deity. If this attitude does not prevail at the start, deep devotion cannot be developed. However, by and by, as one's faith and adoration grow, one comes to feel that one's Beloved is no other than the One. One's intense love and veneration will not allow one any longer to hold a petty conception of Him.**

This needs no comment, but does merit a careful rereading and self-examination to see if Ma's words are being followed by actual endeavor and self-honest scrutiny.

> **The sadhaka's humility and devotion increase; at last he realizes that ultimately the One is in everything and everything in Him. In the One he has now rediscovered the form of his own Beloved. From the seed the tree has grown, and the tree has again yielded the same kind of seed.**
>
> ***Devo bhutwa devam yajet.* "Only by becoming identified with the Lord can one worship Him."**

This is the whole picture in the proverbial nutshell. But Ma alone presents us with such clear and profound nutshells.

If after Self-realization, after one's essential Being has revealed Itself, one still performs the worship of one's particular deity, it means engaging in one's own worship. This is Lila.

Inquirer: Whose Lila?

There is only God's Lila. Whose could it possibly be?

Jai Ma!

TWENTY-THREE

Benares, March 20th, 1949.

Inquirer: If God is not different from the world, why should so much stress be laid on maintaining it?

> **No stress at all is laid on this. Whether the world exists or not, the question does not even arise.**

Reading this I was reminded of a nineteenth-century lecturer who was told by a woman, "I have at last become reconciled to the existence of the universe." His brief response was to the point: "You had jolly well better!"

The question of existence-non-existence, reality-unreality and such like are irrelevant. The questions *Why* Do I Exist? *Who* Am I? and *What* Am I? are the core necessity. And only the yogi will ever find out the answers through direct knowledge-experience. The world can take care of itself, but we have been put in charge of a body-mind-spirit complex through which we are meant to evolve. Doing so should be our main interest.

It is not a matter of intellectualizing and playing with the mind like a bouncing ball. True knowing is beyond the mind. Just a step or so, but still: beyond. Sadhana is the only way beyond, though the ego-mind is able to work up a lot of false ways to distract us. The sum is this: We must work on ourselves. In the brilliant Pogo comic strip there was a panel in which someone said: "We have met the enemy and they are us!"

The Bhagavad Gita explains what is needed very well: "What is man's will and how shall he use it? Let him put forth its power to uncover the Atman, not hide the Atman: man's will is the only friend of the Atman: his will is also the Atman's enemy. For when a man is self-controlled, his will is the Atman's friend. But the will of an uncontrolled man is hostile to the Atman, like an enemy. That serene one absorbed in the Atman masters his will, he knows no disquiet in heat or in cold, in pain or pleasure, in honor, dishonor" (Bhagavad Gita 6:5-7). "The recollected mind is awake in the knowledge of the Atman" (Bhagavad Gita 2:69). The adept yogi rests in his own Self.

Inquirer: Some hold the opinion that the vision of the Munis who attained to Brahman was incomplete, because they lost the world. They further contend that the world will remain as it is in name and form. This seems as impossible as for a stone cup to be described as golden.

> **Those who hold these opinions have not attained to Oneness. They have kept themselves aloof from the world and yet speak of saving it. Although they do not know what the existing world is actually like, they want to establish a new kingdom. By realizing that the whole universe is THAT, and nothing but THAT, it is transformed. This much may be said.**
>
> **To declare that the world ever remains what it is now means that the world as such is still perceived. Moreover, what have I gained or lost by discussing the world? There is no question of denying the existence of the world by declaring that it is alien from God; and there is no question either of whether it exists or not.**
>
> **It is said that He is in diversity as well as in oneness–just like water and ice. Where water is called ice, that is to say, where space and form appear, there form is also He. Why do you not grasp this? Vapor as vapor will never become water as such.**

Careful and thoughtful reading is needed here. Then we will have gotten the right idea.

Now let's plunge into a lengthy exchange.

Inquirer: So far as theory of evolution holds good, there is diversity as well as identity.

Someone else: Worldly knowledge is of the many, and the Knowledge of Reality (Brahmajnana) is of Oneness; how can both exist together in the same place?

Inquirer: The oneness of Reality is not in contradiction to multiplicity. Generally speaking one can distinguish four planes:

(1) The world alone appears, in other words, diversity; this is the plane of ignorance.

(2) At times the world or the many appear and at other times Oneness, which is Reality; this is the plane of nirvikalpa samadhi in yoga.

(3) The world appears, reposing within the Brahman.

Inquirer: There is no world! This is how it appears. When light removes darkness, how can darkness be still perceived? Brahman is everyone's fulfillment and nobody's obstacle. That which is Chaitanya (Pure Consciousness) is Itself this and that object. But according to the people mentioned above, there are two: Form, as well as Pure Consciousness. However, I should say, what appears as form is nothing but Pure Consciousness.

Even so, you have to speak of form?

Inquirer: Yes, I speak of form, because I see its essence. My son is acting the part of Rama, yet I know that he is my son. If the knowledge of the world does not persist when Brahman is realized, the possibility of jivanmukti, which is a fact, cannot be established, for the simple reason that for such a one contact with the world is impossible. For him fire and water are both expressions of the one Brahman; consequently he might swallow fire instead of drinking water.

According to some doctrines, perfection has not been attained so long as "this" (the world) is perceived. There is a stage beyond it where there is no more duality, and one becomes established on the plane of Oneness. This should be understood to represent the fourth of the four planes previously mentioned. (These planes are different from the seven planes spoken of in yoga.) I consider the third plane the highest; namely the play of duality rooted in Oneness. In other words, on this plane there is oneness in duality and duality in oneness. He who is liberated may nevertheless come out into the world and seem to act like an ordinary man, while his Realization remains perfectly intact. *Sarvam kalvidam Brahman*–All this is Brahman–and *neti, neti* are not contradictory in the least.

On this plane, the whole and the part exist in the same place; although there is a difference between the two, namely, the whole and the parts: flowers and leaves are different, yet they belong to the same tree. This is why I will not acknowledge the difference of one part from the other, nor of the parts from the whole. Am I wrong when I understand it in this way?

> **Whatever is said is correct from the standpoint from which it is said. In dhyana or samadhi there comes a stage where there is no possibility even of perceiving a second besides the One. There, the behavior that arises out of duality cannot occur. What is referred to here, is a state in which there is no movement, although there appears to be. How can movement be possible here? When such a person is seen acting, someone may perhaps remark: "He has descended in order to do some particular work." When an M.A. reads the a b c does he thereby lose his status as an M.A.? There is a state, where nothing can possibly appear as a "second."**

We must realize this.

> **Having dived into the Ganges, one is bound to be wholly drenched. When established in Pure Being, one does not stray from it anymore.**

This is a most important statement. Enlightenment does not come and go, increase or decrease. Illumination is permanent because the individual is irrevocably established in total union with Absolute Consciousness that Itself is Absolute Unity and changeless. But there are two expressions it is good to consider. First is that the consciousness that has entered the Ganga of Supreme Consciousness is totally united with that consciousness, not just in unity but in union–in absolute oneness/identity with That. Furthermore, establishment in Pure Being is total and permanent. Nothing remains to be experienced or attained. As the ancient verse says: "This is the Purna [Full/Complete]. That is the Purna. If we take the Purna away from the Purna, the Purna alone remains." For it is a matter of identity of essential being.

> **However, before one's status has ripened to perfect maturity, one may have occasional lapses; but what has once been realized will, as it were, draw one back to itself.**

Therefore he who has truly set his feet upon the Path To The Infinite will not deviate from it or abandon it to any degree whatsoever because it is a matter of one's individual, essential being, his unchangeable essence, in revelation-manifestation. Forward is the only direction the fully awakened sadhaka can move, for it is no longer a matter of affinity or will, but one of eternal, ever-present Identity.

> **At this stage there is oscillation between two directions; yet it is a marvelous state, not one of ignorance.**

Rather, it is one of beginning awakening.

> **The next stage is bhava.**

By "bhava" Ma is referring to bhava samadhi, the superconscious state in which the devotee retains his ego and enjoys communion with the Personal God.

> **One enters and leaves it alternately, becoming immersed, and then floating once more on the surface.**

At this point the sadhaka moves in and out of immersion in this state much as a dyer keeps dipping a cloth in a dye vat, at each dip increasing the intensity and permanence of the color until the desired state of complete coloring is irreversible and therefore permanent.

Going still further, even this state passes, and one becomes absolutely inert like a stone.

By "inert" Ma means totally unaffected, unchanged or unaltered by any subsequent experience of condition–not unconscious or unresponsive. That perfect, irrevocable and permanent transmutation of consciousness becomes the sadhaka's very nature, for he has entered into his Original Being after long wanderings and changes within the field of samsara. But he is now at all times chinmaya: full of consciousness; verily formed of Consciousness Itself. The state of Soham, of I Am That, prevails because it is truly the Original Face of the individual jiva. What has always been is now revealed unchanged and unchangeable.

If one has not arrived at this rock-like inertness, and is still experiencing ecstatic fervor with its ups and downs–this is not a perfect, although a supernormal state. It is like being alternately in a cool room and going outside into the heat. Then comes perfection, complete and final immersion. When this has taken place, he who has achieved it is still seen to move and act as you do, but actually he neither goes anywhere, nor eats, nor does he perceive anything.

This is a totally inner condition, not arising from or dependent on anything external. It is *bhavatitam, trigunarahitam*: beyond states of mind and the three gunas which produce those states. The sadhaka becomes himself The Changeless through the alchemy of sadhana. Yet there is no becoming, since the state is eternal, outside time, space and change. As Ma continually stated, That is beyond words and concepts and therefore cannot be expressed. Yet it can be hinted at enough to enable the awakening consciousness of the sadhaka to grasp and move forward in the realm of awakening that is of course really The Great Return to his original state–and becoming established permanently in the consciousness that is his Self.

Inquirer: This sounds like a contradiction in terms: he eats, yet does not eat; he goes, yet does not go–how can this be?

> **Once immersed, one will have to be stabilized in that condition, where the inner and the outer have fused into one. I eat as you do, go about the same as you do. If one feels that the statement "he eats and yet does not eat" is self-contradictory, then one's "realization" of the Brahman is of a piecemeal variety.**
>
> **There is no ground for contradiction.**
>
> **How can Oneness be limited? By limitation it would be broken up. This is why it was said that there is no question of eating or not eating, and so on. However, it is difficult to understand, even in part, whether someone is asleep or in samadhi. Gold and brass look more or less alike. But when gold has been touched, one is transformed into it.**
>
> **How can one who lives on the plane of the Brahman see petty differences? Due to your partial vision you perceive incongruity. There is in fact no question of having realized or being in ignorance. If someone calls himself a "man of Realization," he thereby assumes a certain position.**
>
> **What does Self-realization signify? Knowledge, all-comprehensive and unlimited in every respect. What you have been, nay, what you are in reality, becomes revealed. From whatever line of approach or attitude of mind anyone may hold any view, everything is right. Just as you say: "He walks without feet, He sees without eyes." If limited by any place or qualification, by any form or mode, be it through inclusion or exclusion–the Realization is not full, not complete. What is expressed from any standpoint is seen from that particular angle, in a particular way; for space and time have remained. This body does not falsify matters, it speaks the exact truth. Everything is correct from the point of view from which it is said.**

This is absolute perfection. How can I touch it with any words of mine?

Inquirer: If as you declare, everything is correct, then suppose someone, wishing to have darshana of Vishwanatha goes to a Durga temple and says "This is Vishwanatha," is this also correct?

> **At a certain level one may rightly say: "Yes, this is Vishwanatha," because at that moment, it will be Vishwanatha. The Vishwanatha now thought of in his mind will reveal Himself as exactly the same as the Vishwanatha limited by time and space. For everything is contained in everything. But it may also be said that Vishwanatha is not in a temple of Durga; Truth can be expressed in many ways. All kinds of replies may be given.**

Yes, and this is an absolutely stupid objection on the part of "Inquirer." Fools flocked around Ma just as wise and learned people did, and the jackasses brayed loudly at times. I started very early on in this commentary to say this but decided to remain "nice." But enough is enough.

Inquirer: If whatever anyone says is correct, why then did Sri Shankaracharya, who was a man of Realization (Brahmajnani), refute the arguments of his opponents?

> **Whenever it is necessary that anything should be done, it will be done without fail. The top of the tree contains its root, because the seeds are everywhere present; there is no contradiction.**

I am sure that did not clarify anything for "Inquirer," but it will for the clear-sighted sadhaka.

Twenty Four

You want to know whether Grace (ahetuka kripa) is without cause or reason? Certainly; for Grace is by its very nature beyond cause or reason.

This is because it is innate in God and in God's creation/manifestation, and in time produces profound inner awareness of God in the aspirant. Everything in the universe is grace. Our very manifestation in this universe is kripa–divine grace and mercy–because its ultimate purpose and effect is conscious union with God in perfect Self-realization, for God is the infinite Self of our finite self. The very purpose of true yoga is the realization-experience and practical manifestation of this reality.

When working, one reaps the fruit of one's actions. If, for instance, you serve your father and he, being pleased with your service, gives you a present, this would be called the fruit of action. One does something and receives something in return.

But the eternal relationship that by nature exists between father and son, does surely not depend on any action. The Supreme Father, Mother and Friend–verily, God is all of these. Consequently, how can there be a cause or reason for His Grace?

You are His, and in whatever way He may draw you to Him, it is for the sake of revealing Himself to you.

This is Living Grace which is our own essential nature as it is the essential nature of God, the Divine Archetype of every sentient–and especially the human–being. The primary action of God toward every sentient being is the drawing of that being upward and finally into the Divine Being which is our eternal Essence. "One's Self, indeed, is the arrow. Brahman is spoken of as the target of that. It is to be hit without making a mistake. Thus one becomes united with it as the arrow [becomes one with the target]" (Mundaka Upanishad 2.2.4).

> **The desire to find Him that awakens in man–who has instilled it into you? Who is it that makes you work for its fulfillment?**
>
> **Thus you should try to arrive at the understanding that everything originates from Him.**

The entire journey to Self-realization is initiated in the depths of our being, is a part of our original makeup which impels us to total realization of the Self which is inseparable from Brahman the Absolute. We can reasonably call it Soham Consciousness, the very consciousness: I Am That. Complete knowledge of this principle is itself Self-realization. It is the beginning, the middle and the end of our evolutionary journey.

> **Whatever power, whatever skill you possess–why, even you yourself–from where does everything arise? And does it not all have for purpose the finding of Him, the destroying of the veil of ignorance?**

Therefore those who do not put their entire focus and endeavor in the attainment of Self-realization are ignoring the sole purpose of their existence. Where will they find any place for themselves in this universe which has been manifested for that purpose if they do not put forth their entire attention and endeavor for that attainment? As Yogananda said, humanity is divided into two types: the wise that seek God and the foolish who do not. To be a true human being is to seek God.

> **Whatever exists has its origin in Him alone. So then, you must try to realize yourself.**

Let's get busy!

> **Are you master even of a single breath? To whatever small degree He makes you feel that you have freedom of action, if you understand that this freedom has to be used to aspire after the realization of Him, it will be for your good.**
>
> **But if you regard yourself as the doer, and God as being far away, and if, owing to His apparent remoteness, you work for the gratification of your desires, it is wrong action.**

Read and remember.

> **You should look upon all things as manifestations of Him.**

This is not possible without the opening of the divine eye, the highest consciousness that is our essential nature. That is why the attainment of liberation (moksha) is called Self-realization. It is true, however, that there are two steps to fulfillment of our eternal destiny. 1) Self-realization and 2) God-realization. They are really two aspects of one thing, but thinking of them as two makes sadhana easier as a concept and practice.

> **When you recognize the existence of God, He will reveal Himself to you as compassionate, or gracious, or merciful, in accordance with your attitude towards Him at the time. Just as, for example, to the humble He becomes the Lord of the Humble.**

Actually the usual term for this aspect of God is Dinabandhu: The Friend Of The Lowly/Humble.

> **If you say: "He is immutable, yet He also acts," you call Him the doer, when in reality He is actionless.**

But we have to speak from the level we are on at the present. We have to be like the son of a friend of mine. He and his mother were watching television, and by special effect a man playing a piano appeared to rise up along with the piano and start making somersaults in the air. His mother said to herself aloud: "I wonder how they do that?" Nicky said: "I know! There's a magician hiding in the piano!"

> **Since your ego sees itself as the doer, you think of Him as equally performing action.**

That is, we project onto God what we perceive in ourself. As the old saying claims, in our limited powers of conception we make God in *our* image.

> **Of course, He is whatever you take Him to be.**

Does this imply that we can cause God to interact with us according to our conception and expectations of Him? We are made in the image of God, but does God make Himself over into our image? Something to ponder.

> **On the other hand, where THAT is, just think: Who is to become the doer of what action, and upon what is he to act?**

Pause and ponder. And then consider:

> **He walks without feet, He sees without eyes, He hears without ears, and eats without a mouth–in whatever way you may describe Him, so He is.**

Just accept it and be in awe of such a sublime reality.

> **When a sadhaka starts worshipping a vigraha (form) of his Beloved, he will in the course of his practice attain to a condition in which the form of his Beloved is beheld, wherever his eyes may fall.**

This occurs in two ways. 1) He will actually see the Beloved's form, or 2) intellectually consider ("see") that all forms are forms of the Beloved.

One is visual, the other is intellectual. Both are valid and may occur simultaneously.

> **Next he comes to realize: "All other deities are contained in my Beloved." He sees that everyone's Lord, in fact all things, are contained in his own Ishta, and that his Ishta also dwells in all deities, as indeed, in everything.**

No comment needed.

> **The sadhaka comes to feel: "As my Lord resides within me, so He, who is present within everyone else, is truly the same Lord. In water and on land, in trees, shrubs and creepers–everywhere in the whole universe abides my Beloved. Further, all the various forms and modes of being that we behold, are they not expressions of my Beloved? For there is none save Him. He is smaller than the smallest, and greater than the greatest."**

No comment is needed here, either.

> **Actuated by your various inborn tendencies, you each worship a different deity.**

The mind is a field of vibrating energy and is attracted to, neutral toward, or repelled, by objects according the affinity of their vibration with his mind-vibration. This produces attraction, neutrality and repulsion/aversion toward virtually every thing, including divine forms.

> **The true progress in one's spiritual experience depends on the sincerity and intensity of one's aspiration.**

Once some disciples of Yogananda asked that he bless them to do/be better. He simply remarked: "You already have my blessing. What is missing is your blessing." Here Ma indicates that true progress in spiritual life comes from the elements put into it by the sadhaka: sincerity and intensity of aspiration.

I hope it is not too tiresome that I frequently cite the statement about the Westward Expansion in nineteenth-century America: "the weak died along the way and the cowards never started," but it fits here. From the very first the sadhaka must be utterly sincere and intense–self-empowered–in his sadhana. This requires a clear-sighted understanding of the implications of taking up spiritual life which is nothing less than total spiritual self-transformation.

A realistic conception of oneself as an aspirant and the nature of the goal to be attained, as well as its manner of attainment, is an absolute requirement for success. Frankly, most "aspirants" are like damp firecrackers: they get lit, spit, fizzle and shake a bit, and then go dead.

As the wise Solomon wrote: "Better is it that thou shouldest not vow, than that thou shouldest vow and not pay" (Ecclesiastes 5:5).

I want to repeat here the words of a hymn I have cited before:

So straight is the gate and so narrow
The way to eternal day,
And few are the pilgrims who find it,
Too great is the price they must pay.

Salvation is free, yet to gain it
The soul must leave all things behind;
Deny self and follow the Savior,
The way straight and narrow to find.

How rugged the path, yet God's glory
Attendeth each soul on that way;
And brighter and brighter it shineth,
Revealing a glad, perfect day.

But it's worth all it costs to be holy,
It is worth all it costs to be true;

God's blessing and honor shall crown thee
With power thy life to endue.

And that power is God's power, so we must be able to handle it, to foster it, to increase it and make it permanent in our lives–for it IS our life.

The true sadhaka lives with wide-open eyes at all times.

The measure of a person's spiritual advance will be reflected in the manifestations that are vouchsafed to him of his Ishta, who will by no means remain inaccessible or separate from His devotee, but let Himself be contacted in an infinite variety of ways.

Now this is no nonsense. And if this does not become the actual experience of the sadhaka then something essential is lacking in him or his sadhana–or both. Here are the points Ma makes:

1) His Ishta devata will be revealed as accessible to and one with him–inseparable from him.

2) In various ways–even of an infinite number–his Ishta devata will be in contact with him, living his life right along with him.

This is not poetry or emotional rhapsody, but simple unvarnished truth. And sadhana that does not produce this result eventually is not true sadhana at all.

Conditioned though you be, you will find the All within you and on the other hand, be able to grasp that your own innate tendencies are also part of this All.

The successful sadhaka will remain what he has been, but will find the Infinite within and without. Further, he will see and experience that every aspect of his being, including his innate qualities, are parts of Infinite Being. For he is one with the Infinite Being.

What has been said here represents one point of view.

Although these are Her words, Ma wants us to realize that there are other viewpoints besides, that we must not think they are all-embracing and all-inclusive. They are part of the Divine Whole which was manifesting in/as Anandamayi Ma.

> **You cannot dissociate yourself from the Whole. The multifarious kinds of beasts, birds, men and so forth–what are they all? What are these varieties of shapes, of modes of being, what is the essence within them? What really are these ever-changing forms?**

Everything is THE ONE.

> **Gradually, slowly, because you are rapt in the contemplation of your Beloved, He becomes revealed to you in every one of them; not even a grain of sand is excluded. You realize that water, earth, plants, animals, birds, human beings, are nothing but forms of your Beloved.**

The Universal Vision does not just blaze forth like a flash of lightning. Since it is a matter of each one's enlightenment, it is truly a gradual and slow–but never reversing or fading–revelation of the All as truly ALL. As Ma points out, it includes everything from smallest to largest, from the most gross to the most subtle. Since everything is The One, we are not seeing true if our inner vision does not embrace and reveal The One in every single particle of relative existence/manifestation.

"Utterly quiet, made clean of passion, the mind of the yogi knows that Brahman: his bliss is the highest. Released from evil his mind is constant in contemplation: the way is easy, Brahman has touched him, that bliss is boundless. His heart is with Brahman, his eye in all things sees only Brahman equally present, knows his own Atman in every creature, and all creation within that Atman. That yogi sees me in all things, and all things within me. He never loses sight of me, nor I of him" (Bhagavad Gita 6:27-30).

Some experience it in this manner–realization does not come to everyone in the same way. There are infinite possibilities.

We should keep this in mind, realizing that realization, or its expression, can be vastly different from sadhaka to sadhaka, that truly "there are infinite possibilities."

Consequently, the specific path along which for any particular person the Universal will reveal itself in its boundlessness remains concealed from the average individual.

Therefore the wise sadhaka is very careful in making an evaluation of another sadhaka's approach or experience. The "average individual," of course, will usually have no relevant impression or opinion whatsoever in this matter of another's sadhana path and its results, much less his own (if any). Consequently, the wise sadhaka fixes his attention on his own sadhana and makes that the focus of his thought and action. "Tend to your own knitting" was the adage I grew up with. Of course, you have to have some knitting of your own to attend to.

What you have just heard in the discourse on the Shrimad Bhagavatam about the universal body of the Lord, which comprises all things–trees, flowers, leaves, hills, mountains, rivers, oceans, and so forth–a time will come, must come, when one actually perceives this all-pervading Universal Form of the One.

So that account is not a wonder to be amazed about and impressed by, but a realization to be actively anticipated and sought after.

The variety of His shapes and guises is infinite, uncountable, without end.

"He who is multi-formed, who constantly creates and destroys these His forms, He is the One whom I adore." To the degree that you grow in the ever fuller and wider recognition

of this truth, you will realize your oneness with each of these numberless forms.

Our perception and understanding of/in these things is a matter of growth, of development, of evolution. Therefore the wise sadhaka daily expands the scope of his highest perceptions through constant japa and meditation.

Sadhana is a very real thing that produces very real effects.

In this immensity there are diverse shapes, diverse modes, manifested in diverse ways, without end, without number–and yet there is end and number.

In the Absolute there is both infinity and finitude. This must be, because duality is the keynote of all relative existence. Of course, in the Absolute Being unity/duality and infinity/finitude are concepts or ever-present potentials. Otherwise nothing could arise from Infinite Being into manifestation. Death has to be inherent in birth. For though the simplistic-minded like to harp on Unity and Oneness, that is only one half of the equation and therefore partial and limited. And, frankly, small-minded and intellectually dim. Without the foundation of yoga sadhana, the higher faculties of the human being cannot possibly come into function and Ma's words cannot possibly be rightly understood, or in the right perspective.

When a sadhaka enters this state, he becomes conscious of the perpetual transformation of all forms and moods. He awakens to true understanding; that is to say, he comes to realize that the Supreme Himself manifests as the power of understanding.

The sadhaka enters–becomes conscious and awakens to–Reality which is both Truth and The True Itself. For he is what he perceives, since knower, knowing and known are one. Otherwise they could not inter-react with/on/in one another. It is crucial for the yogi to understand that if his perceptions and responses are not understood as fundamentally conceptions/

ideations he cannot have a right perspective regarding them. It brings to mind something I read decades ago: "It is not a matter of knowing the truth, but of knowing The True." Further, when he perceives anything his response is recognition of it as The True in manifestation, and even an extension of his own Self (Consciousness). And regarding himself he has but one word: Soham. I AM THAT.

> **When the current of one's thinking that was directed towards worldly matters is reversed and turned inwards, the One Himself becomes revealed as the "secret skill."**

For inner awareness is also inner being, from which arises inner action, which manifests as outer action, which remains essentially internal in being. This is not mere juggling of words, but an attempt to encompass in words what can really only be directly perceived in the depths of one's own being. Therefore all that is external is in essence internal. Otherwise the external could not exist, since only the internal is real.

> **Look at the ever-changing world, where what exists at one moment is non-existent the next, where being is continually entering into non-being–who then is this non-being? Even the non-existent exists.**

There really is no non-being. There is only Being appearing as both manifest and unmanifest, being and non-being. In unity how can duality even be perceived? This is the Great Mystery.

None of this is a matter of awakening or not awakening, of perceiving or not perceiving. It is a matter of BEING. Duality cannot even come into it. The basic need is for the sadhaka to BE. Nothing more.

> **In this connection it must be said that if one wants to find Truth, everything will have to be realized as it is in its own place, without choosing one thing rather than another.**

Evaluation and preference are mayic in essence. The principle of essential Consciousness is the whole.

> **It is a Kingdom without end, in which even what is discerned as non-existence is equally an expression of the One.**

For The One is the sole reality. Existence and non-existence are its lila which exists only in consciousness, not external reality. For there is no external.

> **In Chinmayi, the purely spiritual world, all forms–whatever they be–are ever eternal. Therefore, simultaneously and in the same place, there is non-existence as well as existence, and also neither non-existence, nor existence–and more of the kind if you can proceed further!**

There is no need to intellectually understand this. Only to be (not become) Chinmayi.

> **Very well, just as ice is nothing but water, so the Beloved is without form, without quality, and the question of manifestation does not arise.**

And where, then, is the question of relationship either regarding, toward, or with That?

> **When this is realized, one has realized one's Self.**

Realization is seeing, experiencing and knowing and ultimately: becoming.

> **For, to find the Beloved is to find my Self, to discover that God is my very own, wholly identical with myself, my innermost Self, the Self of my Self.**

Then, according to the exigency of time and circumstance, various possibilities may take effect; as for example, the revelation of mantras and even of the entire Vedas by the ancient Rishis, who were seers of mantras.

All this will occur in consonance with the individual karma and inner disposition of the person concerned.

This final statement is most significant, because we usually consider that the ultimate realization can only occur when "the individual karma and inner disposition of the person concerned" cease to even exist!

When a sadhaka realizes what form and formlessness essentially are, it is indeed a consummate Realization.

He comes to know what bhava is, the inner relation of form to the Shabda Brahman, numerous types of language–endless in variety–and he also realizes language as Shabda Brahman.

Sounds, numberless in kind, manifest themselves before him, each in its own characteristic visual shape; this is so where all forms become visible.

All the same, form is really void; one sees that freedom from form means the realization that form itself is the void.

In this way the world reveals itself as void, before merging into the Great Void (Mahashunya).

No one is going to intellectually understand this because it is a state beyond the mind and intellect, manasa and buddhi. But it can be intuited. Some trace must remain in that Moment, or Ma would not have said this. So there must be a practical understanding/application of this principle at some point.

The void that is perceived within the world is a part of prakriti, and therefore still form. From this void one will have to proceed to the Great Void.

I believe I comprehend this to some degree, but it seems best to let it be.

> **It is the perception of the world, based upon the identification of yourself with body and mind, that has all along been the source of your bondage.**

Fake Vedantists are fond of intoning: I Am That. But their actual basis is what Ma describes in this sentence.

> **A time will come, when this kind of perception will give way before the awakening of universal consciousness, which will reveal itself as an aspect of Supreme Knowledge.**

It is universal, but only an aspect. But we must experience that to truly know it and know both what it is and it is not.

> **When this Knowledge of the Essence of Things has come, what happens to the Essence Itself? Ponder over this!**

This is extremely interesting. Does knowing something affect that thing? We easily consider that the knower is affected, but how can the known become affected by the knowing of the knower? Perhaps it is because knower, knowing and known are one? This is a well-known principle, but Ma's words open a completely new and unsuspected area or aspect to the matter. Of course there is a statement that knowing, known and knower are ultimately one, but Ma seems to propose a further insight to be gained. Ma does not say that our perception of the Essence is modified, but that the knowing of the knower has a very real effect on that Essence we assume is transcendental and beyond possibility of being affected or changed. Does identity with the Essence make it subject to change, real or apparent? Does the Essence change, or does the knower change?

> **When insight into form and the formless dawns in its boundlessness, everything will be uprooted. On transcending**

the level where form, diversity, manifestation exist, one enters into a state of formlessness.

Therefore Ma seems to be implying that formlessness is the primal or original state that is also a power or force of some kind that affects both the seer and the seen.

I think that it/this is a matter of realization, not intellectual elucidation. In the Upanishads many times someone becomes threatened that if they do a certain thing, "your head will fall off." I think that perhaps there are some of Ma's statements that would at least metaphysically result in someone's head symbolically falling off if they attempted to either understand or explain something beyond their comprehension. It might be a state of transcendental insight, but I do not think I should try, lest in time, like a little cousin of mine used to say, "I feel a fool of myself!"

What can this be called? Godhead, the Paramatma Himself.

As the individual self becomes gradually freed from all fetters, which are nothing but the veil of ignorance, it realizes its oneness with the Supreme Spirit (Paramatma) and becomes established in its own Essential Being.

No explanation or exposition is needed. Ma's words are perfection.

Now to another aspect of the matter.

Everyone has his own path. Some, advancing along the line of Vedanta, find, as they progress, the path of a Rishi opening out for them. To others also, whose spiritual practices, worship, or yoga, proceed with the help of images and other intermediary aids, the same path of a Rishi may become disclosed.

In the Bhagavad Gita (5:4-5) we are told: "The yoga of action, say the ignorant, is different from the yoga of the knowledge of Brahman. The wise see knowledge and action as one: they see truly. Take either path and tread it to the end: the end is the same. There the followers of action meet the seekers after knowledge in equal freedom" (Bhagavad Gita 5:5).

> **Yet others, guided by voices and locutions from the unseen, at first hear these voices as audible sounds, but gradually hear them in perfect language, conveying the full significance of what is expressed. By and by it becomes evident that these voices arise from one's own Self, and that they are He Himself, manifesting in that particular way.**

This is most interesting and certainly novel, since usually such phenomena are declared either self-originated or delusional. But Ma affirms that this is a well-established sequence of self-illumination. Naturally, the ego and ignorance being what they are, a spurious version of this can occur to the ignorant and self-deluded. Therefore the wise sadhaka is always cautious and questioning in regard to any phenomena or experience.

> **No matter what be anyone's line of approach, in due course the path of a Rishi or a similar path may open out for him in one manner or another. But at what time this will occur and to whom, is beyond the ken of the ordinary person's understanding.**

This is a valuable principle. As we follow a path, that path can open up or evolve into further paths in differing ways. It is beyond the sadhaka's comprehension, but he must be prepared for its possibility.

> **Well, now suppose a man follows his own specific path, which happens to be the worship of a deity. Who actually is present as that particular deity? Certainly the One, who is the formless Self!**
>
> **Consequently, just as the formless Self is He, so is the concrete object of worship.**

Therefore, worship of both form and formless are completely legitimate, and such worship leads to perception/realization of the Absolute, the Supreme Self. Both abstract and concrete concepts aid in leading the mind to direct perception of the Reality that is both behind and embodied in them.

> **One who by the method of Veddi has become fully established in the Self, may also find the Supreme Reality in the vigraha (form), just as water is contained in ice. He will then come to see that all vigrahas (forms) are really spiritual forms of the One. For what is hidden in ice? Water of course.**

I can find no reference to the word "Veddi," which may be a mispelling of "Vedi," which means the altar on/in which the sacrificial fire is kindled for the Vedic Yajna (Sacrifice). It is certainly believed that such rituals rightly performed by the truly qualified can open them to higher consciousness which can develop into perfect Self-knowledge.

Although that approach is focused on the Formless Reality, Ma says that it can lead to realization of the Divine manifesting as Form. The simile of formless, fluidic water that can be frozen into a solid substance with form is common in Vedantic writings. For the Absolute Being as Pure Consciousness is manifesting in both form and formlessness. The mind of the purified and insightful worshipper can perceive that wood, stone or metal are all manifestations of Divine Consciousness. So it is possible to become established in that Consciousness through worship of images made of wood, stone or metal–especially since modern Quantum Physics has established that matter and consciousness are essentially the same.

> **Where He is present as the All, in that ice there are stages of melting, like solid and semi-solid ice. But in the pure Self the question of stages cannot arise.**

For the Self cannot change and exists beyond the realm of possible change or stages of change.

> **Although ice may be melting, yet it had become ice, and the possibility of its existing as such again is there. Consequently, for Him who Himself manifests in the form of ice, there can be no question of the eternal or the non-eternal.**

For He is Consciousness Itself which is beyond modification or change. It is only vibrating energy, Prakriti, that manifests as form and change.

> **Hence one speaks of dvaita-dvaita** [dvaita-advaita], **signifying that dualism and non-dualism are both facts–just as you are father and son all at once. How can there be a son without a father, or a father without a son?**
>
> **In this way one sees that neither of the two is less important than the other and that here there can be no distinction between higher and lower; there is only equality, sameness.**

That is perfectly clear and comprehensible.

> **However, there is a place where one can actually speak of higher and lower states. Each of the two standpoints is complete in itself.**
>
> **(No simile can be applicable in every detail, therefore take note only of that much for which it is intended.)**

Sometimes we must have to realize that things are as they are, and leave it at that.

> **Thus: both water and ice partake of the nature of eternity.**

That is, they alternate between the states of form [ice] and formless [water], but they are always only water and therefore essentially formless. The state of ice is temporary, but the state of water is constant.

> **Likewise, He is as indubitably with form as He is without.**

There are those whose minds are so obsessed with non-duality as real and duality as unreal, momentary or only apparent, that they simply have to be able to declare which of the two is real, and which is mere appearance, implying that one is real and the other is not. As another cousin of mine used to say: "Children must play."

> **When with form–which is compared to ice–He appears in the guise of countless shapes and modes, each one of them His own Spiritual Form (Chinmayi Vigraha).**

Each one is real, and each one is He in essence. None is the truest or the best or the most real. For all the forms are the One Reality appearing as many.

> **Depending on one's avenue of approach, prominence is given to one particular form.**

This is the activity of the conditioned mind. All forms are the One Undivided Consciousness, but the conditioned individual and his ego just must have a favorite or a best or a most real, etc., etc., etc. But that is also part of the dream existence, not part of the reality.

> **Why should there be so many different religious sects and sub-sects? Through every one of them He gives Himself to Himself, so that each person may advance according to his individual uniqueness.**

Children engage in many forms of make-believe and their parents smile and enjoy seeing them do so. So, the Absolute manifesting as the many allows the many to play and pretend as they will. For, being part of the Absolute, it is a surety that eventually the play will stop, the toys will be put away, and they will awaken into the truth of their Oneness. And each play is a reflection of their individual, unique character that will remain when the costumes are all put away. Duality is as real as Non-duality. For together they are That which includes and transcends both reality and non-duality. As Swami Brahmananda, the great master-disciple of Sri Ramakrishna, liked to say: "Just see the fun!"

> **He alone is water as well as ice. What is there in ice? Nothing but water. According to dvaita-dvaita, duality and non-duality are both facts; expressed from this position, there is form as well as freedom from form.**

No comment is needed on something so marvelously clear.

> **Again, when saying there are both duality and non-duality, where does this kind of statement hold good? There is certainly a level where difference and non-difference are perceived simultaneously.**
>
> **In very truth, He is as much in difference as He is in non-difference.**

There it is!

> **Look, from the worldly point of view, one quite obviously assumes that there are differences. The very fact that you are endeavoring to find your Self, shows, that you accept difference, that, in the manner of the world, you think of yourself as separate.**
>
> **From this standpoint difference undoubtedly exists. But then the world is inevitably heading towards destruction (nasa), since it is not the Self (na Swa), not He (na a). It cannot last for ever.**

Yes.

> **Yet, who is it that appears even in the guise of the ephemeral? Ponder over this! Well then, what goes and what comes?**

It is He Who appears in all appearance and changes in all change. Can the Reality, the Self of our Self, either come and go or not come and go? There is a state that transcends change and duality. But why do we have the compulsion to put all kinds of words and definitions into the mixture? Why can we not see as It Is? We refuse to do so. We can see, but we will to not see. This is simple, willful self-delusion. (Note the small "s" in "self-delusion."

Behold, it is movement as that of the sea (samudra), He expressing Himself (Swa mudra). The waves are but the rising and the falling, the undulation of the water, and it is water that forms into waves (taranga)–limbs of His own body (tar anga)–water in essence.

What is it that makes the same substance appear in different forms, as water, ice, waves? This again is asked from a particular plane of consciousness.

Reflect and see how much of it you can grasp!

It is impossible that in all things, even illusions and delusions, there will not be some reality, for only The Real exists. So observation of the unreal may yield glimpses of The Real.

No simile is ever valid in all respects.

This is only reasonable, but there are people who nit-pick and think they are completely invalidating a statement or simile because they can find an obscure aspect that is inconsistent or contrary to the general interpretation. Ignore them. Truth is not their aim, only resistance.

What lesson have you actually derived from it? Find out!

Extremely simple as this seems to be, it is profound and necessary principle. Everything that deserves our attention adds to our understanding or comprehension. If we have not learned from it, we may need to reconsider its possible significance or meaning. So we need to always look for the lesson or principle it embodies. Learning from life is not a mere truism, it is a crucial necessity. We are often disgusted or displeased with something that seems to be worthless or useless, but we should study it to make sure we are not missing valuable insight or information. It is normal to want to "just forget it" sometimes, but it may not be wise. Will power is often needed to make ourselves look objectively at something that elicits aversion from us, but we must do so, always. Life itself is our main teacher, including that which we dislike or reject before giving it intense scrutiny and analysis. Looking at something is good, but looking *into* it is also important.

Ma is implying that everything has a lesson or significance for us, and it is essential to discover completely what that might be.

What you thought of as with form you have understood to be formless.

Duality persists even if it is not apparent to us. So to understand and profit from something we must see if its seeming opposite carries a meaning or value, as well as its usual understanding.

Further, all form arises from the formless and resolves into the formless. So form and formlessness exist potentially in everything.

However, the realization of Truth cannot come through this process of speculation–this also you will certainly come to see.

There is relative truth and absolute Truth. We must become aware of both the potential and the limitation of every intellectual concept or conclusion. Certainly logic and intelligence have great potential, but they are limited by their very nature. Insight and intuition can carry us far beyond their usual scope, especially that which is based on the direct experiential knowledge that arises from or is based on sadhana as it reveals the Truth that is at the root of all things and perceptions.

The aforesaid implies that He eternally manifests, displaying form and quality, and yet is without form and quality; and still further, that the question of attributes and attributelessness cannot arise since there is solely the One-without-a-second.

Intuition-insight–direct and open perception that arises from/in our essential consciousness–is the highest form of knowing and the most trustworthy. However, there is the matter of producing it at will and then interpreting it correctly and fully and incorporating it into our practical life, inner and outer.

In the highest state implied in the final words, knower and known are One.

You speak of the Absolute as Truth, Knowledge, Infinity. In pure advaita no question of form, quality, or predication–be it affirmative or negative–can possibly arise.

When you say: "This indeed is He and that also is He," you have limited yourself by the word "also," and as a result assume the separateness of the thing referred to. In the One there can be no "also." The state of Supreme Oneness cannot be described as "THAT, and also something other than THAT." In the attributeless Brahman there can be no such thing as quality or absence of quality–there is only the Self alone.

Suppose you hold that He is with quality, embodied. When you become wholly centered in the particular form you adore, then formlessness does not exist for you–this is one state (sthiti). There is another state where He appears with attributes as well as without. There is yet another state where difference as well as non-difference exist–both being inconceivable–where He is quite beyond thought.

Besides, one can take the stand of the Vedic Karmakanda.

This and all that has been said above, is within the Supreme State, of which it is said that, even though the Whole is taken from the Whole, the Whole remains unimpaired. There can be no additions and no subtractions; the wholeness of the Whole remains unaltered.

Whatever line you may follow represents a particular aspect of it. Each method has its own mantras, its own methods, its beliefs and disbelief–to what purpose? To realize Him, your own Self.

Who or what is this Self? Depending on your orientation, you find Him, who is your own Self, in the relation of a perfect servant to his Master, of a part to the Whole, or simply as the One Self (Atma).

Look, if one believes in Swayam [Self-existent] Bhagavan, His Divine Power (Shakti) is already taken for granted.

Here you distinguish between Bhagavan and Bhagavati, between God as male and His Power as female. Yet from one standpoint there is no question of male or female, while from another the Divinity is conceived as divided into these two aspects.

The Eternal Virgin (Kumari) does not depend on anyone, She is the One Itself as POWER.

Where the Supreme Reality is conceived as Shakti. It is recognized as Pure Existence (Sattwa)–with form or without form–Power alone constituting Its Essence. This represents yet another standpoint.

When bhava (the mood to create) manifests as kriya (action), then only can form emerge. This also is a way of seeing it.

Further, if you think of Bhagavati Herself as Shakti, there are untold manifestations of Her Infinite Power.

Again, Mahashakti is the root-cause of everything–of creation, preservation, dissolution. Just as in the case of a tree, boughs and branches spring forth from its root, so all kinds and orders of deities, angels, archangels, and so forth, come into being as the manifestations of that Power.

The specific character of Shiva is a transcendence of all change and mutation, symbolized by a sava–corpse, which signifies that in the death of death lies Immortality, namely Swa.

Where creation, preservation and dissolution occur, He is present as becoming and He Himself preserves the universe as what is called Mahavishnu.

As regards the various cosmic positions, He is indeed in all of them, manifesting Himself in diverse ways, and as the formless. In each of them all the rest are contained, and in this multi-formity behold the One!

When you gaze at one form you cannot see any other, but in each of them the All is present, and every form reveals the One.

In the void there is fullness, and in fullness the void.

There are possibilities of every kind and description, but the root is the One, the Great Light. He is infinite.

Even when speaking merely of one path–how can the end of it be found? Yet, when the individual is unable to proceed any further, then there seems to be an end.

What is Pure Existence (Sattwa)? The Self, the Supreme Spirit, call it what you will. That which you variously name God (Bhagavan), Divine Majesty, Glory or Splendor–is only He, the One.

Very well, God is immutable, the non-doer (akarta), since He does not act. Only one who engages in action may be described as the doer of that action. Since He Himself is present in all causes and effects, how can one speak of Him as controlling or not controlling them?

Thus, here He is actionless.

But where His maya is, where the display of His Divine Power and Majesty is perceived, and where nature function according to fixed laws, who manifests there? The One of course.

Mutable and immutable–these one-sided views of yours, belong to the veil of ignorance. You speak of Him as the doer or non-doer, trying to limit Him to the one or the other. From your angle of vision it is but natural to perceive differences. He is whatever you take Him to be; you see Him according to your way of thinking, and as you portray Him, so He is.

As long as the curtain, the veil of ignorance exists, one is bound to see and hear in this restricted way. Until the obscuration is removed, how can one expect the revelation of Truth to occur in its entirety? When the veil is rent asunder, the fact will be disclosed that even the rending of the veil, in fact all that exists or occurs anywhere, is but He Himself.

Very well, the many creeds and sects serve the purpose that He may bestow Himself on Himself along various channels–each has its own beauty–and that He may be discovered as immanent, revealing Himself in countless ways, in all shapes, and in the formless.

As the Path, He attracts each person to a particular line, in harmony with his inner dispositions and tendencies.

The One is present in each sect, even though in some cases there appears to be conflict among them, due to the limitations of the ego. This body however, does not exclude anything. He, who follows one particular creed or sect, will have to proceed right up to the point where he knows all that it stands for in its entirety.

When advancing along one line, in other words, when adhering to one particular religion, faith or creed–which you conceive as distinct and as conflicting with all the others–you will, first of all, have to realize the perfection to which its Founder points and then what is beyond will of itself become revealed to you.

What has just been explained is applicable in the case of each of the various sects; yet it is of course true that, if one remains satisfied with whatever can be achieved by following one line, the Goal of human life has not been attained. What is required is a Realization that will uproot conflict and divergence of opinion, which is complete and free from inherent antagonism.

If it be anything less than that, it means that one's experience is partial, incomplete. In the event of true Realization, one can have no quarrel with anyone–one is fully enlightened as to all faiths and doctrines, and sees all paths as equally good. This is absolute and perfect Realization. So long as there is dissension, one cannot speak of attainment. Nevertheless, one should undoubtedly have firm faith in one's Ishta and pursue one's chosen path with constancy and single-mindedness.

> **As to the fruit of action. Just consider, where along whatever line of approach effort is sustained without a break and with undivided concentration on the one Goal, who will thus be revealed? He, the Indivisible One!**
>
> **But even in action as such, the Perfect One stands Self-revealed. This is the real significance of each action, of the striving, which is the innate characteristic of the individual. Man's true nature prompts him to do actions that give it expression, his true nature awakens in him the urge to perform actions of this type. Man's true nature, Sva, Swayam, Atma–call it by any name–it is the Supreme, I myself.**

In conclusion the only thing I can say is this in the words of the Great Prophet Isaiah (40:5):

The Mouth Of The Lord Hath Spoken It

Did you enjoy reading this book?

Thank you for taking the time to read *The Eternal Wisdom of Anandamayi Ma.* If you found it meaningful, or if it inspired you, or simply gave you something worth pondering, we invite you to leave a short review on Amazon, Goodreads, or anywhere books are shared.

Word of mouth is one of the greatest gifts you can offer to independent publishers, and helps keep this work in motion.

CONTINUE Your Journey Within:
GET YOUR FREE MEDITATION GUIDE

Sign up for the Light of the Spirit Newsletter and get
The Pathway to Awakening: Three Essentials for a Successful Spiritual Life

Get free updates: newsletters, blog posts, and podcasts, plus exclusive content from Light of the Spirit Monastery.

Visit: https://ocoy.org/signup

About the Author

Swami Nirmalananda Giri (Abbot George Burke) is the founder and director of the Atma Jyoti Ashram (Light of the Spirit Monastery) in Cedar Crest, New Mexico, USA.

In his many pilgrimages to India, he had the opportunity of meeting some of India's greatest spiritual figures, including Swami Sivananda of Rishikesh and Anandamayi Ma. During his first trip to India he was made a member of the ancient Swami Order by Swami Vidyananda Giri, a direct disciple of Paramhansa Yogananda, who had himself been given sannyas by the Shankaracharya of Puri, Jagadguru Bharati Krishna Tirtha.

In the United States he also encountered various Christian saints, including Saint John Maximovich of San Francisco and Saint Philaret Voznesensky of New York.

For many years Swami Nirmalananda has researched the identity of Jesus Christ and his teachings with India and Sanatana Dharma, including Yoga. It is his conclusion that Jesus lived in India for most of his life, and was a yogi and Sanatana Dharma missionary to the West. After his resurrection he returned to India and lived the rest of his life in the Himalayas.

He has written extensively on these and other topics, many of which are posted at OCOY.org.

Atma Jyoti Ashram
(Light of the Spirit Monastery)

Atma Jyoti Ashram (Light of the Spirit Monastery) is a monastic community for those men who seek direct experience of the Spirit through yoga meditation, traditional yogic discipline, Sanatana Dharma and the life of the sannyasi in the tradition of the Order of Shankara. Our lineage is in the Giri branch of the Order.

The public outreach of the monastery is through its website, OCOY.org (Original Christianity and Original Yoga). There you will find many articles on Original Christianity and Original Yoga, including *The Christ of India. Foundations of Yoga* and *How to Be a Yogi* are practical guides for anyone seriously interested in living the Yoga Life.

You will also discover many other articles on leading an effective spiritual life, including *Soham Yoga: The Yoga of the Self* and *Spiritual Benefits of a Vegetarian Diet*, as well as the "Dharma for Awakening" series–in-depth commentaries on these spiritual classics: the Bhagavad Gita, the Upanishads, the Dhammapada, the Tao Teh King and more.

You can listen to podcasts by Swami Nirmalananda on meditation, the Yoga Life, and remarkable spiritual people he has met in India and elsewhere, at http://ocoy.org/podcasts/

Join over 35,000 subscribers and watch over 350 videos on these topics and more, including recordings of online satsangs where Swami Nirmalananda answers various questions on practical aspects of spiritual life. A new series of talks on the Bhagavad Gita has also been added.

Visit our Youtube channel here:
Youtube.com/@lightofthespirit

Reading for Awakening

Light of the Spirit Press presents books on spiritual wisdom and Original Christianity and Original Yoga. From our "Dharma for Awakening" series (practical commentaries on the world's scriptures) to books on how to meditate and live a successful spiritual life, you will find books that are informative, helpful, and even entertaining.

Light of the Spirit Press is the publishing house of Light of the Spirit Monastery (Atma Jyoti Ashram) in Cedar Crest, New Mexico, USA. Our books feature the writings of the founder and director of the monastery, Swami Nirmalananda Giri (Abbot George Burke) which are also found on the monastery's website, OCOY.org.

We invite you to explore our publications in the following pages.

Find out more about our publications at
lightofthespiritpress.com

BOOKS ON MEDITATION

Soham Yoga
The Yoga of the Self

A complete and in-depth guide to effective meditation and the life that supports it, this important book explains with clarity and insight what real yoga is, and why and how to practice Soham Yoga meditation.

Discovered centuries ago by the Nath yogis, this simple and classic approach to self-realization has no "secrets," requires no "initiation," and is easily accessible to the serious modern yogi.

Includes helpful, practical advice on leading an effective spiritual life and many Illuminating quotes on Soham from Indian scriptures and great yogis.

"This book is a complete spiritual path." –Arnold Van Wie

Light of Soham
The Life and Teachings of Sri Gajanana Maharaj of Nashik

Gajanan Murlidhar Gupte, later known as Gajanana Maharaj, led an unassuming life, to all appearances a normal unmarried man of contemporary society. Crediting his personal transformation to the practice of the Soham mantra, he freely shared this practice with a small number of disciples, whom he simply called his friends. Strictly avoiding the trap of gurudom, he insisted that his friends be self-reliant and not be dependent on him for their spiritual progress. Yet he was uniquely able to assist them in their inner development.

The Inspired Wisdom of Gajanana Maharaj
A Practical Commentary on Leading an Effectual Spiritual Life

Presents the teachings and sayings of the great twentieth-century Soham yogi Gajanana Maharaj, with a commentary by Swami Nirmalananda.

The author writes: "In reading about Gajanana Maharaj I encountered a holy personality that eclipsed all others for me. In his words I found a unique wisdom that altered my perspective on what yoga, yogis, and gurus should be.

"But I realized that through no fault of their own, many Western readers need a clarification and expansion of Maharaj's meaning to get the right understanding of his words. This commentary is meant to help my friends who, like me have found his words 'a light in the darkness.'"

Inspired Wisdom of Lalla Yogeshwari
A Commentary on the Mystical Poetry of the Great Yogini of Kashmir

Lalla Yogeshwari was a great fourteenth-century yogini and wandering ascetic of Kashmir, whose mystic poetry were the earliest compositions in the Kashmiri language. She was in the tradition of the Nath Yogi Sampradaya whose meditation practice is that of Soham Sadhana: the joining of the mental repetition of Soham Mantra with the natural breath.

Swami Nirmalananda's commentary mines the treasures of Lalleshwari's mystic poems and presents his reflections in an easily intelligible fashion for those wishing to put these priceless teachings on the path of yogic self-transformation into practice.

Dwelling in the Mirror

A Study of Illusions Produced By Delusive Meditation And How to Be Free from Them

Swami Nirmalananda says of this book:

"Over and over people have mistaken trivial and pathological conditions for enlightenment, written books, given seminars and gained a devoted following.

"There are those who can have an experience and realize that it really cannot be real, but a vagary of their mind. Some may not understand that on their own, but can be shown by others the truth about it. For them and those that may one day be in danger of meditation-produced delusions I have written this brief study."

Books on Yoga & Spiritual Life

An Eagle's Flight

A Yogi's Spiritual Autobiography

Swami Nirmalananda Giri shares with rare honesty the struggles, insights, and blessings that have shaped his spiritual life.

Written with his usual insight, vividness, and humor, this book presents stories of his encounters with Anandamayi Ma, Swami Sivananda of Rishikesh and many other saints and yogis.

Satsang with the Abbot

Questions and Answers about Life, Spiritual Liberty, and the Pursuit of Ultimate Happiness

The questions in this book range from the most sublime to the most practical. "How can I attain samadhi?" "I am married with children. How can I lead a spiritual life?" "What is Self-realization?" "How important is belief in karma and reincarnation?"

In Swami Nirmalananda's replies to these questions the reader will discover common sense, helpful information, and a guiding light for their journey through and beyond the forest of cliches, contradictions, and confusion of yoga, Hinduism, Christianity, and metaphysical thought.

Foundations of Yoga

Ten Important Principles Every Meditator Should Know

An introduction to the important foundation principles of Patanjali's Yoga: Yama and Niyama

Yama and Niyama are often called the Ten Commandments of Yoga, but they have nothing to do with the ideas of sin and virtue or good and evil as dictated by some cosmic potentate. Rather they are determined by a thoroughly practical, pragmatic basis: that which strengthens and facilitates our yoga practice should be observed and that which weakens or hinders it should be avoided.

Yoga: Science of the Absolute

A Commentary on the Yoga Sutras of Patanjali

The Yoga Sutras of Patanjali is the most authoritative text on Yoga as a practice. It is also known as the Yoga Darshana because it is the fundamental text of Yoga as a philosophy.

In this commentary, Swami Nirmalananda draws on the age-long tradition regarding this essential text, including the commentaries of Vyasa and Shankara, the most highly regarded writers on Indian philosophy and practice, as well as I. K. Taimni and other authoritative commentators, and adds his own ideas based on half a century of study and practice. Serious students of yoga will find this an essential addition to their spiritual studies.

The Benefits of Brahmacharya

A Collection of Writings About the Spiritual, Mental, and Physical Benefits of Continence

"Brahmacharya is the basis for morality. It is the basis for eternal life. It is a spring flower that exhales immortality from its petals." Swami Sivananda

This collection of articles from a variety of authorities including Mahatma Gandhi, Sri Ramakrishna, Swami Vivekananda, Swamis Sivananda and Chidananda of the Divine Life Society, Swami Nirmalananda, and medical experts, presents many facets of brahmacharya and will prove of immense value to all who wish to grow spiritually.

Living the Yoga Life

Perspectives on Yoga

"Dive deep; otherwise you cannot get the gems at the bottom of the ocean. You cannot pick up the gems if you only float on the surface." Sri Ramakrishna

In *Living the Yoga Life* Swami Nirmalananda shares the gems he has found from a lifetime of "diving deep." This collection of reflections and short essays addresses the key concepts of yoga philosophy that are so easy to take for granted. Never content with the accepted cliches about yoga sadhana, the yoga life, the place of a guru, the nature of Brahman and our unity with It, Swami Nirmalananda's insights on these and other facets of the yoga life will inspire, provoke, enlighten, and even entertain.

Spiritual Benefits of a Vegetarian Diet

The health benefits of a vegetarian diet are well known, as are the ethical aspects. But the spiritual advantages should be studied by anyone involved in meditation, yoga, or any type of spiritual practice.

Diet is a crucial aspect of emotional, intellectual, and spiritual development as well. For diet and consciousness are interrelated, and purity of diet is an effective aid to purity and clarity of consciousness.

The major thing to keep in mind when considering the subject of vegetarianism is its relevancy in relation to our explorations of consciousness. We need only ask: Does it facilitate my spiritual growth–the development and expansion of my consciousness? The answer is Yes.

Books on the Sacred Scriptures of India

The Bhagavad Gita for Awakening

A Practical Commentary for Leading a Successful Spiritual Life

Drawing from the teachings of Sri Ramakrishna, Jesus, Paramhansa Yogananda, Ramana Maharshi, Swami Vivekananda, Swami Sivananda of Rishikesh, Papa Ramdas, and other spiritual masters and teachers, as well as his own experiences, Swami Nirmalananda illustrates the teachings of the Gita with stories which make the teachings of Krishna in the Gita vibrant and living.

From *Publisher's Weekly*: "[The author] enthusiastically explores the story as a means for knowing oneself, the cosmos, and one's calling within it. His plainspoken insights often distill complex lessons with simplicity and sagacity. Those with a deep interest in the Gita will find much wisdom here."

The Upanishads for Awakening

A Practical Commentary on India's Classical Scriptures

The sacred scriptures of India are vast. Yet they are only different ways of seeing the same thing, the One Thing which makes them both valid and ultimately harmonious. That unifying subject is Brahman: God the Absolute, beyond and besides whom there is no "other" whatsoever. The thirteen major Upanishads are the fountainhead of all expositions of Brahman.

Swamiji illumines the Upanishads' value for spiritual seekers from the unique perspective of a lifetime of study and practice of both Eastern and Western spirituality.

The Bhagavad Gita–The Song of God

Often called the "Bible" of Hinduism, the Bhagavad Gita is found in households throughout India and has been translated into every major language of the world. Literally billions of copies have been handwritten or printed.

The clarity of this translation by Swami Nirmalananda makes for easy reading, while the rich content makes this the ideal "study" Gita. As the original Sanskrit language is so rich, often there are several accurate translations for the same word, which are noted in the text, giving the spiritual student the needed understanding of the fullness of the Gita.

All Is One

A Commentary On Sri Vaiyai R. Subramanian's Ellam Ondre

Swami Nirmalananda's insightful commentary brings even further light to Ellam Ondre's refreshing perspective on what Unity signifies, and the path to its realization.

Written in the colorful and well-informed style typical of his other commentaries, it is a timely and important contribution to Advaitic literature that explains Unity as the fruit of yoga sadhana, rather than mere wishful thinking or some vague intellectual gymnastic, as is so commonly taught by the modern "Advaita gurus."

Sanatana Dharma

The Eternal Religion

Sanatana Dharma, commonly called Hinduism, is not just beautiful temples, colorful festivals, gurus and unusual beliefs. It is, simply put, "The Way Things Are" on a cosmic scale. It is the facts of existence and transcendence.

Swami Nirmalananda has edited for the modern reader a book originally printed nearly one hundred years ago in Varanasi, India, for use as a textbook by students of Benares Hindu University. Its original title was *Sanatana Dharma, An Advanced Text Book of Hindu Religion and Ethics*.

A Brief Sanskrit Glossary

A Spiritual Student's Guide to Essential Sanskrit Terms

This Sanskrit glossary contains full translations and explanations of hundreds of the most commonly used spiritual Sanskrit terms, and will help students of the Bhagavad Gita, the Upanishads, the Yoga Sutras of Patanjali, and other Indian scriptures and philosophical works to expand their vocabularies to include the Sanskrit terms contained in these, and gain a fuller understanding in their studies.

Vivekachudamani The Crest-Jewel of Discrimination For Awakening

A Commentary on Shankara's Classic on Advaita Vedanta

Beyond theory, this commentary offers practical insights for those seeking true spiritual growth, making it an essential guide for both beginners and advanced practitioners of Vedanta.

Whether you are a seasoned yogi or new to the path of spiritual awakening, this book will illuminate your journey, helping you discern the path to higher awareness amidst the clutter of modern spiritual clichés.

Dive into this classic text reimagined for contemporary seekers and transform your understanding of self and reality.

Books on Original Christianity

The Christ of India

The Story of Original Christianity

"Original Christianity" is the teaching of both Jesus and his Apostle Saint Thomas in India. Although it was new to the Mediterranean world, it was really the classical, traditional teachings of the rishis of India that even today comprise the Eternal Dharma, that goes far beyond religion into realization.

In *The Christ of India* Swami Nirmalananda presents what those ancient teachings are, as well as the growing evidence that Jesus spent much of his "Lost Years" in India and Tibet. This is also the story of how the original teachings of Jesus and Saint Thomas thrived in India for centuries before the coming of the European colonialists.

May a Christian Believe in Reincarnation?

Discover the real and surprising history of reincarnation and Christianity.

A growing number of people are open to the subject of past lives, and the belief in rebirth–reincarnation, metempsychosis, or transmigration–is commonplace. It often thought that belief in reincarnation and Christianity are incompatible. But is this really true? May a Christian believe in reincarnation? The answer may surprise you.

"Those needing evidence that a belief in reincarnation is in accordance with teachings of the Christ need look no further: Plainly laid out and explained in an intelligent manner from one who has spent his life on a Christ-like path of renunciation and prayer/meditation."—Christopher T. Cook

The Unknown Lives of Jesus and Mary

Compiled from Ancient Records and Mystical Revelations

"There are also many other things which Jesus did, the which, if they should be written every one, I suppose that even the world itself could not contain the books that should be written." (Gospel of Saint John, final verse)

You can discover much of those "many other things" in this unique compilation of ancient records and mystical revelations, which includes historical records of the lives of Jesus Christ and his Mother Mary that have been accepted and used by the Church since apostolic times. This treasury of little-known stories of Jesus' life will broaden the reader's understanding of what Christianity really was in its original form.

The Gospel of Thomas for Awakening

A Commentary on Jesus' Sayings as Recorded by the Apostle Thomas

When the Apostles dispersed to the various area of the world, Thomas travelled to India, where evidence shows Jesus spent his Lost Years, and which had been the source of the wisdom which he had brought to the "West."

The Christ that Saint Thomas quotes in this ancient text is quite different than the Christ presented by popular Christianity. Through his unique experience and study with both Christianity and Indian religion, Swami Nirmalananda clarifies the sometimes enigmatic sayings of Jesus in an informative and inspiring way.

The Odes of Solomon for Awakening

A Commentary on the Mystical Wisdom of the Earliest Christian Hymns and Poems

The Odes of Solomon is the earliest Christian hymn-book, and therefore one of the most important early Christian documents. Since they are mystical and esoteric, they teach and express the classical and universal mystical truths of Christianity, revealing a Christian perspective quite different than that of "Churchianity," and present the path of Christhood that all Christians are called to.

"Fresh and soothing, these 41 poems and hymns are beyond delightful! I deeply appreciate Abbot George Burke's useful and illuminating insight and find myself spiritually re-animated." –John Lawhn

The Aquarian Gospel for Awakening (2 Volumes)

A Practical Commentary on Levi Dowling's Classic Life of Jesus Christ

Written in 1908 by the American mystic Levi Dowling, The Aquarian Gospel of Jesus the Christ answers many questions about Jesus' life that the Bible doesn't address. Dowling presents a universal message found at the heart of all valid religions, a broad vision of love and wisdom that will ring true with Christians who are attracted to Christ but put off by the narrow views of the tradition that has been given his name.

Swami Nirmalananda's commentary is a treasure-house of knowledge and insight that even further expands Dowling's vision of the true Christ and his message.

Robe of Light

An Esoteric Christian Cosmology

In *Robe of Light* Swami Nirmalananda explores the whys and wherefores of the mystery of creation. From the emanation of the worlds from the very Being of God, to the evolution of the souls to their ultimate destiny as perfected Sons of God, the ideal progression of creation is described. Since the rebellion of Lucifer and the fall of Adam and Eve from Paradise flawed the normal plan of evolution, a restoration was necessary. How this came about is the prime subject of this insightful study.

Moreover, what this means to aspirants for spiritual perfection is expounded, with a compelling knowledge of the scriptures and of the mystical traditions of East and West.

Wandering With The Cherubim

A Commentary on the Mystical Verse of Angelus Silesius–The Cherubinic Wanderer

Johannes Scheffler, who wrote under the name Angelus Silesius, was a mystic and a poet. In his most famous book, "The Cherubinic Wanderer," he expressed his mystical vision.

Swami Nirmalananda reveals the timelessness of his mystical teachings and The Cherubinic Wanderer's practical value for spiritual seekers. He does this in an easily intelligible fashion for those wishing to put those priceless teachings into practice.

"Set yourself on the journey of this mystical poetry made accessible through this very beautifully commentated text. It is text that submerges one in the philosophical context of the Advaita notion of Non Duality. Swami Nirmalananda's commentary is indispensable in understanding higher philosophical ideas, for Swami's language, while readily approachable, is rich in deep essence of the teachings."–Savitri

Christian Non-Dualism

A Commentary on Theologia Germanica

What if the roots of Christian mysticism held teachings as profound as those found in the East? What if a single medieval text, long forgotten by mainstream theology, offered a clear and proven path to inner union with God?

Christian Non-Dualism is a revelatory commentary on *Theologia Germanica*, a 14th-century mystical masterpiece that has gone through nearly 200 editions but is almost unknown today. With depth, clarity, and spiritual authority, Swami Nirmalananda Giri unveils the text's rich insights into ego-surrender, divine grace, and the path to inner revelation.

Spirit & Life–The Four Gospels for Awakening

A Practical Commentary on the Life and Teachings of Jesus Christ

Spirit & Life offers a powerful, practical commentary on a harmony of the Gospels, and is not a mere biography but a spiritual revelation consisting of both the life and the teachings of Jesus.

Far from being a conventional or doctrinal study, this book invites readers into the inner life of the soul, where Jesus is not only the Master Teacher, but the awakened Self within. With clarity and reverence, the author examines the inner meaning of the canonical Gospels, unveiling their universal message of illumination, liberation, and union with God.

A two volume set, beautifully illustrated.

Books on Buddhism & Taoism and More

The Dhammapada for Awakening

A Commentary on Buddha's Practical Wisdom

Swami Nirmalananda's commentary on this classic Buddhist scripture explores the Buddha's answers to the urgent questions, such as "How can I find find lasting peace, happiness and fulfillment that seems so elusive?" and "What can I do to avoid many of the miseries big and small that afflict all of us?" Drawing on his personal experience, the author sheds new light on the Buddha's eternal wisdom.

"Swami Nirmalananda's commentary is well crafted and stacked with anecdotes, humor, literary references and beautiful quotes from the Buddha. I have come to consider it a guide to daily living." –Rev. Gerry Nangle

The Tao Teh King for Awakening

A Practical Commentary on Lao Tzu's Classic Exposition of Taoism

"The Tao does all things, yet our interior disposition determines our success or failure in coming to knowledge of the unknowable Tao."

Lao Tzu's classic writing, the *Tao Teh King*, has fascinated scholars and seekers for centuries. Swami Nirmalananda offers a commentary that makes the treasures of Lao Tzu's teachings accessible and applicable for the sincere seeker.

Bio-Magnetic Therapy

Healing in Your Hands

In *Bio-Magnetic Therapy* Swami Nirmalananda teaches the techniques to strengthen your vitality and improve the body's natural healing ability in yourself and in others with specific methods that anyone can use.

Bio-Magnetic Therapy is a simple and natural way to increase the flow of life-force into the body for general good health and to stimulate the supply and flow of life-force to a troubled area that has become vitality-starved through some obstruction. It does not cure; it simply aids the body to cure itself by supplying it with curative force.

How to Read the Tarot

A Practical Method Using the Rider-Waite Deck

Discover Swami Nirmalananda's unique method of reading the Tarot specifically for use with the Rider-Waite deck, with detailed instructions on how to use the cards to develop your intuition for understanding the meanings of the cards. Illustrated with color plates of each of the cards of the Rider-Waite deck with full explanations of their symbolism.

Light on the Path for Awakening

A Commentary on Mabel Collins' Spiritual Classic

In the last quarter of the nineteenth century, Mabel Collins printed a small book on the beginnings of the spiritual quest entitled Light On The Path. She did not consider herself the author but only the transmitter.

This commentary carefully analyzes her transcription, for those who would make the Great Journey must know both the path and how to travel upon it.

Light on the Path explains the nature of discipleship and the qualities of a worthy disciple. The master of such a disciple is the disciple's own divine Self which draws its existence from the Supreme Self: God.

More Titles

Light from Eternal Lamps

The Gnosis of the Ten Commandments and Beatitudes

www.ingramcontent.com/pod-product-compliance
Lightning Source LLC
LaVergne TN
LVHW020040110826
845155LV00029B/565

* 9 7 8 1 9 5 5 0 4 6 4 5 9 *